The Savior
the Priesthood
and You

The Savior
the Priesthood
and You

1973-74 Course of Study for the Melechizedek Priesthood Quorums

Published by The Church of Jesus Christ of Latter-day Saints, Salt Lake City, Utah

Contents

Section Five: You Are the Patriarch in Your Home

Foreword

TO ALL MELCHIZEDEK PRIESTHOOD HOLDERS AND PROSPECTIVE ELDERS

The purpose of this Priesthood course of study is to help you learn your duty in order that you will be a better follower of Christ as a father, husband, student, worker, friend and neighbor, and to help you become a better representative of the Priesthood in your everyday living.

THE FOCUS OF THIS COURSE

In the meridian of time our Savior asked the following question of a group of Priesthood holders: "What manner of men ought ye to be?" And then he answered his own question: "Verily I say unto you, even as I am." (3 Nephi 27:27.) Again the Savior admonished, "Follow me, and do the things which ye have seen me do." (2 Nephi 31:12.)

The focus of this course is upon the Savior and also upon the Priesthood as it relates to you and to the decisions you make and the actions you take in your everyday living. What is the basis for your decision making? What are the standards that determine the actions you take?

The introductory lesson for this manual is entitled, "What Would Jesus Do?" This question is repeated in the application section of every lesson. It is to be a reminder and a standard to you in helping you make decisions and in choosing a course of action.

The lessons are about the Priesthood, with emphasis on the great strength and power that comes to the person who learns his calling in the Priesthood and then magnifies that calling. They should help you to pattern your life after the Savior, with Him as your model. Much of this manual is material previously used for the 1966 Melchizedek Priesthood course of study. You will note that the year's study is composed of thirty-four lessons plus the introductory lesson. This lesson structure puts greater responsibility upon the quorum Priesthood leaders and instructors to emphasize the practical application of the lesson materials in meeting your needs as an individual and in meeting the needs of the quorum.

HOW YOU WILL DERIVE THE MOST FROM THIS COURSE OF STUDY

DAILY PRAYERFUL MEDITATION ON THE SCRIPTURES

One specific practice resulting from the use of this course of study would be for you to spend time in daily prayerful meditation on the scriptures. You should not just read the scriptures, but should "*ponder* [them] in your hearts" (Moroni 10:3), "*feasting* upon the word[s] of Christ" (2 Nephi 31:20) and *treasuring* up the words of the Lord (see Joseph Smith 1:37) found in the scriptures as well as those spoken by the living prophets. (Read carefully the "Introductory Lesson" by President Marion G. Romney to see more fully the great need for daily scriptural study.)

In order for the real power of this course to be felt in your life, you should come to quorum meeting having read the lesson, thus preparing yourself to receive the word by the spirit of truth. (See D&C 50:17-22.)

Introductory
Lesson
What Would Jesus Do?

What Would Jesus Do?

LESSON OBJECTIVE

As you read this material, you as a Priesthood holder should feel motivated to:

1. Ponder the significance of using "What would Jesus Do?" criterion in your everyday decision-making.

2. Establish for yourself a daily scripture reading habit, in which you will strive to prayerfully meditate and seek the will of your Heavenly Father concerning your life.

3. Review the message at the front of this manual, "To All Melchizedek Priesthood Holders and Prospective Elders," and the Contents pages.

LESSON DEVELOPMENT

Read the following article by President Marion G. Romney, a reprint from *The New Era*, September 1972. As you read the article, determine how President Romney answered for himself these questions:

1. What would Jesus do?
2. How did Jesus discover the Father's will? What two things did He persistently do?
3. How did President Romney apply this understanding to everyday decision-making in his life?

WHAT WOULD JESUS DO?

During my early teens a small book or pamphlet titled "What Would Jesus Do?" came into my hands. I do not now remember the name of the author, nor do I remember what he said. The title, however, has been in my mind ever since. The question posed epitomized the desire I had had from my childhood. Countless times as I have faced challenges and vexing decisions I have asked myself "What would Jesus do?" Fortunately, I was exposed early in life to the standard works of the Church. The elementary school I attended was a Church school.

Theology was one of the subjects we were required to study daily. Books being scarce, the scriptures were used as texts. It was therefore natural for me, as I pondered the question, "What would Jesus do?" to turn to the scriptures in search of the answer. There in the Gospel as recorded by St. John, I found the clear and certain answer: *Jesus would always do the will of his Father.* This he himself repeatedly declared.

As he taught in the temple, the Jews "marvelled, saying, How knoweth this man letters, having never learned?

"Jesus answered them, and said, My doctrine is not mine, but his that sent me.

"He that speaketh of himself seeketh his own glory; but he that seeketh his glory that sent him, the same is true, and no unrighteousness is in him.

". . . he that sent me is true; and I speak to the world those things which I have heard of him.

". . . I do nothing of myself; but as my Father hath taught me, I speak these things.

"And he that sent me is with me: the Father hath not left me alone; for I do always those things that please him.

"I and my Father are one." (John 7:15, 16, 18; 8:26, 28, 29; 10:30.)

". . . Verily, verily, I say unto you, The Son can do nothing of himself, but what he seeth the Father do: for what things soever he doeth, these also doeth the Son likewise." (John 5:19.)

Having learned that Jesus would always do the will of his Father, *my next objective was to find out what Jesus would do to ascertain the will of his Father. Searching the New Testament, I discovered that one thing he did was to thoroughly familiarize himself with what his Father had declared his will to be as recorded in the Old Testament.* That he did this is evidenced by the fact that in his statements as recorded in the New Testament, Jesus quoted or cited scriptures from the Old Testament more than one hundred times.

Finally, and most importantly, I learned that he communed constantly with his Father through prayer. This he did not only to learn the will of his Father but also to obtain the strength to do his Father's will. He fasted and prayed forty days and forty nights at the beginning of his ministry. (Matt. 4:2; Mark 1:13; Luke 4:2.) He prayed all night just before choosing his twelve apostles. (Luke 6:12-13.) He prayed in the Garden of Gethsemane. (Matt. 26:39.) It would seem that during his earthly ministry he never made a major decision or met a crisis without praying.

From the record of his struggle in Gethsemane—

". . . Father, if thou be willing, remove this cup from me; nevertheless not my will, but thine, be done.

"And being in an agony he prayed more earnestly: and his sweat was as it were great drops of blood falling down to the ground." (Luke 22:42, 44)— We learn that although it was not always easy nor pleasant for him to do his Father's will, he always did it.

Speaking to the Prophet Joseph 1800 years later concerning his Gethsemane ordeal, Jesus said:

"Which suffering caused myself, even God, the greatest of all, to tremble because of pain, and to bleed at every pore, and to suffer both body and spirit—and would that I might not drink the bitter cup, and shrink—

"Nevertheless, glory be to the Father, and I partook and finished my preparations unto the children of men." (D&C 19:18-19.)

Relying upon the foregoing and companion scriptures, *I decided in my youth that for me the best approach to the solution of problems and the resolving of questions would be to proceed as Jesus proceeded: foster an earnest desire to do the Lord's will; familiarize myself with what the Lord has revealed on the matters involved; pray with diligence and faith for an inspired understanding of his will and the courage to do it.*

By following this pattern, Jesus lived a perfect life. We cannot, of course, equal his performance. We can, however, make greater progress toward it by emulating him than in any other way.

The accomplishments of such men as Nephi and the Prophet Joseph Smith have given me courage to try. Each of those great men embarked upon this course early in life.

Near the beginning of his record, Nephi wrote:

"And it came to pass that I, Nephi, being exceeding young, nevertheless . . . having great desires to know of the mysteries of God, wherefore, I did cry unto the Lord; and behold he did visit me, and did soften my heart that I did believe all the words which had been spoken by my father. . . ." (1 Ne. 2:16.)

His appreciation of the value of the scriptures in learning the will of the Lord is evidenced by his thoughts when the angel told him to slay Laban in order to get the brass plates.

"And now, when I, Nephi, had heard these words, I remembered the words of the Lord which he spake unto me in the wilderness, saying that: Inasmuch as thy seed shall keep my commandments, they shall prosper in the land of promise.

"Yea, and I also thought that they could not keep the commandments of the Lord according to the law of Moses, save they should have the law.

"And I also knew that the law was engraven upon the plates of brass." (1 Ne. 4:14-16.)

After he obtained the record, he searched it. (1 Ne. 5:21.)

In his fifteenth year the Prophet Joseph, to learn the Lord's will as to which church he should join, searched the scriptures. Upon reading James, first chapter, fifth verse, he prayed about it. Every Latter-day Saint knows the answer that came, as recorded in the Pearl of Great Price, Joseph Smith 2.

The most satisfying solutions to problems and the best answers to questions that I have been able to make in my own life, I have arrived at as follows:

1. From my youth I have searched the scriptures.

2. I have tried to honestly face the challenge or question presented with a sincere desire to solve it as Jesus would solve it.

3. I have, through diligent study and prayer, sought to weigh alternatives in light of what I knew about gospel principles.

4. I have made a decision in my own mind.

5. I have then taken the matter to the Lord, told him the problem, told him that I wanted to do what was right in his view, and asked him to give me peace of mind if I have made the right decision.

This, I think, is in harmony with the pattern Jesus set by precept and example during his ministry on the earth and with the 9th section of the Doctrine and Covenants where, through the Prophet Joseph Smith, the Lord said to Oliver Cowdery:

". . . you have not understood; you have supposed that I would give it unto you, when you took no thought save it was to ask me.

"But, behold, I say unto you, that you must study it out in your mind; then you must ask me if it be right, and if it is right I will cause that your bosom shall burn within you; therefore, you shall feel that it is right.

"But if it be not right you shall have no such feelings, but you shall have a stupor of thought. . . ." (D&C 9:7-9.)

When I feel the burning in my bosom, I conclude that I have done as Jesus would have me do under the circumstances. (Marion G. Romney, "What Would Jesus Do?" *The New Era*, September 1972, pp. 4-6. Italics added.)

Now that you have read of the effects upon President Romney of using the criterion, "What Would Jesus Do?" you may want to consider the potential effect of this criterion in your own life. President Joseph Fielding Smith has reminded all Priesthood holders that the significance of the Priesthood is "to do what he [Jesus] would do if he were personally present."

We are the Lord's agents; we represent him; he has given us authority which empowers us to do all that is necessary to save and exalt ourselves as well as his other children in the world.

We are ambassadors of the Lord Jesus Christ. Our commission is to represent him. We are directed to preach his gospel, to perform the ordinances of salvation, to bless mankind, to heal the sick and perhaps perform miracles, *to do what he would do if he were personally present—and all this because we hold the holy priesthood.* (*CR,* April 1971, p. 47. Italics added.)

Here is your challenge this year as Priesthood holders—*do what Jesus would do if He were present!* The 1973-74 course of study will provide you with the opportunity to apply this criterion. This manual's title, *The Savior, the Priesthood and You,* was carefully chosen to link your *daily actions* together with the *Priesthood you hold* and with *the Savior.* Each lesson contains a section entitled, "Application: What Would Jesus Do?" Your challenge will be to apply the material in such a way that you can ascertain what Jesus would do, and then commit yourself to a similar course of action. Take a moment now and examine a lesson to see how this will be done.

Also review the message at the front of this manual: "To All Melchizedek Priesthood Holders and Prospective Elders." Note the encouragement to prayerfully meditate on the scriptures daily as a means of determining our Heavenly Father's will.

The application section of each lesson will suggest some areas of scripture study for you. It is hoped that you will use this and other scripture readings for personal scripture study.

Turn now to the Contents page and scan the lesson titles and the subject matter of the lessons. Now select two or three lessons to look over, and you will note that each lesson after this introductory lesson follows this format:

1. Lesson Title
2. Lesson Follow-up
3. Lesson Objective

4. Introduction
5. Lesson Development

What Would Jesus Do?

T his course of study has been designed to provide you with a greater comprehension of the meaning of your Priesthood—to do what Jesus would do if he were personally present. Your Priesthood will be a blessing to you and to those about you as you strive to righteously put into action this principle and other principles associated with your Priesthood callings.

Section

11

Priesthood Gives You a Partnership With God

A God of Power and Love

LESSON OBJECTIVE

The Priesthood holder should feel motivated to (1) comprehend the character and attributes of God, our Heavenly Father, and (2) prayerfully consider what he might do to acquire these same godlike attributes in his own life.

INTRODUCTION

Suppose you were going on a long journey over territory which was entirely new to you. You knew the journey was going to be strewn with danger all the way; challenges, unpredictable hardships, threatening consequences, disappointments, successes, hosts of oppositions of all kinds, and innumerable risks. Suppose too you had the responsibility of taking care of your family, your wife and children, of getting them safely to your destination.

What would you be willing to do to be granted access to the knowledge and power of the only person who knew the way?

You *are* on such a journey. There are great risks. You are responsible for your family. You do have access to the only source of knowledge and power to get you and yours to your hoped-for destination. God is He who knows the way.

LESSON DEVELOPMENT

WHAT IS GOD LIKE?

From the days of Adam, God has manifested himself periodically unto mankind and clearly revealed that He is a personal being and possesses personal characteristics and attributes. God's superiority to man does at present preclude the possibility of man's fully comprehending God. Yet He has nonetheless let us know that as a personage He possesses characteristics and attributes which man himself possesses.

It is suggested here that the class instructor place two headings on the chalkboard:

Characteristics of God   **Statement or Incident Where Each Characteristic Is Shown**

Now class members could be invited to recall characteristics of God and tell where each is revealed. The instructor could list the answers in the two columns on the chalkboard.

Let us now consider something of the character of God and His attributes as revealed through His prophets.

THREE PERSONAGES IN THE GODHEAD

James E. Talmage has given us this clear statement of our understanding of the Godhead:[1]

Three personages comprising the great presiding council of the universe have revealed themselves to man: (1) God the Eternal Father; (2) His Son, Jesus Christ; and (3) the Holy Ghost. That these three are separate individuals, physically distinct from each other, is demonstrated by the accepted records of divine dealings with man. On the occasion of the Savior's baptism, John recognized the sign of the Holy Ghost; he saw before him in a tabernacle of flesh the Christ, unto whom he had administered the holy ordinance; and he heard the voice of the Father.[2] The three personages of the Godhead were present, manifesting themselves each in a different way, and each distinct from the others. Later the Savior promised His disciples that the Comforter,[3] who is the Holy Ghost, should be sent unto them by His Father; here again are the three members of the Godhead separately defined. Stephen, at the time of his martyrdom, was blessed with the power of heavenly vision, and he saw Jesus standing on the right hand of God.[4] Joseph Smith, while calling upon the Lord in fervent prayer, saw the Father and the Son, standing in the midst of light that shamed the brightness of the sun; and one of them declared of the other, "This is My Beloved Son. Hear Him!" Each of the members of the Trinity is called God;[5] together they constitute the Godhead.

GOD IS ALL POWERFUL

Elder Talmage writes further of the great powers of God:

There is no part of creation, however remote, into which God

---

[1]Talmage, James E., *The Articles of Faith*, Salt Lake City, The Church of Jesus Christ of Latter-day Saints, 1957 (36th Edition), pp. 39-40.

[2]Matthew 3:16, 17; also Mark 1:9-11; Luke 3:21-22.

[3]John 14:26, 15:26.

[4]Acts 7:55, 56.

[5]I Corinthians 3:6; John 1:1-14; Matthew 4:10; I Timothy 3:16; I John 5:7; Mosiah 15:1, 2.

cannot penetrate; through the medium of the Spirit the God-head is in direct communication with all things at all times. . . . The senses of each of the Trinity are of infinite power; His mind is of unlimited capacity; His powers of transferring Himself from place to place are infinite; plainly, however, His person cannot be in more than one place at any time. Admitting the personality of God, we are compelled to accept the fact of His materiality; indeed an "immaterial being," under which meaningless name some have sought to designate the condition of God, cannot exist, for the very expression is a contradiction of terms.[6]

GOD IS MERCIFUL

In one place Moses says: "And the Lord passed by before him [Moses], and proclaimed, The Lord, The Lord God, merciful and gracious, long-suffering, and abundant in goodness and truth, Keeping mercy for thousands, forgiving iniquity and transgression and sin, and that will by no means clear the guilty; . . .'" (Exodus 34:6-7.)

In a moving passage Nehemiah rehearses the obstinacy of Israel and among other things records: ". . . but thou art a God ready to pardon, gracious and merciful, slow to anger, and of great kindness, and forsookest them not. . . . Nevertheless they were disobedient, and rebelled against thee, and cast thy law behind their backs, and slew thy prophets which testified against them to turn them to thee, and they wrought great provocations. . . . Yet many years didst thou forbear them, and testifiedst against them by thy spirit in thy prophets: yet would they not give ear: therefore gavest thou them into the hand of the people of the lands. (Nehemiah 9:17, 26, 30.)

King Benjamin, the great Nephite prophet, was aware of the character of God and His attributes when he recounted: ". . . the goodness of God, and his matchless power, and his wisdom, and his patience, and his long-suffering towards the children of men; . . ." (Mosiah 4:6.)

WHAT DOES THIS POWER MEAN TO YOU?

Class members may wish to comment on how a knowledge of God's great power can strengthen them as they exercise His Priesthood in:
1. Administering to the sick.
2. Calling upon Him in prayer before discharging a Priesthood assignment.
3. Asking His blessings on their homes through family prayer.

---

[6]Talmage, James E., *The Articles of Faith*, Salt Lake City, The Church of Jesus Christ of Latter-day Saints, 1957 (36th Edition), pp. 42-43.

GOD HAS GREAT LOVE

Another manifestation of the character of God is His love. In John's first epistle he speaks of God as the very personification of love. He says: "He that loveth not knoweth not God; for God is love. In this was manifested the love of God toward us, because that God sent his only begotten Son into the world, that we might live through him. Herein is love, not that we loved God, but that he loved us, and sent his Son to be the propitiation for our sins. Beloved, if God so loved us, we ought also to love one another." (1 John 4:8-11.)

In a remarkable passage regarding the Father's love, the Son's love, and their joy, and man's love and joy, the Lord declared to His ancient Palestinian apostles: "As the Father hath loved me, so have I loved you; continue ye in my love. If ye keep my commandments, ye shall abide in my love; even as I have kept my Father's commandments, and abide in his love. These things have I spoken unto you, that my joy might remain in you, and that your joy might be full. This is my commandment, That ye love one another, as I have loved you. Greater love hath no man than this, that a man lay down his life for his friends." (John 15:9-13.)

In these few representative passages of scripture the Lord reveals many things to us regarding the character of the Father and the Son. The Lord describes Himself as Almighty, i.e., all powerful, as knowing all things, long-suffering, merciful, slow to anger, and as a God of love. Then, not only does God love His children and realize that they make mistakes, but He is patient with them. God is both just and merciful. If men will not repent and accept God's mercy through the power of the atonement, then they must satisfy the demands of justice themselves, which the scriptures denominate the wrath of God. (See D&C 19:16-19.)

Through the ages God's love has been manifested as typified in the words of the Christ when He said; ". . . how often would I have gathered thy children together, even as a hen gathereth her chickens under her wings, and ye would not!" (Matthew 23:37.) He bore the incomparable weight of the sins of the world in Gethsemane and suffered death on the cross out of love for mankind and His Father. God has done and continues to do all that He can do for us. The responsibility now lies with man to do what he will for himself.

Class members might discuss how we can learn to love better from God's example:

1. Our wives.
2. Our children.
3. Our neighbors.
4. The person who has sinned.
5. Our enemies.

GOD WANTS US TO ATTAIN GODHOOD

Inasmuch as God is our Father He has provided us with a plan which is designed to help us become as He is. He has revealed that it is His work and glory to bring to pass the immortality and eternal life of man. (Moses 1:39.)

In addition to this general goal and objective for man, the Lord has revealed other explicit goals which might be experienced by His children. Several specific ones are: that man might live an abundant life (John 10:10), that he might become perfect (Matthew 5:48), that he might have peace (John 16:33, Philippians 4:7), that he might have joy (2 Nephi 2:25), and that he might even pass beyond the angels and become a god. (D&C 132:20.)

Essentially, then, the Lord wants us to become as He is, and to share His glories. He has said: "These things have I spoken unto you, that *my joy* might remain in you, and that *your joy* might be full." (John 15:11. Italics ours.)

GOD HAS GIVEN US THE MEANS TO ATTAIN GOALS

Not only has the Lord made these goals known to us, but He has provided the means whereby they can be realized. They are not mere idealistic abstractions. They are actual realities which are within the grasp of all of God's children who will humbly accept the Lord and gratefully follow His generous counsel. One of the high and inestimable privileges man has been promised is that he may know God. The Lord said: "And I will pray the Father, and he shall give you another Comforter, that he may abide with you forever; Even the Spirit of truth; whom the world cannot receive, because it seeth him not, neither knoweth him: but ye know him; for he dwelleth with you, and shall be in you. . . . He that hath my commandments, and keepeth them, he it is that loveth me: and he that loveth me shall be loved of my Father, and I will love him, and will manifest myself to him. . . . If a man love me, he will keep my words: and my Father will love him, and we will come unto him, and make our abode with him." (John 14:16, 17, 21, 23.)

In order to restore His Gospel to the earth the Lord restored His Holy Priesthood. You have had the Priesthood conferred upon you and have been given specific rights, privileges, powers, etc., which pertain to your particular calling and ordination. The Priesthood may be a major means through which God's blessings may be manifested in our lives—in *your* life.

Priesthood holders should be ever mindful that women share in the blessings of the Priesthood. As John A. Widtsoe has written: "The

Priesthood is for the benefit of all members of the Church. Men have no greater claim than women upon the blessings that issue from the Priesthood and accompany its possession."[7]

---

[7]Widtsoe, John A., *Priesthood and Church Government*, Salt Lake City, Deseret Book Company, 1961, p. 83.

What Would Jesus Do?

It is evident from the Savior's life that He understood the character and attributes of our Heavenly Father. This comprehension, which came as a result of His study of the scriptures and earnest prayer, led Jesus to a state of perfection in these same attributes. "Show us the Father," inquired Philip. "Have I been so long time with you, and yet hast thou not known me, Philip? he that hath seen me hath seen the Father." (John 14:8-9.)

Similarly, what might the Priesthood holder do to develop these characteristics and positive attributes of God? For example, the Priesthood holder might ask: How can I become more merciful and loving in my life? How can I use God's power to bless others? Am I just in my dealings with others in business affairs? Am I just and loving in my home with my wife and children?

Prayerfully ponder these scriptures: D&C 93: 11-20; D&C 4:1-7; Moroni 7:39-48.

SPECIAL INSTRUCTIONS TO THE TEACHER

Make certain that the focus of your lesson is on how the Priesthood holder might acquire the characteristics and attributes of God. Emphasize D&C 4:7 and Moroni 7:48.

Try to relate experiences that illustrate this principle.

Our Priesthood Heritage

LESSON FOLLOW-UP

Quorum members might be asked to relate any insights that they gained as a result of focusing on understanding God's character and attributes so that these same attributes might become a part of their lives.

LESSON OBJECTIVES

The Priesthood holder should feel motivated to (1) understand the significance of Priesthood keys as they have been restored from ancient to modern prophets and (2) meditate on the relationship between these keys and his own responsibilities as a husband, father, or home teacher.

INTRODUCTION

What is the Priesthood? "It is the rule and government of God, whether on earth or in the heaven; and it is the only legitimate power, the only authority that is acknowledged by Him to rule and regulate the affairs of His kingdom."[1]

"It is nothing more nor less than the power of God delegated to man by which man can act in the earth for the salvation of the human family in the name of the Father and the Son and the Holy Ghost, and act legitimately; not assuming that authority, not borrowing it from generations that are dead and gone, but authority that has been given in this day in which we live by ministering angels and spirits from above, direct from the presence of Almighty God."[2]

LESSON DEVELOPMENT

Because of the pressures of daily life and the apparently inherent

[1] *Journal of Discourses*, Vol. 1, p. 224.
[2] Smith, Joseph F., *Gospel Doctrine* (Fifth Edition), Salt Lake City, Deseret Book Company, 1939, pp. 139-140.

"pull" of the mortal world, sometimes it is easy for one to lose his focus upon eternal things and lose a long-range perspective, becoming fully absorbed in the affairs of the present, if not the moment. This is true with reference to the Priesthood or some of its aspects. It is possible to become so absorbed in certain details, or issues or problems of limited scope, that one may at least momentarily forget how great the Priesthood is in duration and influence. If one can be aroused from this mortal lethargy and awakened to a realization of the incomparable magnitude of the Gospel and the Priesthood with its immortal power, he cannot be other than grateful for it and moved to bring himself into a more complete harmony with the Gospel, and God, its author.

THE GOSPEL IS ETERNAL

The Gospel is eternal, or is from eternity to eternity, and we should never lose sight of the fact that the period of time in which we live does no exist in isolation, but is an integral part of eternity. The Gospel has a comprehensive past as well as an all-encompassing future. We are a part of something great and marvelous.

This world was organized by the power of God for the sake of His spirit children. Even from the creation, Adam held the power and authority of the Holy Priesthood.

ADAM FIRST TO RECEIVE THE PRIESTHOOD

The Prophet Joseph Smith declared: "The Priesthood was first given to Adam; he obtained the First Presidency, and held the keys of it from generation to generation. He obtained it in the Creation, before the world was formed, as in Genesis 1:26, 27, 28. He had dominion given him over every living creature. He is Michael the Archangel, spoken of in the Scriptures. Then to Noah, who is Gabriel; he stands next in authority to Adam in the Priesthood; he was called of God to this office, and was the father of all living in this day, and to him was given the dominion. These men held keys first on earth, and then in heaven."[3]

Throughout the ages God has given mortals the opportunity to participate in and enjoy His divine influence. He has raised up many to be blessed with special keys and callings in the Holy Priesthood.

OTHERS WHO HELD KEYS

Adam, or Michael, held the keys of the Priesthood from generation to generation. Noah, or Gabriel, also held the keys of the Priesthood.

[3]Smith, Joseph Fielding, Compiler, *Teachings of the Prophet Joseph Smith* (Second Edition), Salt Lake City, Deseret News Press, 1940, p. 157.

To Elijah, He "committed the keys of the power of turning the hearts of the fathers to the children, and the hearts of the children to the fathers, that the whole earth may not be smitten with a curse." (D&C 27:9.)

To Peter, James and John, He committed the keys of the ministry during the dispensation in which they were mortals. (D&C 27:12. See also John 15:16.) Peter, James and John held the keys of the dispensation of the fulness of times, our dispensation. (See D&C 27:13 and 128:20.)

Of Peter, James, and John, the Lord also said: "Unto whom I have committed the keys of my kingdom, and a dispensation of the gospel for the last times; and for the fulness of times, in the which I will gather together in one all things, both which are in heaven, and which are on earth." (D&C 27:13.) Joseph Smith and Oliver Cowdery held these, but they got them from Peter, James, and John as D&C 128:20 shows.

In addition to these and others who have held special keys there have been some who have had special callings. Certainly Abraham, Isaac, and Jacob with their remarkable covenants with Jehovah are appropriate examples. Perhaps the plainest statement of the covenant is that recorded in the Book of Abraham. It reads:

My name is Jehovah, and I know the end from the beginning; therefore my hand shall be over thee.

And I will make of thee a great nation, and I will bless thee above measure, and make thy name great among all nations, and thou shalt be a blessing unto thy seed after thee, that in their hands they shall bear this ministry and Priesthood unto all nations;

And I will bless them though thy name; for as many as receive this Gospel shall be called after thy name, and shall be accounted thy seed, and shall rise up and bless thee, as their father;

And will bless them that bless thee, and curse them that curse thee; and in thee (that is, in thy Priesthood) and in thy seed (that is, thy Priesthood), for I give unto thee a promise that this right shall continue in thee, and in thy seed after thee (that is to say, the literal seed, or the seed of the body) shall all the families of the earth be blessed, even with the blessings of the Gospel, which are the blessings of salvation, even of life eternal. (Abraham 2:8-11.)

From the Creation, through past generations, unto our own day, the Lord has provided and preserved the keys of the Holy Priesthood that His children might enjoy the rights, privileges, and blessings associated therewith. Likewise, through special callings and covenants, such as those with Abraham, Isaac, and Jacob, the Lord has made provision for the continued guidance and blessing of His spirit children. It is through and because of these keys, covenants, powers, and blessings that the Gospel is made available to us.

AN ACTIVITY FOR THE CLASS

(At this point the class instructor might write these names on the board and ask class members to tell the role of each in giving us our Priesthood heritage today: Adam, Noah, Elijah, Abraham, Jacob, John the Baptist, Peter, James and John.)

WE HOLD SAME PRIESTHOOD AS ADAM

Adam, Enoch, Noah, Abraham, Isaac, Jacob, Elijah, Joseph, Peter, James, John, Moroni and others having held the Holy Priesthood of God were all given the opportunity to participate within a divine influence. Each man who holds the Priesthood today has the same opportunity if he keeps himself in harmony with that influence. Each one who holds an office in the Priesthood should cherish and cultivate the Spirit and strive never to let himself take his opportunities for granted and become indifferent.

TAKE UPON YOU MY WHOLE ARMOR

In a wonderful revelation to the Prophet Joseph Smith in which the Lord recounted some of those who have held keys of the Priesthood in the various dispensations, He gave a marvelous admonition. Although only certain ones on the earth hold keys, and those according to proper settings apart, by extension that admonition of the Lord is to every man who is given the high privilege of holding an office in the Holy Priesthood. The Lord said:

> Wherefore, lift up your hearts and rejoice, and gird up your loins, and take upon you my whole armor, that ye may be able to withstand the evil day, having done all, that ye may be able to stand.

> Stand, therefore, having your loins girt about with truth, having on the *breastplate of righteousness*, and your feet shod with the preparation of the gospel of peace, which I have sent mine angels to commit unto you;

> Taking the *shield of faith* wherewith ye shall be able to quench all fiery darts of the wicked;

> And take the *helmet of salvation*, and the *sword of my Spirit*,

which I will pour out upon you, and my word which I reveal unto you, and be agreed as touching all things whatsoever ye ask of me, and be faithful until I come, and ye shall be caught up, that where I am ye shall be also. Amen. (D&C 27:15-18. Italics ours.)

One may not hold any keys of the Priesthood, but he or she should have full appreciation of the fact that had the Lord not preserved those keys through the dispensations and restored the Priesthood and its keys in our time, he or she could not share in the rights, privileges and blessings that he or she does. (We should ever be mindful that the women and children of the Church share in the blessings of the Priesthood.)

GO FORWARD, NOT BACKWARD

The Prophet Joseph Smith asks:

Brethren, shall we not go on in so great a cause? Go forward and not backward. Courage, brethren; and on, on to the victory! Let your hearts rejoice, and be exceedingly glad. Let the earth break forth into singing. Let the dead speak forth anthems of eternal praise to the King Immanuel, who hath ordained, before the world was, that which would enable us to redeem them out of their prison; for the prisoners shall go free.

Let the mountains shout for joy, and all ye valleys cry aloud; and all ye seas and dry lands tell the wonders of your Eternal King! And ye rivers, and brooks, and rills, flow down with gladness. Let the woods and all the trees of the field praise the Lord; and ye solid rocks weep for joy! And let the sun, moon, and the morning stars sing together, and let all the sons of God shout for joy! And let the eternal creations declare his name forever and ever! And again I say, how glorious is the voice we hear from heaven, proclaiming in our ears, glory, and salvation, and honor, and immortality, and eternal life; kingdoms, principalities, and powers!

Behold, the great day of the Lord is at hand; and who can abide the day of his coming, and who can stand when he appeareth? . . . (D&C 128:22-24.)

What Would Jesus Do?

The Priesthood authority is your opportunity to participate with Jesus in bringing about His purposes in the world.

Do you know what He would have you do? Have you recently considered your patriarchal blessing to determine His will concerning you? Ask yourself: What relationship do the Priesthood keys have to my responsibility as a husband? A father? A home teacher? As a holder of the Priesthood, what can I do, as the patriarchs of old did, to bless those about me?

Consider these scriptural passages: D&C 107:53-56; Moses 6:52-62.

SPECIAL INSTRUCTIONS TO THE TEACHER

1. Help the class member distinguish between the Priesthood and the keys of the Priesthood (See Joseph F. Smith, *Gospel Doctrine*, p. 136.) 15th Edition.

2. Have class members identify which keys were restored by the ancient prophets to Joseph Smith, and the significance of these keys today.

3. Help the class members to see the significance of the keys of the Priesthood as they relate to their callings as husbands and fathers.

INSTRUCTIONAL MATERIALS

The Restoration of Keys

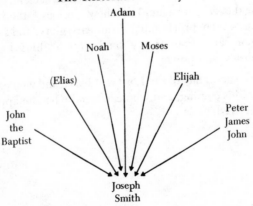

References: D&C 13, 27, 128; *Teachings of the Prophet Joseph Smith* p. 157.

The Priesthood When Jesus Taught

LESSON FOLLOW-UP

Quorum members might be asked to relate specifically the kinds of applications they made from the challenge in lesson two, What would Jesus do?

LESSON OBJECTIVES

Priesthood holders should feel motivated to (1) acquire a deeper understanding of the Priesthood at the time of Jesus and (2) organize as a quorum a meaningful activity designed to extend Priesthood power and blessings to other quorum members.

INTRODUCTION

To begin this lesson, the class instructor might write on the chalkboard these names, and ask class members to describe their understanding of the functioning of each before the coming of Christ and during His ministry:

Aaronic Priesthood
or   **Melchizedek Priesthood**
Levitical Priesthood

(This discussion should not exceed five minutes.)

Now, let the class proceed with the lesson discussion, noting how answers to the questions unfold.

LESSON DEVELOPMENT

THE LORD TAKES THE HIGHER PRIESTHOOD FROM ISRAEL

From the days of Adam through the ministry of Moses there was a continuous lineage of those who held the Melchizedek Priesthood. (D&C 84:6-16.) In the dispensation of Moses "the Lord confirmed a priesthood also upon Aaron and his seed, throughout all their generations, which priesthood also continueth and abideth forever with the priesthood which is after the holiest order of God." (D&C 84:18.)

The Lord has revealed in our day that Moses taught the children of Israel plainly and diligently that which it was necessary for them to know and do that they might be sanctified and behold the face of God. "But they hardened their hearts and could not endure his presence; therefore, the Lord in his wrath, for his anger was kindled against them, swore that they should not enter into his rest while in the wilderness, which rest is the fulness of his glory.

"Therefore, he took Moses out of their midst, and the Holy Priesthood also;

"And the lesser priesthood continued, which priesthood holdeth the key of the ministering of angels and the preparatory gospel,

"Which gospel is the gospel of repentance and of baptism, and the remission of sins, and the law of carnal commandments, which the Lord in his wrath caused to continue with the house of Aaron among the children of Israel until John. . . ." (D&C 84:24-27.)

When the revelation says the Lord took Moses and the Holy Priesthood out of their midst, it means that because he took Moses the Holy Priesthood went in course of time. When Moses went there were still holders of the higher Priesthood in Israel, but Moses took the keys, and without the keys no one could authorize others to be ordained to offices in the Melchizedek Priesthood; hence this Priesthood soon ceased to be among men.

Once when the Prophet Joseph Smith was asked if the Melchizedek Priesthood was taken away with Moses he responded by saying: "All Priesthood is Melchizedek, but there are different portions or degrees of it. That portion which brought Moses to speak with God face to face was taken away; but that which brought the ministry of angels remained. All the prophets had the Melchizedek Priesthood and were ordained by God himself."[1] By this we are to understand that the Aaronic Priesthood is embraced within and is part of the higher order.

Thus we see that because of the perversity of Israel the Melchizedek Priesthood (or the higher portion of it), which had continued among men from Adam until the dispensation of Moses, was taken from Israel with Moses. After that time, although prophets were raised up from

---

[1]Smith, Joseph Fielding, *Teachings of the Prophet Joseph Smith*, Salt Lake City, Deseret News Press, 1938, pp. 180-181.

time to time who were given the Melchizedek Priesthood, as were Isaiah, Jeremiah and Elijah, generally the people of Israel were without the Melchizedek Priesthood and were under the jurisdiction of the Aaronic Priesthood. That is, that portion of the Priesthood which remained was Aaronic. Aaron had been given the keys of that lesser Priesthod, and his sons were called to minister with him in the priest's office.

In anticipation of removing Moses and the higher Priesthood from among Israel after the Lord had chosen Aaron and his sons to minister to him as priests, he relieved the firstborn males of the various tribes of Israel of their Priesthood duties and replaced them with the males of the tribe of Levi. Thus the new organization consisted of Moses, who held the keys of the Melchizedek Priesthood; Aaron, who held the keys of the lesser Priesthood; and Aaron's sons who were priests with him; and the Levites who also held the lesser Priesthood.

AARONIC AND LEVITICAL PRIESTHOOD

President Joseph Fielding Smith, speaking of the Aaronic and Levitical callings, says: "The Aaronic Priesthood is divided into the *Aaronic* and the *Levitical*, yet it is but one Priesthood. This is merely a matter of designating certain duties within the Priesthood. The sons of Aaron, who *presided* in the Aaronic order, were spoken of as holding the *Aaronic Priesthood;* and the sons of Levi, who were not sons of Aaron, were spoken of as the *Levites*. They held the *Aaronic Priesthood* but served under, or in a lesser capacity, than the sons of Aaron."[2]

In ancient Israel the principal place of worship was the tabernacle of the congregation. Because Israel was required to journey for many years, the tabernacle had been designed as a portable structure. The express calling of the Levites was to be in charge of and porters of the tabernacle. Their duties were more of a temporal nature than were those of the sons of Aaron, or the presiding priests. The latter were expressly charged to have care of the sanctuary and the altar—the holy places. (Numbers 18:1-6.)

As long as Aaron presided in the lesser Priesthood he functioned under the direction of Moses, who held the keys of the Melchizedek Priesthood. But when Eleazar, Aaron's oldest living son, received the keys of the lesser Priesthood, and Moses was taken out of Israel, he (Eleazar) became God's mouthpiece to Israel.

[2]McConkie, Bruce R., Compiler, *Doctrines of Salvation:* Sermons and Writings of Joseph Fielding Smith, Salt Lake City, Bookcraft, 1956, Vol. III, p. 86.

The priests of Aaron and the Levites ministered in their respective callings without serious conflict until the death of Solomon. But with the division of Israel into the Northern Kingdom (or Israel) and the Southern Kingdom (or Judah) and with King Jeroboam's establishing an idolatrous worship and making "priests of the lowest of the people, which were not of the sons of Levi," a critical situation arose. (See I Kings 12:31.)

The authorized priests, no longer being permitted to function in the Northern Kingdom, made their way back into the kingdom of Judah and with that exodus "the history of the Lesser Priesthood in the kingdom of Israel was ended. Never again, so far as we know, did the tribe of Levi function as a group in the Aaronic Priesthood among the Ten Tribes."[3]

PRIESTHOOD REMAINS WITH JUDAH

In time the Ten Tribes were taken into captivity and eventually lost. But the Priesthood remained in force in the kingdom of Judah. However, through many difficulties there was a legitimate succession in the Priesthood.

Lee A. Palmer wrote: "With the exception of the time when the office of high priest in the Aaronic Priesthood passed from the house of Eleazar to Eli of the house of Ithamar, and eventually, back to the house of Eleazar, through Zadok, it appears that the high office descended in legitimate succession from Aaron forward to the time of Onias III, 175 B.C."[4]

JOHN THE BAPTIST AND THE PRIESTHOOD

After Onias III there were legitimate priests who continued to function, but the office of high priest was sold and bought and otherwise polluted.

John's birth was an event of signal importance and it, like that of the Lord, was announced by angelic visitation. His father was Zacharias, one of the faithful priests of Aaron, for only they were permitted to burn incense at the altar,[5] and his mother was Elisabeth, one "of the daughters of Aaron." (Luke 1:5.)

The Lord, in our own day, speaking of John, has said he was "filled with the Holy Ghost from his mother's womb.

[3]Palmer, Lee A., *Aaronic Priesthood Through the Centuries*, Salt Lake City, Deseret Book Company, 1964, p. 106.

[4]*Ibid.*, p. 153.

[5]Flavius Josephus; *Antiquities of the Jews;* Book IX, Ch. 10:4.

"For he was baptized while he was yet in his childhood, and was ordained by the angel of God at the time he was eight days old unto this power, to overthrow the kingdom of the Jews, and to make straight the way of the Lord before the face of his people, to prepare them for the coming of the Lord, in whose hand is given all power." (D&C 84:27-28.)

It is significant to recall that when John was born, the keys of the Melchizedek Priesthood were not among the Jews.

John's role as the priest who held the keys of the Aaronic Priesthood was different from that of his predecessors in that office. For 1,500 years they had ministered at the altar in the sanctuary with burnt offerings and sacrifices. He was concerned primarily with heralding the coming of the Lord, calling all men to repentance and performing the initiatory ordinance of the Gospel, and preparing men to receive the power of the Holy Ghost from Him who was mightier than he.

In the Sermon on the Mount the Lord announced that He had come to fulfill the law. (See Matthew 5 and 6 esp.)

DISCIPLES HELD PRIESTHOOD

Prior to the time the Lord gave His Sermon on the Mount, and several months prior to their ordination as apostles, some of His disciples had been ordained priests or to some office in the Melchizedek Priesthood, for they were authorized to perform baptisms.[6]

Later twelve of the disciples were chosen and ordained apostles. In a meeting with the Twelve at Caesarea Philippi the Lord promised the keys of the kingdom of heaven would be given. A week later, when he took Peter, James and John with Him up onto a high mountain, He was transfigured before them, and Moses and Elijah (Elias in the New Testament record) appeared unto them. The Prophet Joseph Smith declared that it was on that occasion that the Lord, Moses and Elijah bestowed the keys of the Priesthood upon Peter, James and John. These keys were later given to all of the Twelve, so that each apostle had power to bind on earth and seal in heaven. (Matthew 18:18.) (See Matthew 16:13-20; 17:1-13.)

The New Testament also contains a record of there having been other officers in the Church: namely, prophets, evangelists, seventies, elders, bishops, priests, teachers, and deacons.

_____
[6]See Clark, J. Reuben, Jr., *Our Lord of the Gospels,* Salt Lake City, Deseret Book Company, 1957, pp. 43, 51; and J. Reuben Clark, Jr., *On the Way to Immortality and Eternal Life,* Salt Lake City, Deseret Book Company, 1950, p. 358.

LESSER AND HIGHER PRIESTHOODS SERVE TOGETHER

The Lord has given unto us the following passage of modern revelation which indicates one specific way in which the lesser Priesthood functioned in relation to the Melchizedek Priesthood in the ancient church. The Lord counsels: "And if any man among you be strong in the Spirit, let him take with him him that is weak, that he may be edified in all meekness, that he may become strong also.

"Therefore, take with you those who are ordained unto the lesser priesthood, and send them before you to make appointments, and to prepare the way, and to fill appointments that you yourselves are not able to fill.

"*Behold, this is the way that mine apostles, in ancient days, built up my Church unto me.*" (D&C 84:106-108. Italics ours.)

APPLICATION

What Would Jesus Do?

By His example, Jesus showed us that the Priesthood was given to men in order to help them bless others. Its ultimate to help men enter the rest of the Lord, or the fulness of his glory. (See D&C 84:24.)

Your priesthood quorum or group may wish to consider these activities for bringing the Priesthood's power and blessings to other Priesthood bearers:

1. A plan for regularly taking Priesthood discussions to homebound Priesthood holders through the home teachers assigned to them.

2. A program of writing regularly to Priesthood bearers away with the armed forces, at college, or on missions or isolated otherwise.

3. A plan, through home teaching, to better encourage inactive quorum members to attend these Priesthood meeting discussions.

Study and ponder D&C 84.

1. The focus of the background material should be to help the Priesthood holder understand that the Melchizedek Priesthood enables one to enter the rest of the Lord and that this blessing is available only in and through the Melchizedek Priesthood.

2. Allow sufficient time for a discussion on a quorum project or activity to help others.

INSTRUCTIONAL MATERIALS

Chalkboard illustration comparing the Melchizedek and Aaronic orders:

D&C 84:27

Melchizedek (Full Gospel)	Aaronic (Preparatory Gospel)
1. Faith in Jesus Christ	1. Faith in Jesus Christ
2. Repentance	2. Repentance
3. Baptism for remission of sins	3. Baptism for remission of sins
4. The gift of the Holy Ghost	

The Priesthood Is Restored

LESSON FOLLOW-UP

Quorum members could be asked to report on what steps they have taken to bring more of the blessings of the Priesthood to others, such as the homebound, those away, and the inactive. (This discussion should not exceed five minutes.)

LESSON OBJECTIVES

The Priesthood holder should feel motivated to (1) *acquire a deeper understanding of the restoration of the Priesthood, and* (2) *obtain the spirit and power of Elijah as it relates to his own family, living and dead.*

INTRODUCTION

Have you ever thought about the responsibility that rests upon an ambassador or other diplomat who has been empowered to act in behalf of a nation of men? Have you ever considered the authority of an executive in one of the large corporations or industries of the world and the responsibility incumbent upon him? Perhaps you yourself have an occupation which imposes awesome authority and responsibility upon you in the daily or periodic decisions you are obliged to make! Granted the authority and responsibility suggested here are of momentous import and involve many implications, but how do these compare with or relate to the authority and responsibility of one who holds the Holy Priesthood of God?

(The class teacher at this point could write on the chalkboard these names: John the Baptist; Moses; Elias; Elijah; Peter, James and John.

Then class members might be asked to tell how their Priesthood has been affected by visits in this dispensation of these heavenly visitors.)

23

RESTITUTION OF ALL THINGS

Anciently Peter called men to repentance and said there would be a time of refreshing which would come with the second coming to the earth of Jesus the Christ. Peter also spoke of "the times of restitution of all things, which God hath spoken by the mouth of all the holy prophets since the world began." (Acts 3:19-21.)

At present we are concerned with two principal things Peter said: (1) that there would be "times of restitution" or an age of restoration, and (2) in this age of restoration God would restore all things spoken by the mouth of all his holy prophets since the world began.

THE FATHER AND THE SON VISIT JOSEPH

In the spring of 1820 God the Eternal Father and Jesus Christ the Son of God—the Redeemer of man—appeared to Joseph Smith, Jr., in the woods near Palmyra, New York. They gave him initial instructions in preparation for his modern prophetic calling. In September of 1823, and periodically at least through June of 1829, Moroni, a resurrected being, visited Joseph Smith. Moroni revealed the Book of Mormon to him and further prepared him for his prophetic call. Moroni had been a record keeper and prophet of the ancient inhabitants of the American continent.

Even as John the Baptist received the word of God in the wilderness under angelic guidance, so was Joseph Smith taught by heavenly teachers.

JOHN THE BAPTIST COMES

When the period of initial preparation was completed and the Lord was ready for His youthful prophet to act with authority in His name, He sent John the Baptist to him with the keys of the Aaronic Priesthood. It was on May 15, 1829, that John came. John the Baptist indicated "that he acted under the direction of Peter, James and John, who held the keys of the Priesthood of Melchizedek." (Joseph Smith 2:72.) John laid his hands upon the heads of Joseph Smith and his associate, Oliver Cowdery. Then John said: "Upon you my fellow servants, in the name of Messiah, I confer the Priesthood of Aaron, which holds the keys of the ministering of angels, and of the gospel of repentance, and of baptism by immersion for the remission of sins; and this shall never be taken again from the earth until the sons of Levi do offer again an offering unto the Lord in righteousness." (Joseph Smith 2:69.)

Thus, John, who was especially raised up by God to hold the keys of the Aaronic Priesthood and to prepare the way for the Christ, restored the Aaronic Priesthood. The keys of this lesser Priesthood involve "the ministering of angels and the preparatory gospel; Which gospel is the gospel of repentance and of baptism, and the remission of sins, . . ." (D&C 84:26-27.)

THE HIGHER PRIESTHOOD RESTORED

Shortly after the restoration of the Aaronic Priesthood, Joseph and Oliver received the Melchizedek Priesthood from Peter, James, and John.

In a revelation later, the Lord referred to Peter, James, and John, and said: ". . . whom I have sent unto you, by whom I have ordained you and confirmed you to be apostles, and especial witnesses of my name, and bear the keys of your ministry and of the same things which I revealed unto them; Unto whom I have committed the keys of my kingdom, and a dispensation of the gospel for the last times; and for the fulness of times, in the which I will gather together in one all things, both which are in heaven, and which are on earth." (D&C 27:12-13.)

FOUR GREAT VISIONS

On April 3, 1836, after the completion of the Kirtland Temple, four great visions were given to Joseph Smith and Oliver Cowdery. In the first vision the Lord Jesus Christ appeared and accepted the temple as His house.

Modern holy writ declares: "After this vision closed, the heavens were again opened unto us; and Moses appeared before us, and committed unto us the keys of the gathering of Israel from the four parts of the earth, and the leading of the ten tribes from the land of the north.

"After this, Elias appeared, and committed the dispensation of the gospel of Abraham, saying that in us and our seed all generations after us should be blessed.

"After this vision had closed, another great and glorious vision burst upon us; for Elijah the prophet, who was taken to heaven without tasting death, stood before us, and said:

Behold, the time has fully come, which was spoken of by the mouth of Malachi—testifying that he [Elijah] should be sent, before the great and dreadful day of the Lord came—

To turn the hearts of the fathers to the children, and the children to the fathers, lest the whole earth be smitten with a curse—

Therefore, the keys of this dispensation are committed into your hands; and by this ye may know that the great and dreadful day of the Lord is near, even at the doors. (D&C 110:11-16.)

ELIJAH'S IMPORTANT MISSION

President Joseph Fielding Smith informs us: "The higher ordinances, the greater blessings which are essential to exaltation in the kingdom of God, and which can only be obtained in certain places, no man has a right to perform except as he receives the authority to do it from the one who holds the keys . . . Elijah restored to this Church and, if they would receive it, to the world, the keys of the sealing power; and that sealing power puts the stamp of approval upon *every ordinance* that is done in this Church and *more particularly those that are performed in the temples of the Lord.*"[1] Further: "Some members of the Church have been confused in thinking that Elijah came with the keys of baptism for the dead or of salvation for the dead. Elijah's keys were *greater* than that. They were the keys of *sealing,* and *those keys of sealing pertain to the living and embrace the dead who are willing to repent.*"[2]

In a revelation concerning the Twelve Apostles given to the Prophet Joseph Smith after the conferral of keys at the Kirtland Temple, the Lord indicated the power of the Priesthood was given unto the First Presidency and the Twelve "for the last time, in the which is the dispensation of the fulness of times." He then declared they held the power, "in connection with all those who have received a dispensation at any time from the beginning of the creation; . . ." and said, "For verily I say unto you the keys of the dispensation, which ye have received, have come down from the fathers, and last of all, being sent down from heaven unto you." (D&C 112:30-32.)

In an epistle written by Joseph Smith he names many of those from the ancient world who visited him on various occasions and then records: ". . . And the voice of Michael, the archangel; the voice of Gabriel, and of Raphael, and of divers angels, from Michael or Adam down to the present time, all declaring their dispensation, their rights, their keys, their honors, their majesty and glory, and the power of their priesthood; giving line upon line, precept upon precept; here a little, and there a little; giving us consolation by holding forth that which is

---

[1]McConkie, Bruce R., Compiler, *Doctrines of Salvation:* Sermons and Writings of Joseph Fielding Smith, Salt Lake City, Bookcraft, 1956. Vol. III, p. 129.

[2]*Ibid.*, p. 130.

to come, confirming our hope!" (D&C 128:21. See also D&C 132:45-47.)

Thus all of the keys of the Holy Priesthood from previous dispensations were restored to the earth at the beginning of this, the last dispensation of the Gospel.

THE TWELVE RECEIVE THE KEYS

Prior to the martyrdom of the Prophet Joseph Smith he bestowed all of the keys and authorities which he held upon all of the members of the Council of the Twelve. President Joseph Fielding Smith says: "All members of the Council of the Twelve since that day have also been given all of these keys and powers. But these powers cannot be exercised by any one of them *until*, if the occasion arises, he is called to be the *presiding officer* of the Church. The Twelve, therefore, in the setting apart of the President do not give him any additional priesthood, but *confirm* upon him that which he has *already* received; they *set him apart* to the office, which it is their right to do."[3] Therefore the keys of the Priesthood are preserved from generation to generation. They are held by each member of the Council of the Twelve, although there is only one man on the earth at a time who holds those keys of the Priesthood in the sense that he can exercise or use them in their fulness. In their nature keys are the right and power of presidency, and since only one man can preside over all others, only one man can "hold," meaning use and exercise, all of the keys at any one time. (D&C 132:7.)

It is not necessary however for one to hold the keys of the Priesthood, that is, become President of the Church, in order to have a fulness of the Priesthood. As President Smith says: "If we want to receive the fulness of the Priesthood of God, then we must receive the fulness of the ordinances of the house of the Lord and keep his commandments. . . . *No man can get the fulness of the Priesthood outside of the temple of the Lord.* . . . Every man who is faithful and will receive these ordinances and blessings obtains a fulness of the Priesthood, and the Lord has said that 'he makes them equal in power, and in might, and in dominion.' "[4]

Thus in the restoration of the Melchizedek Priesthood, with its various keys and authorities, the Lord has provided the means that men may not only repent and be baptized, but that they may go to the temples of the Lord and receive the higher ordinances and a fulness of the Priesthood, so that if they are faithful to their covenants they may become joint heirs with Jesus Christ.[5]

---

[3]*Ibid.*, p. 155.

[4]*Ibid.*, pp. 131-132.

[5]*Documentary History of the Church*, Salt Lake City, Deseret News, 1909, Vol. V, p. 424.

Hence, the restitution of all things, prophesied by Peter, belongs to the age of the world in which we live. Each man who holds the Melchizedek Priesthood has a tremendous blessing, a great potential. Through righteousness he may become a joint heir with Jesus the Christ. What greater blessing can a man ask?

APPLICATION:

What Would Jesus Do?

One of the greatest purposes of our Savior having the priesthood keys restored was to seal families together for time and eternity. Thus the mission of Elijah is to turn the hearts of the children to their fathers. (See D&C 2:2.) This pertains significantly *to the living* as well as the dead.

As you contemplate this, ask yourself:

1. Am I holding home evenings regularly in my home as a means of turning my children's hearts to me, and my heart to them?

2. Do I hold an active temple recommend and use it regularly?

3. Do I have a Book of Remembrance and have I assisted or am I assisting my children to prepare theirs?

4. What am I doing in behalf of my forebears in genealogical research or in temple work?

Read and ponder; D&C 68:25-28; D&C 128; 132:7, 15-25.

SPECIAL INSTRUCTIONS TO THE TEACHER

1. Your testimony regarding the restoration of the Priesthood will help strengthen your brethren.

2. You may want to show the filmstrip, *The Restoration of the Priesthood.*

3. Emphasize that Elijah's mission pertains significantly to the living as well as the dead. Show quorum members that they have a responsibility now to turn their hearts to their children and to their parents as well as turning the hearts of their children to them. Illustrate the ways this can be done.

ILLUSTRATION

ELIJAH'S MISSION

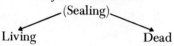
(Sealing)

Living · Dead

1.	Placing family first	1.	Genealogical research
2.	Teaching children the gospel	2.	Temple work

1. Placing family first
2. Teaching children the gospel
   a. Regular family prayer
   b. Regular family home evening
   c. Teaching moments
   d. Example
3. Honoring parents, wife, children

1. Genealogical research
2. Temple work

INSTRUCTIONAL MATERIALS

Meetinghouse library pictures and filmstrip:
OPO32 The Restoration of the Aaronic Priesthood Monument
ISO19 Joseph Smith's First Vision
ISO23 Authority Restored
Filmstrip: *The Restoration of the Priesthood*

Section

2

Your Priesthood
Represents
Authority

Every Man Is a Steward

LESSON FOLLOW-UP

One or two class members could be called upon to report briefly what they have done during the last week to exercise their rights as Priesthood holders, relating to the authority restored by Elijah.

(This discussion should not exceed five minutes.)

LESSON OBJECTIVES

The Priesthood holder should feel motivated to (1) obtain a clear understanding of the place of stewardship in the Priesthood, and (2) determine specific ways in which he can improve in his stewardship responsibilities.

INTRODUCTION

To introduce the lesson, the teacher might ask class members to describe some of the ways they serve as stewards—in their employment, in community affairs, in the Church, and in their families.

LESSON DEVELOPMENT

THE FULNESS OF THE EARTH IS YOURS

The ancient psalmist sang: "The earth is the Lord's, and the fulness thereof; the world, and they that dwell therein." (Psalms 24:1.)

In our own dispensation of the Gospel, after giving counsel regarding certain commandments, the Lord declared: "Verily I say, that inasmuch as ye do this, the fulness of the earth is yours, the beasts of the field and the fowls of the air, and that which climbeth upon the trees and walketh upon the earth; Yea, and the herb, and the good things which come of the earth, whether for food or for raiment, or for houses, or for barns, or for orchards, or for gardens, or for vineyards. Yea, all things which come of the earth, in the season thereof, are made for the benefit and the use of man, both to please the eye and to gladden the heart; Yea, for food and for raiment, for taste and for smell, to strengthen the body and to enliven the soul. And it pleaseth God that he hath given all these things unto man; for unto this end were they made to be used, with judgment, not to excess, neither by extortion." (D&C 59:16-20.)

The earth itself was organized as an abode for man, a place where God's spirit children could gain bodies of flesh and bones, be richly blessed, prove themselves, and prepare for even further progress. (Abraham 3:22-26.) The Book of Mormon prophets call this life a probationary state.

EACH PERSON IS A STEWARD

Inasmuch as the earth is the Lord's, and He prepared it for man's habitation and blessing, and this life is a probationary state for the development of God's children, men are accountable to God in all things. In a word, *each person is a steward.*

When the Gospel was restored through Joseph Smith, from the early Kirtland period through the Nauvoo period, the Lord gave His prophet revelations on the subject of stewardship. Particularly during what is called the Kirtland period, special instructions and charges were revealed to the Prophet regarding the law of consecration and stewardship. (See esp. D&C 42, 51, 70, 72, and 78.) The law as it was given and required of the Saints at that time enabled them to operate what is known as the United Order. That is, the United Order was the vehicle used in that day to aid in living the law of stewardship. Our immediate concern is not with the detailed requirements of the United Order, to which we are not at present subject and are therefore not benefactors, but with the general principle or law of stewardship, *which is binding* upon us, and in appropriate measure upon all mankind.

In many places in the scriptures we are told that every man will be judged according to his own works. (For example: Matthew 16:27; Revelation 20:13; 1 Nephi 15:33; D&C 19:3.) Stewardship in a sense is a more specific and precise formulation of the concept of responsibility incumbent upon all men.

After relating what is known as the parable of the unjust steward to the Jews, the Lord made the following declaration: "He that is faithful in that which is least is faithful also in much: and he that is unjust in the least is unjust also in much. If therefore ye have not been faithful in the unrighteous mammon, who will commit to your trust the true riches? And if ye have not been faithful in that which is another man's, who shall give you that which is your own?" (Luke 16:10-12.)

Among the principles taught here are these:

(1) If one cannot be faithful in a small stewardship he will not be entrusted with a larger one.

(2) If one cannot discharge a responsible management and use of his worldly goods for righteous purposes, he will not be entrusted with eternal values.

(3) If one is not faithful in the care of those things which belong to the Lord but which He has permitted him to use, he will not be given a permanent or eternal inheritance of his own.

STEWARDSHIP AND JUDGMENT

One of the most impressive statements the Lord made regarding the final judgment concerns the law of stewardship. He said when the Son of Man comes in His glory, He will separate men from one another "as a shepherd divideth his sheep from the goats." The basis of the division which He describes in this account is the use one makes of what he has in rendering service to others. Those who are faithful in the use of what they have in rendering service to others are the doers of the word, the faithful stewards, the sheep, as it were, and will receive eternal life. On the contrary, those who are unfaithful, selfish, careless and indifferent in the use of what they have, and do not render service commensurate with their ability, are the non-doers of the word, the unfaithful stewards, the goats, as it were. They will "go away into everlasting punishment." (Matthew 25:31-46.)

In our own day the Lord has reaffirmed the same principle with unequivocal force. He said: "If any man shall take of the abundance which I have made, and impart not his portion, according to the law of my gospel, unto the poor and the needy, he shall, with the wicked, lift up his eyes in hell, being in torment." (D&C 104:18.)

In addition to teachings expressly concerning care of the poor and rendering service, the Lord gave other instructions which constitute part of the general law of stewardship. For example, Jesus said: "And take heed to yourselves, lest at any time your hearts be overcharged with surfeiting [overindulgences], and drunkenness, *and cares of this life*, and so that day come upon you unawares. For as a snare shall it come on all them that dwell on the face of the whole earth." (Luke 21:34-35.) "For the Son of Man is as a man taking a far journey, who left his house, and *gave authority to his servants, and to every man his work*, and commanded the porter to watch. Watch ye therefore: for ye know not when the master of the house cometh, at even, or at midnight, or at the cockcrowing, or in the morning: Lest coming suddenly he find you sleeping." (Mark 13:34-36. Italics ours.)

PARABLE OF THE POUNDS

One of the most comprehensive statements the Lord has made on the law of stewardship is His wonderful parable of the ten pounds. Here He speaks of a "certain nobleman" who was going into a far country to receive a kingdom for himself, and before leaving he called each of his ten servants and gave to each one pound. Upon receiving his kingdom he returned and asked his servants to give an account of what they had done with their respective stewardships. One servant had increased his pound to ten and was given authority over ten cities. Another servant had increased his pound to five and was given authority over five cities. A third servant had done nothing with his pound and offered a poor excuse for having done so; consequently his pound was taken from him and given to him who had ten. In addition to the three categories of faithfulness or the lack of it here described, the parable also included mention of citizens of the kingdom who rejected the nobleman as their king. When the servants gave their accounting, those who rejected the king were slain. (Luke 19:11-28.) These four categories suggest what the Lord described to the Prophet Joseph Smith in the vision of the three degrees of glory. That is, those who are valiant and faithful to their stewardships will be heirs of the celestial kingdom of glory. Those who are good but less valiant and faithful of their stewardships will be heirs of the terrestrial glory. Those who are not valiant at all to their stewardships will lose them but will eventually be heirs of the telestial glory. Those citizens of the kingdom who "hate" the Lord and rebel against Him will be condemned to perdition. (See D&C 76.)

EVERYONE HAS A STEWARDSHIP

No one is justified in assuming that because he is not a bishop or stake president or something else he is without a stewardship. Everyone has a stewardship. The Lord has said: "For it is expedient that I, the Lord, should make every man accountable, as a steward over earthly blessings, which I have made and prepared for my creatures." (D&C 104:13.) Furthermore, "All those who reject the testimony of the elders of Israel will be held responsible and will have to give an accounting for their stewardship, just as we will give an accounting of our stewardship as elders and teachers of the people."[1]

---

[1]McConkie, Bruce R., Compiler, *Doctrines of Salvation:* Sermons and Writings of Joseph Fielding Smith; Salt Lake City, Bookcraft, 1956, Vol. III, p. 117.

Every man who bears the Melchizedek Priesthood has the responsibility to be faithful to his covenants irrespective of the callings or lack of special callings he may have in the Church. President Joseph Fielding Smith has said: *"The apostle is under no greater commandment to be true to his covenant and membership in the Church than is the ordinary elder, or seventy, or any other individual holding the Priesthood.* It is true the apostle has a greater responsibility, or calling, in the Priesthood, but no greater responsibility to be true to Gospel principles and commandments. Especially is this so, if the elder has received the ordinances of the house of the Lord. . . .

"The punishment for the violation of this covenant of the Priesthood will come as readily and as surely upon the ordained elder as it will upon the apostle in the Church, who may turn away into forbidden paths and to the neglect of duty."[2]

SEVERAL FACTORS IN STEWARDSHIP

There are several factors which contribute to the various magnitudes of stewardship a man has. Such factors are time, talent, means, and opportunities. Surely each individual is a custodian of the years of mortality with which he is blessed and is going to be accountable for the use of those years. Likewise each one is the custodian of his intellectual and other personal skills and endowments and is going to be accountable for the use he makes of them. We have already discussed parables of the Lord's in which He made it very clear that each person is a steward over his possessions, his temporal wealth, be it little or much, and is going to be held responsible for what he does with it. And, no doubt, each one will be made to give an account for what he has made of his opportunities, be they of the nature of environment, associations, education, positions or various other situations.

Each man who has had the Melchizedek Priesthood conferred upon him should realize that his authority to act is commensurate with his stewardship. He should examine his own life to clearly determine the nature of his stewardship and likewise determine specific ways in which he can improve in the administration of his affairs and make a firm resolve to do so. He should seek the aid of the Spirit of the Lord to help him do so.

JOY COMES TO THE FAITHFUL STEWARD

Each of us should try to be conscious always of these *promises* of

[2]*Ibid.*, pp. 119-120.

the Lord: "And whoso is found a faithful, a just, and a wise steward shall enter into the joy of his Lord, and shall inherit *eternal life.*" (D&C 51:19.)

"And he that is a faithful and wise steward shall inherit *all things.*" (D&C 78:22.)

". . . for it is required of the Lord, at the hand of every steward to render an account of his stewardship, both in time and in eternity. For he who is faithful and wise in time is accounted worthy to inherit the *mansions* prepared for him of my Father." (D&C 72:3-4. Italics ours.)

APPLICATION

What Would Jesus Do?

The Lord has given each of us stewardships. We have the stewardships related to holding the Priesthood, being a husband and father, and being a member of the Church. We should ask ourselves, what would Jesus have us do with these stewardships He has given us? How am I doing in my stewardship to my wife, to my children, in my Church assignments, with my money, with my lands, with health, with my talents and gifts? Am I relying on the Spirit of the Lord for help and guidance?

Read and ponder: D&C 72:3-4; D&C 51:19; Matthew 25:14-30; D&C 50:13-34.

SPECIAL INSTRUCTIONS TO THE TEACHER

You may want to ask a quorum member to prepare and present the Parable of the Pounds.

Discuss stewardship responsibilities as they relate to (1) the home, (2) the quorum, (3) home teaching, and (4) other Church responsibilities.

Discuss: What does it mean to render an account of your stewardship? Ask: How does one do this today?

Assign two or three class members to trace their Priesthood lineage to Peter, James and John at the beginning of the next week's class. (See Introduction, lesson six.)

Meetinghouse Library picture:

OP198 Earth From Afar. Can be used at the beginning of the lesson to emphasize that the Lord created the earth.

Priesthood — a Sacred Gift

LESSON FOLLOW-UP

Inquire of the quorum members if pondering their responsibilities as stewards has helped them in their relationship with their families and with their Church assignments. Have them give specific illustrations.

(This discussion should not exceed five minutes.)

LESSON OBJECTIVE

Priesthood holders should be motivated to contemplate what the Priesthood can mean in their personal lives.

INTRODUCTION

It was suggested in the previous lesson that the teacher assign two or three class members to begin this week's discussion by tracing their Priesthood lineage to Peter, James and John.

Each person assigned could also tell a trait in the character of each person in his Priesthood lineage which he would like to emulate in honoring and strengthening his Priesthood.

LESSON DEVELOPMENT

HOW DOES ONE RETAIN PRIESTHOOD POWER?

After one has once received the Holy Priesthood, how is he to maintain its influence and power in his personal life?

(The teacher at this point may ask class members to name some of the ways they can keep the Priesthood's power alive in their own lives. Then the teacher could proceed with the discussion.)

First, the man who holds the Priesthood should faithfully do all of the things that he knows he should do and avoid all of those things which are repugnant to the Spirit of the Lord. For example, he knows that he should be honest, true, chaste, benevolent, virtuous, patient, kind, considerate, forgiving, helpful, loving, and that he should do good to all men. Perhaps he may need to examine carefully some of his conduct, or possible conduct, and modify it in view of these principles.

Second, the man who holds the Priesthood should study the teachings of the former prophets in the scriptures and elsewhere. He should also ponder the words which come from the living oracles of God. The Lord has raised up living prophets for the blessings of His people and surely those who have received the Holy Priesthood should cherish the living word.

Third, one who holds the Priesthood should so conduct his own life that he is continuously in harmony with the Spirit of the Lord. As President Brigham Young said: "It is your privilege and duty to live so that you know when the word of the Lord is spoken to you and when the mind of the Lord is revealed to you."[1] Furthermore, after naming the high priests, seventies, elders, bishops, priests, teachers, and deacons, President Young said: "It is their duty to live so that they know and understand the mind and will of the Lord concerning the people to whom they administer, as much as it is mine to know the mind and will of the Lord concerning the entire people. And it is *the duty of every father and mother to live so that they may have the mind and will of the Lord concerning their duties to their families.* If they are not called to exercise the Priesthood which they hold, more than to administer to their children, it is their duty to live so as to know how to teach, lead, and advise their children."[2] (Italics ours.)

Fourth, one who holds the Priesthood should participate fully in the kingdom. He should observe faithfully the rules, commandments and covenants of the Gospel. He should attend his meetings. He should actively engage in genealogical work; and he should attend temple sessions frequently if a temple is within a reasonable distance of his residence. He should have in his heart the desire to spread the Gospel and guide others into the Church. He should cooperate in the pronouncement of President David O. McKay: "Every member a missionary." He should be honest in all of his financial contributions to the kingdom, such as tithes, fast offering, building fund, missionary fund, and welfare. He should actively participate, not only financially, but physically, if possible, in sustaining the welfare program of the Church.

And fifth, one who holds the Priesthood should sustain the brethren. He should sustain his quorum leaders, his ward leaders, his stake leaders, and the general Church officers, and the General Authorities of the Church. In a revelation through the Prophet Joseph Smith, the Lord revealed at least in part what it means to sustain the brethren. He said: "Therefore, strengthen your brethren in all your conversation, in all

[1] *Journal of Discourses*, Vol. 18, p. 72.
[2] *Ibid.*, p. 71.

your prayers, in all your exhortations, and in all your doings." (D&C 108:7.)

PRIESTHOOD IS A SACRED GIFT

The Holy Priesthood is a sacred gift of God, and is given to men for the express purpose of building God's kingdom and rendering service to one's family and fellowmen, and if one is faithful in the performance of these things, it will be a means to his own exaltation. The Priesthood is not to be used for selfish purposes. President Lorenzo Snow said: "We have the same Priesthood that Jesus had, and we have got to do as He did, to make sacrifices of our own desires and feelings as He did, perhaps not to die martyrs as He did, but we have got to make sacrifices in order to carry out the purposes of God, or we shall not be worthy of this Holy Priesthood and be saviors of the world."[3]

MANY CALLED, FEW CHOSEN

There is no more powerful and sublime statement as to how an individual can maintain the authority of the Priesthood in his *personal* life than that which came through the Prophet Joseph Smith. It reads: "Behold, there are many called, but few are chosen. And why are they not chosen? Because their hearts are set so much upon the things of this world, and aspire to the honors of men, that they do not learn this one lesson—That the rights of the priesthood are inseparably connected with the powers of heaven, and that the powers of heaven cannot be controlled nor handled only upon the principles of righteousness. That they may be conferred upon us, it is true; but when we undertake to cover our sins, or to gratify our pride, our vain ambition, or to exercise control or dominion or compulsion upon the souls of the children of men, in any degree of unrighteousness, behold, the heavens withdraw themselves; the Spirit of the Lord is grieved; and when it is withdrawn, Amen to the priesthood or the authority of that man. Behold, ere he is aware, he is left unto himself, to kick against the pricks, to persecute the saints, and to fight against God.

"We have learned by sad experience that it is the nature and disposition of almost all men, as soon as they get a little authority, as they suppose, they will immediately begin to exercise unrighteous dominion. Hence many are called, but few are chosen.

"No power or influence can or ought to be maintained by virtue of the Priesthood, only by persuasion, by long-suffering, by gentleness and meekness, and by love unfeigned; By kindness, and pure knowledge, which shall greatly enlarge the soul without hypocrisy, and without guile." (D&C 121:34-42.)

---

[3]*Ibid.*, Vol. 23, pp. 341-342.

What Would Jesus Do?

T he principle of personal sacrifice is evident in the life of our Savior as He ministered among men. Others' needs were more important than His own. How might you apply this same principle to those in your watchcare? You might want to type or print President Lorenzo Snow's quotation on a card to be carried in your wallet. Refer to this to remind you that your Priesthood is "to do as He did."

Read and ponder D&C 121:34-42; Alma 13:1-31: D&C 84:33-43.

SPECIAL INSTRUCTIONS TO THE TEACHER

1. Discuss the oath and covenant of the Priesthood as it relates to receiving the Melchizedek Priesthood. (D&C 84:35-41.)

The Oath of the Priesthood	The Covenant of the Priesthood	
God	Man	God
Solemn and sworn promise of Deity that those who keep their part of the covenant shall inherit all things according to the covenant.	Solemnly agrees: 1. To magnify his calling. 2. To keep the commandments. 3. To live by every word from God. 4. To walk in paths of righteousness and virtue.	Agrees: 1. To give an inheritance of exaltation and Godhood in His presence.

2. Challenge quorum members to write the quotation of Lorenzo Snow on a small card and place it in their wallets.

3. Discuss how the principle of sacrifice relates to their personal lives, such as in being a husband, a father, or in doing Priesthood work.

INSTRUCTIONAL MATERIAL

Meetinghouse library picture:
OP033-Priesthood Ordinations

Through the Law, the Lord Governs

LESSON FOLLOW-UP

Ask: How many took the challenge to record President Lorenzo Snow's statement on a card for their wallet? Have one or two quorum members report its effects upon them.

LESSON OBJECTIVES

The Priesthood holder should feel motivated to: (1) determine the need for the authority and power of the Priesthood; (2) Consider how he can use the authority and power of his Priesthood to bless his family and others.

INTRODUCTION

If possible the class leader might invite an attorney to begin the lesson discussion with a five-minute talk on how law governs in the affairs of men. These thoughts might be helpful:

Suppose someone came to your home. Upon your opening the door to him he entered and began to go from room to room examining anything that seemed of interest to him. Or, suppose a group of men came to your home, entered, and began to remove your home furnishings and other personal possessions. Or, suppose someone came to your home and demanded that your wife and children go with him. Suppose someone declared himself a senator from a given state and attempted to enter the federal senate. In these and endless other examples the underlying question one would ask is: "By what right or authority. . . ?"

LESSON DEVELOPMENT

THERE IS LAW IN ALL THINGS

Cities have laws. States and provinces have laws. Nations have laws. There are even international laws. Through the centuries, philosophers, scientists, and others have sought to discover and formulate the laws of both the animate and inanimate realms of the natural world. Thus it appears that the vast complex of things we call the universe is a mass of law. Regarding the universality of law, the Lord revealed the following to the prophet Joseph Smith: "All kingdoms have a law given; And there are many kingdoms; for there is no space in which there is no kingdom; and there is no kingdom in which there is no space, either a greater or a lesser kingdom. And unto every kingdom is given a law; and unto every law there are certain bounds also and conditions." (D&C 88:36-38.)

Laws then are not only universal but have their bounds (limitations) and conditions. It is unreasonable for men to have this principle verified day after day, year after year, generation after generation in their experiences of the social, physical, and other dimensions of life, and then assume that God operates totally devoid of law and is promiscuous in His relations with mankind.

In every age of the world's history when the Gospel has been upon the earth, there have been persons whom the Lord has especially chosen and authorized to act in His name. No man has the legal right to act for or in behalf of another man or men in civil matters unless he has been duly commissioned and authorized to so act. Similarly it is highly presumptuous, to say the least, to assume that anyone, irrespective of his moral worth, can take it upon himself to speak or act in behalf of God when he has not been duly commissioned and authorized by God according to the law which God Himself has established.

Long before the 19th century the voices of the prophets had been silenced. The written word of the dead prophets retained some of its vitality. The light of Christ which enlightens every man who comes into the world stimulated some men to seek the Lord and His righteousness. Yet there were no living oracles of God and the gifts, keys, and powers which accompany them. There was no authoritative voice among men. The redeeming power of the Gospel could not be administered.

In 1820, when the Father and the Son appeared to Joseph Smith in the First Vision, the Lord unequivocably and categorically renounced the existing sects of the world.

JOSEPH CALLED BY FATHER AND SON

The Father and the Son personally called Joseph to be the instrument through which the fulness of the everlasting Gospel would be restored. Joseph well understood that which his successors were eventually to understand, attested by President Joseph F. Smith in 1904: "I am not leading the Church of Jesus Christ, nor the Latter-day Saints, and I want this distinctly understood. No man does. Joseph did not do it; Brigham did not do it; neither did John Taylor. Neither did Wilford Woodruff, nor Lorenzo Snow, and Joseph F. Smith, least of them all, is not leading the Church of Jesus Christ of Latter-day Saints, and will not lead it. They were instruments in God's hands in accomplishing what they did. God did it through them. We are only instruments whom God may choose and use to do his work. All that we can do we should do to strengthen them in the midst of weaknesses, in the great calling to which they are called. But remember that God leads the work. It is His. It is not man's work."[1]

MUST BE CALLED AS WAS AARON

Inasmuch as this is God's work, not man's, God chooses whom He will as His instruments. Paul stated this clearly when he wrote: "And no man taketh this honour unto himself, but he that is called of God, as was Aaron." (Hebrews 5:4.) Aaron was called by revelation through God's prophet. The Lord said unto him: "And take thou unto thee Aaron thy brother, and his sons with him, from among the children of Israel, that he may minister unto me in the priest's office, even Aaron, Nadad, and Abihu, Eleazar and Ithamar, Aaron's sons." (Exodus 28:1.)

On the evening of the last supper, the Lord reminded His apostles: "Ye have not chosen me, but I have chosen you, and ordained you, that ye should go and bring forth fruit, and that your fruit should remain: . . ." (John 15:16.)

BAPTISM BY AUTHORITY

In 1830, having been directed to do so, the Prophet organized the Church. There were some individuals who wanted to enter the Church without rebaptism, in consequence of which the Lord gave a brief but very important revelation regarding the authority He recognized. It reads: "Behold, I say unto you that all old covenants have I caused to be done away in this thing; and this is a new and an everlasting covenant, even that which was from the beginning. Wherefore, although a man should be baptised an hundred times it availeth him nothing, for you cannot enter in at the strait gate by the law of Moses, neither by your dead works. For it is because of your dead works that I have caused this last covenant and this church to be built up unto me, even as in days of old. Wherefore, enter ye in at the gate, as I have com-

---

[1]Smith, Joseph F., *Gospel Doctrine* (Fifth Edition), Salt Lake City, Deseret Book Company, 1939, pp. 138-139.

manded, and seek not to counsel your God. Amen." (D&C 22.)

The Lord informs us that although the covenant He revealed was new to the world when it was revealed, in reality it is an everlasting covenant. All former covenants are done away, and irrespective of the number of times one were baptized without legitimate authority it would still be considered dead works. His authority is necessary if the work is to be valid and acceptable.

Anciently Paul rebaptized some folks at Ephesus when there was a question regarding the legitimacy of their previous baptism. (Acts 19: 1-7.)

Furthermore, with the full establishment of the Lord's Church, both among the Nephites and in the present dispensation, it was necessary that all those who had been baptized previously by legitimate authority for a remission of sins be baptized again for admission into the Church. (See 3 Nephi 19:11-13.)[2] In these instances the question, however, was not one of authority. The persons involved had been baptized by legal administrators who had authority so to act. But their baptism had been for the remission of sins and not for admission to the Church because there was no organized Church at the time. When the Church was later organized they were rebaptized to become members of it. There is no ordinance of rebaptism in the Church in the normal or usual course of events.

Thus the Lord was not speaking idly in the Sermon on the Mount nor in the revelation to Joseph Smith, when He said men must enter at the "strait gate," and that "Because *strait is the gate, and narrow is the way,* which leadeth unto life, . . . few there be that find it." (Matthew 7:13-14. Italics ours.)

GOSPEL IS FOR ALL PEOPLE

When the Lord re-established His Church in Palestine, under the direction of the Melchizedek Priesthood, He charged the Twelve to go only to the lost sheep of the house of Israel with their message of salvation. (Matthew 10:5-6.) After the resurrection, when the law of Moses was no longer to be fulfilled, but had been fulfilled, the Gospel was no longer restricted to Israel. On the mountain in Galilee, the Resurrected Lord charged His apostles: "Go ye therefore, and teach all nations, baptizing them in the name of the Father, and of the Son, and of the Holy Ghost." (Matthew 28:19.) And immediately prior to his ascension, He

---

[2]*History of the Church of Jesus Christ of Latter-day Saints,* Salt Lake City, Deseret Book Company, Vol. I, p. 76.

repeated His charge when He said, ". . . and ye shall be witnesses unto me both in Jerusalem, and in all Judea, and in Samaria, and unto the uttermost part of the earth." (Acts 1:8.)

Similarly, in our own dispensation, the Lord has announced in vigorous language that His message is to all people, those that are afar off, even to those in the islands of the sea, "For verily the voice of the Lord is unto all men, . . ." (D&C 1:1-2. See entire section.)

PRIESTHOOD NECESSARY FOR EXALTATION

In order for men to obtain exaltation they must not only receive the Gospel, they must receive the Melchizedek Priesthood, and not only the Melchizedek Priesthood but the fulness of the Priesthood, meaning the fulness of the blessings of the Priesthood which can be obtained only in the temples of the Lord through the holy endowment and the sealing ordinances of the Priesthood. (D&C 131:104. Also see D&C 132:5-8.)

The Gospel is eternal law, and has been provided by God for the blessing of His children who are willing to receive it. It is so ordered that it is not only necessary that the keys of the Priesthood be upon the earth, that is, that there be a prophet, but it is necessary for those who want to be members of God's family and have their own individual families preserved as a part of that eternal patriarchal order, to receive and be faithful to all the covenants the Lord has revealed.

APPLICATION:

What Would Jesus Do?

The authority of the Priesthood has been given to us by the laying on of hands. By virtue of the Priesthood we are in a better position to guide and bless our families. What would Jesus Christ have us do with our Priesthood in our families? Ask yourself: Do I bless my wife and children when they are sick? Do I give my children a Father's blessing prior to their going to school or in the services to help them in their coming challenges? What responsibility do we have in regard to family prayers and family home evening because of the Priesthood authority we hold?

Read and ponder: D&C 93:40-15; I Samuel 3.

Share with class members the following illustration which demonstrates the principle of Hebrews 5:4.

"As Was Aaron"			
Scripture	Priesthood Pattern	Called by Prophet?	Ordained by Laying on of Hands?
Hebrews 5:4 Exodus 28:1-3, 41.	Aaron and sons	Yes Verse 1	Yes Verse 41
Numbers 27:18-20, 22-23 Deuteronomy 34:9	Joshua	Yes	Yes
John 15:16	Peter James John	By Christ	Yes
Acts 13:2-3	Paul Barnabas	Yes	Yes
Joseph Smith 2:68-71	Joseph Smith	Yes	Yes

You may want to call on a few of the quorum members to bring to class their Priesthood line of authority and share it with the class.

You may want the class members to volunteer experiences where they used their authority of the Priesthood.

Channels of Authority

LESSON FOLLOW-UP

Have one or several quorum members relate how they use their Priesthood authority to bless family members or persons under their stewardship. Call for specific illustrations.

LESSON OBJECTIVES

Priesthood holders should feel motivated to: (1) Achieve a clear understanding of the channels of authority in the Church. (2) Sustain the leadership of the Church on a local, stake and General Authority level.

INTRODUCTION

To open the discussion the teacher might ask class members who hold the following positions to trace the channels of supervision for their positions to the First Presidency: home teachers, Sunday School teachers, genealogical workers.

LESSON DEVELOPMENT

CHURCH CREATED THROUGH THE PRIESTHOOD

Where there is no Priesthood, there is no true Church. A close examination of the Priesthood and the Church will reveal, however, that they are not identical and that there is a real and significant distinction between them.

The Priesthood is the power by which the Church is brought into being and the source of any authority to act in the name of the Lord. The Priesthood may exist on the earth without the Church, as it did between May 15, 1829, and April 6, 1830, but the Church cannot exist upon the earth without the Priesthood.

PRIESTHOOD AUTHORITY STRUCTURE OF THE CHURCH

The Priesthood authority structure of the Church is as follows: The senior apostle upon the earth and his two counselors constitute the Quorum of the First Presidency and preside over the entire Church.

The Council of the Twelve consists of twelve high priests who have also been ordained apostles, and they constitute a presiding quorum directly under the First Presidency.

A special but nonadministrative officer is the Patriarch to the Church.

The First Presidency, the Council of the Twelve, and the Patriarch to the Church are sustained as Prophets, Seers, and Revelators.

An unspecified number of high priests may be set apart as Assistants to the Twelve, but they are not ordained apostles, and they do not constitute a quorum.

The First Council of Seventy consists of seven seventies who preside particularly over all of the seventies and who exercise certain administrative authority under the direction of the First Presidency and the Council of the Twelve.

These quorums and officers are designated General Authorities because they preside over no local unit but over all of the Priesthood upon the earth.

Among the General Authorities is another group designated the Presiding Bishopric. It consists of three high priests who have been ordained bishops, one of whom is sustained as the Presiding Bishop and the others as his counselors. The Presiding Bishopric advises the First Presidency and Council of the Twelve in all duties pertaining to bishops, including the Aaronic Priesthood and temporal matters.

To assist the General Authorities in the performance of their duties regarding stakes and missions are Regional Representatives of the Twelve and Mission Representatives of the Council of the Twelve and the First Council of Seventy.

KEYS BESTOWED UPON APOSTLES

The Prophet Joseph Smith and Oliver Cowdery received the keys of the Priesthood from various personages who were sent to the earth by the Lord for the express purpose of restoring those keys to the earth. The Prophet bestowed all of the keys he held upon all of the members of the Council of the Twelve. Upon his death, therefore, the keys of the priesthood were not lost.

Under the inspiration of heaven the First Presidency and the Twelve have the authority to call and ordain and set apart other General Authorities as necessary.

Similarly the First Presidency and the Twelve call stake presidents, stake patriarchs, and bishops as necessary. Under their direction, either they, or other appointed General Authorities, ordain and set apart these officers as necessary.

Stake presidencies perform their duties under the direction and jurisdiction of the First Presidency and the Council of the Twelve.

PRESIDENCY PRESIDES IN STAKE

All of the Melchizedek and Aaronic Priesthood in the relatively small geographical units upon the earth designated as stakes are presided over by three high priests who are set apart (not ordained) as presidents. One is set apart as the president, the others are counselors. The president, not the counselors, also has conferred upon him all the keys necessary to direct the affairs of the stake. In addition to presiding over all of the Priesthood in the stake, those three high priests have a specific calling to preside over the quorum consisting of all the high priests who live in that stake.

To assist the stake presidency in all duties regarding the Melchizedek and Aaronic Priesthood in the stake over which they preside, there are twelve high priests designated as the high council. With authorization from the Council of the Twelve and the First Presidency there may be alternate high councilors.

A special but nonadministrative officer is the patriarch to the stake. He is ordained to the office of patriarch and set apart to function in the particular stake in which he resides. Under certain circumstances there may be more than one patriarch authorized to function in a given stake.

A quorum of seventy in a given stake consists of all of the seventy within the stake and they are presided over by seven of their number. Elders residing in one or more wards within a stake are organized into a quorum and are presided over by three of their members. There are as many quorums of elders in a stake as their numbers warrant.

When it is advisable to do so, a stake presidency recommends to the First Council of Seventy that certain elders in their stake be ordained to the office of seventy. Also, a stake presidency may recommend to the First Council of Seventy that certain brethren be set apart as presidents of a given quorum.

A stake presidency is authorized to confer the Melchizedek Priesthood upon a man and ordain him to the office of elder, or direct others

54

having the Melchizedek Priesthood to do so. They have the responsibility and authority, when necessary, to choose an elder to preside over a given quorum of elders, and to set him apart as president and confer upon him all of the keys of authority which appertain to that office and calling. The counselors to the president of the quorum are also set apart by the stake presidency, but no keys are conferred upon them. The keys belong only to the president.

The stake presidency presides over all of the Priesthood, Melchizedek and Aaronic, within a given stake. As Melchizedek Priesthood officers, they are particularly charged with directing the work of the Melchizedek Priesthood quorums of the stake.

PRESIDENCY PRESIDES IN MELCHIZEDEK PRIESTHOOD QUORUM

As has already been stated, the Melchizedek Priesthood quorums in a stake are presided over by presidencies. These presidencies are responsible to sit in council with the quorum members and teach them according to the covenants. The quorum is the primary source of instruction for fathers and others to learn their duties. Home teachers are Priesthood representatives of the quorum charged with watching over and strengthening the home through the father by encouraging him to attend to his family duties.

The bishop of the ward also uses this priesthood channel in learning of all family needs pertinent to his stewardship.

All of those who hold the Aaronic Priesthood in a geographical unit designated as a ward are presided over by three high priests. One of them is ordained bishop and set apart to preside over a particular ward, and the other two high priests are set apart as counselors. The bishop also, but not the counselors, has conferred upon him all of the keys necessary to direct the affairs of the ward and is also set apart as president of the priests quorum. It is not proper to refer to a counselor as "bishop" unless at some previous time he has been ordained a bishop.

A quorum of priests consists of forty-eight priests presided over by the bishop of the ward in which they reside.

A quorum of teachers consists of twenty-four teachers, presided over by three of their members.

A quorum of deacons consists of twelve deacons, presided over by three of their members.

All Aaronic Priesthood and unordained brethren who are adults are called prospective elders and attend the elders quorum meetings and activities. In this respect the elders quorum assists the bishop.

BISHOP GOVERNS IN WARD

When a bishop finds a man qualified to receive the Melchizedek Priesthood, it is his prerogative to recommend to the stake presidency, who preside over that Priesthood, that such a person have the Melchizedek Priesthood conferred upon him. The bishop, in his capacities as president of the Aaronic Priesthood in the ward, has no authority to confer the Melchizedek Priesthood upon another, but as a high priest, acting under the direction of the stake presidency, he could confer the Melchizedek Priesthood and ordain those who have been approved to receive such.

The bishop and his counselors have the authority to confer the Aaronic Priesthood upon those who are qualified to receive it and to ordain them to the appropriate offices: deacon, teacher, or priest. The bishopric also has the responsibility and authority to provide a president and two counselors for each deacons and teachers quorum. As the bishop holds the keys of the Aaronic Priesthood in the ward, it is his place to set apart the presidents of the deacons and teachers quorums and confer upon them the keys necessary to perform their respective duties. Either he or his counselors may then set apart the counselors in those quorums.

Although ward bishoprics receive counsel from the Presiding Bishopric, essentially they perform their duties under the direction and jurisdiction of the presidency of the stake in which they live.

FATHER PRESIDES IN HOME

The basic unit of the Church is the family. Ideally, each family should be presided over by the father, who bears the Melchizedek Priesthood. It is his duty, along with his wife, to teach his family the gospel of Jesus Christ. (Doctrine and Covenants 68:25.) Auxiliaries and other organizations augment this teaching, but the primary responsibility rests with the father.

Home teachers assist the quorum and ward in watching over the family—not to teach the Gospel message only but also "be with and strengthen" the family. (See D&C 20:47-55.)

Briefly stated, this is the channel of authority in the Priesthood upon the earth.

What Would Jesus Do?

A principle that is very evident as one reads the scriptures is that Jesus respects His appointed channel of authority on the earth. For example, when Saul of Tarsus was stopped on the road to Damascus, instead of personally instructing him or sending Saul to the First Presidency, He sent him to the presiding elder at Damascus, Ananias. (See Acts 9:10-17.)

Similarly, each Priesthood holder should respect the Lord's channel of authority. Analyze how you can better sustain your quorum leaders and bishopric, your stake presidency, and the General Authorities. Identify some concrete ideas for yourself.

Read and ponder: D&C 107:1-20; Ephesians 4: 11-15.

SPECIAL INSTRUCTIONS TO THE TEACHER

1.   Illustrate the Priesthood channel of authority in the Church. Emphasize how this structure exists to bless the families of the Church.

2.   Ask for or relate stories or experiences that illustrate that when one respects the Lord's channel of authority, one is blessed, but when this principle is violated, apostasy sometimes occurs.

Note: You may wish to ask a musically qualified class member to review the hymn "O Men of God!" found in lesson nine and come prepared to instruct the class in singing the hymn during that lesson period.

Section

3

The Priesthood Brings the Power of God to You

The Gospel and You

Ask class members to discuss some of the specific ways in which they sustained Church leaders during the past week.

(This discussion should not exceed five minutes.)

LESSON OBJECTIVE

The Priesthood holder should feel motivated to live the Gospel in its fulness as a means of becoming more Christlike.

INTRODUCTION

The Priesthood is the power to act in the name of God. It is the power to go forth, believing completely that we are called of God to be His representatives on this earth and to be His partner in all our thoughts and deeds. Jesus brought us the keys of righteousness. He gave us the holy sacrament that we might take upon us His name, "and always remember him and keep his commandments. . . ." (D&C 20:77.) He has promised us eternal progression toward Godhood if we will walk in His footsteps. He has invited each of us, individually, to share the Celestial Kingdom with Him and our Heavenly Father.

The Gospel is personal. It is personified in the life of the Savior. When we commit ourselves to walk in the steps of Jesus, we commit ourselves to live the principles He taught.

LESSON DEVELOPMENT

Here is a hymn to help us catch the spirit of this commitment. May we suggest that class members sing the hymn together. .

61

O MEN OF GOD!

Male voices in unison

Words and music by
LORIN F. WHEELWRIGHT

1. O men of God! Our pow-er is the Priest-hood!
2. O men of God! Who pray for re-ve-la-tion,
3. O men of God! Our cov-en-ant is ho-ly,
4. O men of God! Be-come the liv-ing ser-mon!

We hold to-day, The keys of heav'n re-stor'd.
Firm in our hands Let's hold the I-ron Rod.
Come, let's re-new The oath by which we live:
Pro-claim a-far The truth that makes us free!

Also available in T.T.B.B.

Hark   to   the   call: Go   forth and live the   Gos -   pel!
Feast   on   the   Word,   Re - cor - ded in   the   Scrip - ture,
"By   love un - feign'd,   I'll ex - er - cise do - min -   ion—
Come   serve the   Lord,   Let ev - 'ry word of   Je   -   sus

Act   in   the   name   Of   Je - sus Christ our   Lord!
Feast   on   the   Word,   The   ho - ly word of   God.
I   will   o - bey!   My   sa - cred word I   give."
Shine   in   our   souls,   For   all the world to   see!

HOW DOES A MAN OF GOD DIFFER FROM
A MAN OF THE WORLD?

To understand the revolutionary movement that Jesus initiated, and one to which we completely subscribe as members of the priesthood, let us compare what He said with the prevailing notions of men. Here are a few points of contrast:

Jesus Taught	The World Believes
We are to love our enemies and bless them that abuse us.	We are to love our friends and fight our enemies.
The path and gate to salvation are narrow.	It is safest to follow the crowd.
It is as difficult for the rich to enter the kingdom of heaven as for a camel to go through the eye of a needle.	Wealth is esteemed above all else. It is the rich who are powerful and happy.

Mark Twain once observed that it was not the sayings of Jesus that he did not understand which bothered him, but the ones he *did* understand. How could Jesus run counter to so much of what we call "human nature"?

A man of God shares an overwhelming love with his fellow men. This is one reason a man of God is fundamentally different or "peculiar." Yet, that is precisely the quality of virtue that maintains the power of the Priesthood. *To act as Jesus would act, we must think as He thought*—and this applies to our understanding of God's love. We must love our fellowman as God loves us. This is the marked difference between a man of God and a man of the world.

WHAT IS CHRIST'S "GOOD NEWS" THAT WE SHARE?

The Gospel is the Good News of God's Word. We sometimes think of it as strictly "old," and we may fail to catch the invigorating freshness of its message. Let us discuss some of the fundamental principles which seem to be overlooked amid commonplace expressions of belief. Let us take a fresh look as though we were hearing the Good News for the first time—the Gospel restored!

Class members could be asked to give some of their ideas on what makes the Gospel *good* and what makes it *news*.

Compare these thoughts with the following:

Equality. When we see a man of God follow in Christ's footsteps, we see a person who acts differently from other men. This has been notable both in our times and in the Ancient Church. Such a man shows genuine affection and concern for his fellowman. He shares his substance, his home, his goodwill, his opportunities—all that he has. There is a brotherhood and sisterhood in the Church which is unlike that in all other organizations. There is a sense of equality that transcends barriers of occupation, race, national origin, political party, or wealth. There is a universality in the Church that makes all citizens equal in the Kingdom of God. In days of tension and discrimination, this is the kind of Good News to cheer men's souls.

Joy. There is a joy in the hearts of Christ's followers which transcends the pleasures of ordinary people. It is a feeling of glory shared with the angels who sang, "Peace on earth, goodwill to men." It is the exultant spirit which characterizes the Mormon Tabernacle Choir—a quality of rejoicing that is found nowhere else.

Confidence. The fear of death haunts no true follower of Christ. We know that death has no sting. It is not a great void to be dreaded and to cause remorse and grief. This freedom from the fear of death creates courage to face the inevitable. The early Christians met the lions in the Roman circus with prayers and songs. The pioneers of our day met travail with a joyous hymn, "And if we die before our journey's through, Happy day, all is well!" Our funerals are generally in the form of a commemoration of a life well lived and worthy of a glorious future rather than a resolute acceptance of a black reality. Christ taught us that death is but a return to our heavenly home. To be welcomed home is Good News.

Peace of Mind. Jesus brought a healing balm to men's troubled minds. He taught them how to free themselves from the poison of a selfish ego—from self-destroying self-centeredness. Peace of mind is a most distinguishing mark upon any man in this twentieth century. Our missionaries glow with it. They lose themselves in the destiny of others. Our Priesthood Welfare Program lifts us beyond personal profit to the broader sharing of group enterprise. Our Relief Society and many of our quorum activities pull us out of our shells and expose our souls to the radiant energy of serving others. These "other-centered" activities help us overcome our "self-centered" natures. And as we walk more vigorously in the footsteps of Jesus, we find that there is no medicine like unselfish service to cure the mental depression of self-pity. Our hymn books contain no "blues." Instead, they are filled with songs that urge us to put our shoulders to the wheel. Jesus gave us this great secret of mental health which brings good feeling and peace of mind, to all men of God. This is Good News—and men hunger for it.

A Fresh Start. Those who discover the futility of sin and seek to purge their souls of haunting regret welcome the good word that there is a way to be born again—a way to shed the dead past. Deep in the souls of some men are unhealed sores of smothered conscience, bad motives, memories of wrongs committed, and cankers of revenge. This prison of sorrows is hopeless without a chance to repent—and that is exactly what Christ offers as a boon to those who will humble themselves, seek forgiveness, make restitution, and follow Him. He leads the way to a new feeling of cleanliness and purification. He says that faith can make us whole. The look of new hope that comes into the eyes of the convert is the glow of a fresh start, and it is like fresh green shoots on a tree in springtime. To someone who has frozen in the cold of a long winter, this is Good News. To someone who has thirsted in the desert, this is Good News.

Purpose. After wandering aimlessly through a morass of theories and philosophies, men cry for direction. Why are we here? Where did we come from? Where are we going? These perplexing enigmas rack their minds and frustrate their actions. They try all kinds of dissipation, seeking that ever-fleeting bluebird of happiness. After looking into a black night, they discover the star of Bethlehem, and it leads them to the Son of God. He opens their eyes to see a different heaven—one where all men have an abode according to their merit; one where justice will reward the righteous; one where men can continue to learn and grow in knowledge and power until they become as God. The beauty of a Celestial Kingdom is painted upon the canvas of their minds in just enough detail to create a great longing. To a wanderer looking for a haven and finding a way to heaven, this is the very best of Good News.

WHAT IS THE MEANING OF THE "GOOD NEWS" FOR US?

We have explored six "promises" of the Gospel: equality, joy, confidence, peace of mind, a fresh start, and purpose. Are they really attainable? Jesus said they were if we would change our basic attitudes and radiate a love toward other men as God radiates His love toward us. He told us to abandon the "human nature" or worldly men, and take on the garments of God. He spared little leeway in his measure of godliness. He said, "Be ye therefore perfect, even as your Father which is in heaven is perfect." (Matthew 5:48.) And to make clear His meaning in the minds of His disciples He said, ". . . I am the way, the truth and the life: no man cometh unto the Father, but by me." (John 14:6.) Jesus tells us in these words that to gain the fruits of the Gospel's promise, we must be perfect, even as He showed us how to be perfect. Therefore, the Gospel becomes the way to perfection, and we follow that way insofar as we follow Christ. So, the Good News means that our life's work is cut out for us—we are to perfect ourselves.

WHAT ARE THE DISCIPLINES OF PERFECTION?

The Discipline of Knowledge. The fact that we believe in the perfectibility of man exemplifies the high value we place upon learning and the products of learning which are knowledge and wisdom. To each is given the opportunity of eternal progression. As God now is, man may become, but he can do so no faster than he gains knowledge. These are our fundamental convictions. But is all knowledge of equal value, regardless of the subject? A fundamental discipline of spiritual growth is to "Seek ye *first* the kingdom of God and his righteousness . . ." (Matthew 6:33.) Another discipline of knowledge is that no one can give it to us; we must gain it for ourselves. President Joseph F. Smith said it this way: "If I have learned something through prayer, supplication, and perseverance in seeking to know the truth, and I tell it to you, it will not be knowledge unto you."[1]

Another discipline of knowledge is the requirement of expression. Languages of all kinds—verbal, artistic, mathematical, graphic—are means of communication by which we clarify our thought, share it, and record it for future reference. Knowledge grows through the refinement of expression, and God has made clear that we should strive to master it.

The Discipline of Faith. Of necessity our knowledge is limited; yet the demands for action require decision. What shall guide us when our knowledge is incomplete? God has told us we should live by faith—by "the substance of things hoped for, the evidence of things not seen." (Hebrews 11:1.) He has told us that ". . . if our earthly house of this tabernacle were dissolved, we have a building of God, an house not made with hands; eternal in the heavens. . . . Therefore we are always confident, . . . (For we walk by faith, not by sight.)" (II Corinthians 5:1, 6, 7.) This discipline requires of us a trust in God and the acceptance of His message through His prophets. It requires a willingness to believe in the unseen world of Spirit, to accept inspiration and revelation from that world, and to purge ourselves of all sin which destroys divine communication.

The Lord has given us the Priesthood to refine our powers of discernment, and he has given us agency to choose our own way. The cen-

---

[1]Smith, Joseph F., *Gospel Doctrine*, Salt Lake City, Deseret Book Company, 1919, p. 52.

tral purpose of our earthly existence is to progress in our sensitivity to spiritual values and to cultivate the spiritual strength to exercise faith so that we can choose the way to spiritual exaltation. The overwhelming presence of the visible, tangible world blinds us to the invisible, spiritual world. The discipline of keeping our spiritual eyes open and our hearts in tune is the discipline of faith. It requires a discipline of obedience to laws we cannot amend. Our religious devotions, our sacred ordinances, our holy temples, and our willingness to wait upon the Lord, all help us to gain this discipline. Hence, they are essential to our perfection.

The Discipline of Christian Love. It is natural to man to love his own: his family, his countrymen, his companions, his associates. But when Christ came with a message of loving our enemies, loving Samaritans, loving sinners, loving the halt and the lame, He challenged us to develop a new kind of discipline—one that we call *Christian love.* The Jews had long praised God for His love—for delivering them from their oppressors. It was a new kind of love which Christ personified, which He called upon all men to feel and share, and which Paul describes in his Epistle to the Corinthians. The translators had difficulty in finding an English word that was equivalent to the meaning, and in the King James version used "charity." Regardless of the word, the meaning is clear and the discipline is demanding. In fact, Paul says, "though I have the gift of prophecy, and understand *all mysteries,* and *all knowledge,* and though I have *all faith,* so that I could remove mountains and have not charity [Christian Love] I am nothing." (I Corinthians 13:2. Italics ours.) He says that "though I bestow all my goods to feed the poor, and though I give my body to be burned, and have not charity [Christian love], it profiteth me nothing." (I Corinthians 13:3.) The discipline is not just good deeds, but *doing the right things for the right reasons,* and the basic, fundamental reason—even more important than knowledge and faith—is love. Just how does His love feed our souls and inspire our actions? Paul says love

> . . . suffereth long . . . vaunteth not itself, is not puffed up, doth not behave itself unseemly, seeketh not her own, is not easily provoked, thinketh no evil; rejoiceth not in iniquity, but rejoiceth in the truth; beareth all things, believeth all things, hopeth all things, endureth all things. (I Corinthians 13:4-7.)

Paul describes Christian love as the enduring, unfailing, and Godlike quality man can possess. As a discipline it makes us set aside our reservations of ulterior motives. When in conflict with personal gain, love comes first. When in conflict with our cultural pursuits, love comes first. When in conflict with our sense of scholarship and accuracy, love comes first. Even when in conflict with our understanding of prophecy and faith, love comes first. It is this priority that Christ personified. It is this fundamental thinking that we must share if we would be Christlike ourselves. It is the most exacting of all the disciplines leading to perfection. Yet it brings the greatest joy, because it completely identifies us with the Savior and with God, and fills our hearts with Their Holiness and Their Glory.

WHERE DO WE GO FROM HERE?

What can we do as mere mortals, bearing the Priesthood of God and striving for perfection?

Nephi says to us, as he said to his father,

> . . . I will go and do the things which the Lord hath commanded, for I know that the Lord giveth no commandments unto the children of men, save he shall prepare a way for them that they may accomplish the thing which he commandeth them. (I Nephi 3:7.)

With the Lord on our side, with determination in our hearts, and with clear vision in our minds of what we hope to achieve, we can climb the mountain to perfection. We may take only one step at a time, but we can climb it.

Perhaps our next step is to find our own flaws of character and correct them. Perhaps we should learn from Benjamin Franklin and Heber J. Grant how to practice one virtue at a time and keep repeating the process until the virtue becomes habitual. Like one highly successful insurance man (Vash Young) we might devote half a day each week just to talk to young people in trouble. By thinking as Christ thought and by pursuing specific steps of self-improvement, we gain spiritual strength in the disciplines leading to perfection.

APPLICATION

What Would Jesus Do?

A s you reflect on the life of the Savior, you can see that He was perfect in each of the disciplines discussed in this lesson. As you discipline your life so that the thoughts of your day are centered in the Savior, you will find your life taking on a more Christlike focus. Thus, you will gain spiritual strength in the disciplines that lead to perfection.

Read and ponder: Philippians 2:5-11; Alma 37:36-37; II Nephi 32:9; D&C 121:34-46; Proverbs 23:7; D&C 39:6.

SPECIAL INSTRUCTIONS TO THE TEACHER

1. Point out to the quorum members that the process of perfection is learned "line upon line," "precept upon precept," and that man's effort, though essential, is not the process by which man becomes perfected. He must receive "grace for grace" until he receives of the fulness of Christ. (See D&C 93:11-19.)

2. Challenge quorum members to attempt to discipline their minds and hearts to focus upon the Savior each day. Let His life and teachings permeate our decision-making, our leisure time and our family associations.

3. Use a picture of the Savior to remind the quorum of the challenge of this course of study: "What Would Jesus Do?"

INSTRUCTIONAL MATERIALS

OQ135—The Savior (or other meetinghouse library picture of the Lord.)

A Companion Who Helps Us Decide

LESSON FOLLOW-UP

Have one or several quorum members report to the quorum on the results of attempting to discipline their thoughts to the Savior in daily decision-making, in their leisure time and in family associations.

LESSON OBJECTIVE

Priesthood holders should feel motivated to seek the companionship of the Holy Ghost in everyday decision-making.

INTRODUCTION

Let us begin by singing or reading together this favorite Latter-day Saint hymn (Number 110):

1. Choose the right, when a choice is placed before you;
   In the right the Holy Spirit guides;
   And its light is forever shining o'er you,
   When in the right your heart confides.

   Chorus:
   > Choose the right! Choose the right!
   > Let wisdom mark the way before;
   > In its light, Choose the right!
   > And God will bless you evermore.

2. Choose the right! let no spirit of digression
   Overcome you in the evil hour;
   There's the right and the wrong to ev'ry question—
   Be safe through inspiration's pow'r.

3. Choose the right! there is peace in righteous doing;
   Choose the right! there's safety for the soul;
   Choose the right, in all labors you're pursuing;
   Let God and heaven be your goal.

   —James Townsend

71

The Holy Ghost comes to us as a gift, bestowed by the laying on of hands by those in authority. Whether we receive Him and are guided by Him depends on our faithfulness and the searchings of our heart. We need Him and His influence to surmount the evils of this world, and to seek His aid requires an understanding of how He works within us. As Priesthood holders we should speak as we are "moved upon by the Holy Ghost." (D&C 68:3.) In this lesson we shall attempt to cultivate understanding by examining the kinds of choices we face and the commandments of God which tell us how to enjoy the companionship of this Holy Comforter.

LESSON DEVELOPMENT

HOW DO WE PERCEIVE RIGHT AND WRONG?

In the hymn, "Choose the Right," are these words, "There's the right and the wrong to every question—." This may appear to be an oversimplification and needs careful consideration if we are to see more clearly the choice which is implied. We might begin by examining a basic problem of perception. Below is what photographers call a "gray scale." It shows degrees of whiteness and blackness ranging from the extremes of white to black.

This scale, in a sense, is an absolute scale of values. But to serve as such it must be viewed under controlled illumination so each step reflects a predetermined percentage of the light and each step appears to be darker or lighter than its neighbor accordingly.

A skilled photographer will look at a scene to be photographed and visualize it as a wide range of these light values. He will expose and develop his film to capture faithfully all of the highlights, middle tones, and shadows. His judgment will be affected by the weather, and on a cloudy day he will perceive the brightest object as not being as light as on a sunny day. Also, he will see that some objects will have a wider range of reflection than others.

Now, what has this to do with perceiving "right and wrong?" In some situations in our lives it is easier to determine what is right and what is wrong than it is in other situations.

DIVINE HELP IS NEEDED IN MAKING CHOICES

So that we might see more clearly—see the right in varying shades of situations—let us examine several situations. In each case we can look at the proposition with filters of various densities. Let us remember that when a holder of the Priesthood makes any choice he makes it with permanent values in mind, and he needs help to make the right choice. It is the seeking of divine help and the companionship of the Holy Ghost which can lift his choosing from a level of mere expediency to one of making a sensitive moral decision.

For example, below are several statements on behavior. Consider each one, then list what you consider to be permissible or practical exceptions, if any. To assist you in this exercise, some common "exceptions" are listed for the first statement. After weighing these by answering the questions that follow, consider the other two as time permits.

1. I do not work on Sunday, except . . .
   a. When not to do so would create suffering.
   b. When I absolutely have to, to keep my job.
   c. When I am in debt and need the money to meet my obligations.
   d. When the extra money will raise our standard of living (such as music lessons or college tuition for the children.)
   e. When I get behind and need to catch up.
   f. When competition forces me to work.
   g. When I see an opportunity to get ahead of my competition.
   h. When I might lose a sale that is important to my income.

Are there any exceptions which you honestly think would be right in some circumstances and wrong in others? Could guidance from the Holy Ghost help you make a personal decision when considering any of these possible exceptions? Give cases from your own life.

2. I always tell the truth, except . . .
3. I declare all income on my tax returns, except . . .

When considering these and similar problems it may be well to recall the slogan that appeared on the Church posters: "Be honest with yourself."

HOW DOES THE HOLY GHOST
HELP US CHOOSE THE RIGHT?

If you have performed the exercises of "perceiving right and wrong" outlined above, you have experienced some of the pain of making choices. Situations often force us into choosing the "lesser of two evils." Yet, we *must* make choices, and there still are Gospel standards in this world. We cannot rationalize ourselves into beings who are exempt from making moral decisions by saying, "I am what I am, and if God made me this way it's His fault and He can't hold me responsible."

The Holy Ghost can help us choose our course of action. And our relationship with God can be understood by all. The Lord tells us concerning His doctrine:

. . . wherefore, I shall speak unto you plainly, according to the plainness of my prophesying. For my soul delighteth in plainness. (II Nephi 31:2-3.)

Nephi declares:

. . . the voice of the Son came unto me, saying: He that is baptized in my name, to him will the Father give the Holy Ghost, like unto me. . . . (II Nephi 31:12.)

. . . I know that if ye shall follow the Son, with full purpose of heart, acting no hypocrisy and no deception before God, but with real intent, repenting of your sins, witnessing unto the Father that ye are willing to take upon you the name of Christ, by baptism . . then shall ye receive the Holy Ghost; yea, then cometh the baptism of fire and of the Holy Ghost; and then can ye speak with the tongue of angels, and shout praises unto the Holy One of Israel. (II Nephi 31:13.)

And by way of explanation Nephi continues:

. . . And now, how could ye speak with the tongue of angels save it were by the Holy Ghost? Angels speak by the power of the Holy Ghost; wherefore, they speak the words of Christ. Wherefore, I said unto you, *feast upon the words of Christ; for behold, the words of Christ will tell you all things what ye should do* . . . behold, again I say unto you that if ye will enter in by the way, and receive the Holy Ghost, it will show unto you all things what ye should do. (II Nephi 32:2-3, 5. Italics ours.)

THE SCRIPTURES GIVE US GUIDANCE

From this scripture and sections eight and nine of the Doctrine and Covenants we gain a knowledge of how to obtain help from the Holy Ghost. When the Prophet Joseph Smith petitioned the Lord to enable Oliver Cowdery to translate from the plates, the Lord said:

I will tell you in your mind and in your heart, by the Holy Ghost, which shall come upon you and which shall dwell in your heart. (D&C 8:2.)

When Oliver Cowdery experienced difficulty, the Lord answered his questions by saying,

. . . you have not understood; you have supposed that I would give it unto you, when you took no thought save it was to ask me. (D&C 9:7.)

Summarizing from these teachings we learn the steps outlined for us to receive guidance from the Holy Ghost:

1. Repent, with full purpose of heart, acting no hypocrisy or deception.
2. Take upon you the name of Christ by baptism.
3. Receive the gift of the Holy Ghost.
4. Feast upon the words of Christ.
5. Study it out in your mind.
6. Ask God if you are right (with fasting and prayer).
7. Receive confirmation by which "your bosom shall burn within you."

HOW CAN WE WELCOME THE HOLY GHOST?

In seeking spiritual aid we carry a responsibility to create within ourselves a holiness that will welcome the Holy Ghost. We must become clean vessels in which His promptings can be felt. Let us, therefore, make a commitment to cleanse our souls of those sins which repel the Holy Ghost and cultivate those virtues which invite Him. "Let virtue garnish thy thoughts unceasingly. . . ." (D&C 121:45.)

What Would Jesus Do?

L ike unto the Savior, we need to create within ourselves a holiness that will welcome the Holy Ghost. Let us, therefore, make a covenant to cleanse our souls of those sins which repel the Holy Ghost and cultivate those virtues that invite him. Follow the Savior's counsel: "Let virtue garnish thy thoughts unceasingly." (D&C 121:45.)

1. How can I clear my mind of carnal thoughts? What control can I exercise over my environment so that I might be free of licentious mental images? How can I do this by selection of books, magazines, shows, jokes, conversation, work and companions?

2. How can I feast upon the words of Christ? Do I study the scriptures regularly and ponder their teachings? Do I read the current Church publications and welcome their teachings?

Ask yourself the following questions:

Invite the Holy Ghost to help you reach your next important decision. Do so by preparing to welcome Him by cleansing your mind of carnal thoughts and by filling your mind with the words of Christ. Study your problem in the light of the words of Christ. Make a decision. Pray for divine guidance. Seek that "burning" confirmation to your decison.

Ponder: D&C 9:7-9; Matthew 25:1-13; D&C 45: 56-57.

SPECIAL INSTRUCTIONS TO THE TEACHER

1. After singing the song mentioned in the introduction, formulate questions similar to those listed under "Divine help is needed in making choices." Divide quorum into groups and pass one question to each group asking them to respond as indicated in the manual.

2. With the aid of the manual or without, have each group now determine what would be necessary to make the right choice in each given situation.

Meetinghouse Library Pictures:

IP035	Faith in the Lord Jesus Christ
IP036	Repentance
IP037	Baptism by Immersion
IP038	Gift of the Holy Ghost

The Power of Discernment

LESSON FOLLOW-UP

Quorum members might be asked what they have done during the past week to "feast upon the words of Christ" to assist them in obtaining guidance for their decisions.

LESSON OBJECTIVE

Priesthood holders should be motivated to use the Holy Ghost to discern good from evil.

INTRODUCTION

When we studied the guidance of the Holy Ghost (Lesson 10) we found that His companionship comes through invitation and that we must prepare ourselves to receive Him and hear His promptings. One essential step of that preparation is to "feast upon the words of Christ." (II Nephi 32:3.) As we consider further the powers of the Priesthood and as we specifically pursue those powers insofar as they enable us to discern good and evil, let us turn first to the Lord's Prayer. In this prayer we find the basic idea of our lesson:

> Our Father which are in heaven, Hallowed be thy name. Thy kingdom come. Thy will be done in earth, as it is in heaven. Give us this day our daily bread. And forgive us our debts, as we forgive our debtors. And lead us not into temptation, but deliver us from evil: For thine is the kingdom, and the power, and the glory, for ever. Amen. (Matthew 6:9-13.)

LESSON DEVELOPMENT

WHY ARE WE TEMPTED?

Does temptation come from God or Satan? Consider the following passages of scripture and reconcile their seeming contradiction:

a. My brethren, count it all joy when ye fall into divers temptations; Knowing this, that the trying of your faith worketh patience. (James 1:2-3.)

b. Let no man say when he is tempted, I am tempted of God; for God cannot be tempted with evil, neither tempteth he any man: But every man is tempted, when he is drawn away of his own lust, and enticed. (James 1:13-14.)

The Greek word from which Bible scholars translated the English word *temptation* can mean both (a) "external hardship and trial," or it can mean (b) "inner impulse to evil." In the first passage cited above, James uses *temptation* as a necessary experience because it helps man build steadfastness in meeting the *trials* of life. In this sense it builds his faith in God and in His principles of righteousness. As Latter-day Saints, we can understand the *trial* of Joseph Smith as he struggled to learn which church was right. It was the passage immediately following the one cited above that inspired him to "be perfect and entire, wanting nothing," (verse four) and (in verses five and six) led him to seek God:

If any of you lack wisdom, let him ask of God. . . But let him ask in faith, nothing wavering; for he that wavereth is like a wave of the sea driven with the wind and tossed.

The virtue of trial is spoken of by David in the Psalm 7:9-10:

Oh let the wickedness of the wicked come to an end; but establish the just; for the righteous God trieth the hearts and reins. My defense is of God, which saveth the upright in heart.

GOD TRIES US TO STRENGTHEN US

In further answer to the question, "Does temptation come from God or Satan?" we might distinguish between the two meanings of the word and say trials come from God, while temptation comes from Satan. God tries us. Satan seduces us. God tries us to strengthen us. Satan seduces us to weaken us. When God tries us He gives us the strength to overcome, if we have sufficient faith. When Satan tempts us, he aims to lead us to sin, and as James says:

Then when lust hath conceived, it bringeth forth sin; and sin, when it is finished, bringeth forth death. (James 1:15.)

God implores us by trial to choose the right. He says:

I have set before thee this day life and good, and death and evil; . . . therefore choose life, that both thou and thy seed may live: That thou mayest love the Lord thy God, and that thou mayest obey his voice, and that thou mayest cleave unto him: for he is thy life, and the length of thy days: . . . (Deuteronomy 30:15, 19-20.)

In view of these teachings we should welcome *trial* as a test of steadfastness in the right, but we should avoid, with all our might, enticement leading to sin. The companionship of the Holy Ghost helps us to discern between trial and enticement. By "feasting on the words of Christ" we are guided toward goodness and virtue and away from sin and corruption.

JOSEPH'S TEMPTATION

The story of Joseph in Potiphar's house illustrates the subtle ways in which Satan entices us. Because some men have similar temptations in this day, let us review this story as told in Genesis:

And Joseph was brought down to Egypt; and Potiphar, an officer of Pharoah, captain of the guard, an Egyptian, bought him of the hands of the Ishmaelites, which had brought him down thither.

And the Lord has with Joseph, and he was a prosperous man; and he was in the house of his master the Egyptian. And his master saw that the Lord was with him, and that the Lord made all that he did to prosper in his hand. And Joseph found grace in his sight, and he served him: and he made him overseer over his house, and all that he had he put into his hand.

And it came to pass from the time that he had made him overseer in his house, and over all that he had, that the Lord blessed the Egyptian's house for Joseph's sake; and the blessing of the Lord was upon all that he had in the house, and in the field.

And he left all that he had in Joseph's hand; and he knew not ought he had, save the bread which he did eat. And Joseph was a goodly person, and well favoured.

And it came to pass after these things, that his master's wife cast her eyes upon Joseph; and she said, Lie with me.

But he refused, and said unto his master's wife, Behold my master wotteth not what is with me in the house, and he hath committed all that he hath to my hand;

There is none greater in this house than I; neither hath he kept back any thing from me but thee, because thou art his wife: how then can I do this great wickedness, and sin against God?

And it came to pass, as she spake to Joseph day by day, that he hearkened not unto her, to lie by her, or to be with her.

And it came to pass about this time, that Joseph went into the house to do his business; and there was none of the men of the house there within.

And she caught him by his garment, saying, Lie with me: and he left his garment in her hand, and fled, and got him out. (Genesis 39:1-12.)

In discussing Joseph's temptation, the class may wish to consider these points:

POINTS TO PONDER ON JOSEPH

1. Had Joseph yielded to Potiphar's wife that day, do you think that would have been the end of his sin with her?

2. How have we today been benefited through Joseph's refusing to yield to temptation?

3. What are some of the temptations today for Priesthood members in regard to morality?

4. Should brethren of the Priesthood who have been married in the temple be stronger than others in resisting temptations such as came to Joseph?

5. Joseph was tempted by his master's wife. Are there other ways in which Priesthood members are tempted regarding their Church standards in relationship to their employment superors? Are you ever tempted to indulge in these transgressions to please your boss:

    a. Use vulgar language or profanity?

    b. Tell off-color stories?

    c. Take an alcoholic cocktail at a businessmen's social?

    d. Do a dishonest act because you think it might "help your business?

    e. Visit places where the entertainment is not in keeping with your personal standards or those of the Church?

6. What can you do to help strengthen yourself to resist resolutely but graciously when temptations such as these arise?

7. What can you do to help prevent such temptations from occurring?

8. Joseph was willing to suffer a temporary setback (prison term) for being "true to the faith." Are you?

9. Discuss: "The lesson of life is to believe what the years and the centuries say as against the hours."

HOW SHOULD WE MEET TEMPTATION?

Today, we hear enticing voices on all sides telling us that sin is the way to happiness. We see lurid pictures, we witness suggestive dances, we smell the perfume of lust, and we hear the seductive voices of "a new morality" enticing us to believe that chastity and fidelity are out of style. The cry of our generation is "Live it up!" If ever there were evil spirits abroad in the guise of fun, entertainment, and pleasure, that time is now. How can we recognize the evil around us and protect ourselves from its death-dealing power? Let us listen to the prophets.

PRIESTHOOD HELPS WITH DISCERNMENT

Joseph Smith taught us that we would have great difficulty at times to discern whether influences upon us come from God or from the devil. He asked:

> ... who can drag into daylight and develop the hidden mysteries of the false spirits that so frequently are made manifest among the Latter-day Saints? We answer that no man can do this without the Priesthood, and having a knowledge of the laws by which spirits are governed; for as no man knows the things of God, but by the Spirit of God, so no man knows the spirit of the devil, and his power and influence, but by possessing intelligence which is more than human, and having unfolded through the medium of the Priesthood the mysterious operations of his devices; ... A man must have the discerning of spirits before he can drag into daylight this hellish influence and unfold it unto the world in all its soul-destroying, diabolical, and horrid colors; for nothing is a greater injury to the children of men than to be under the influence of a false spirit when they think they have the Spirit of God.[1]

Our trial today is to recognize and resist temptation: to discern good and evil in all its tones of white, gray, and black. One sure test is given us by Alma:

---

[1]Smith, Joseph Fielding, *Teachings of the Prophet Joseph Smith*, Salt Lake City, Deseret Book Company, 1938, pp. 204-205.

Therefore, if a man bringeth forth good works he hearkeneth unto the voice of the Good Shepherd, and he doth follow him; but whosoever bringeth forth evil works, the same becometh a child of the devil. . . . (Alma 5:41.)

Herein lies the secret to righteous living: meet all tests of faith with determination to follow the Good Shepherd, and avoid the enticements of sin by separating yourself from its presence.

APPLICATION

What Would Jesus Do?

J esus was, as Paul taught, ". . . in all points tempted like as we are, yet without sin." (Hebrews 4:15.) His encounter with Satan three times in the wilderness provides us with the perfect example of how temptation may be overcome. (See Matthew 4.) We should ". . . not live by bread alone, but by every word that proceedeth out of the mouth of God." (Matthew 4:4.) We can rebuke temptation and Satan with our Priesthood. (Matthew 4:7.) We should worship the Lord our God and serve Him only.
Contemplate these questions:

What are my major temptations? What are my trials? How can I use the word of the scriptures and the living prophets to overcome my temptations and trials? How can I more faithfully serve the Lord with my Priesthood so that I will obtain the power to overcome temptation?

Develop a plan by which you can use the example of Jesus to overcome your temptations.

Ponder these scriptures: Mathew 4; Alma 5: 38-43; D&C 133:63-74.

SPECIAL INSTRUCTIONS TO THE TEACHER

1. Place the words *temptation* and *trial* on the chalkboard and ask class members to distinguish between the two.

2. Discuss the questions under "Points to Ponder on Joseph."

3. Draw from the experience of Jesus how He overcame the major temptations which came to Him and apply His answer to Satan to each Priesthood holder.

4. Challenge the quorum member to try to determine his major temptations and then develop a plan in accordance with the way Jesus overcame His temptations.

5. You might want to play a recording of "The Lord's Prayer," or have a quorum member play it on the piano.

INSTRUCTIONAL MATERIALS

The song, "The Lord's Prayer."

The Right to Receive Revelation

LESSON FOLLOW-UP

Class members could be asked to tell of any steps they as individuals have taken during the past week to remove temptation from their lives.

(This discussion should not exceed five minutes.)

LESSON OBJECTIVE

The Priesthood holder should feel motivated to seek the knowledge of God and His will through divine revelation.

INTRODUCTION

Let us begin by reciting together two Articles of Faith pertaining to revelation:

7.   We believe in the gift of tongues, prophecy, revelation, visions, healing, interpretation of tongues, etc.

9.   We believe all that God has revealed, all that He does now reveal, and we believe that He will yet reveal many great and important things pertaining to the Kingdom of God.

Spiritual growth of the individual comes through exercise of the powers of the Priesthood. One of these powers is revelation, which, in substance, is a holy communication from God to man.

To the atheist, communication from God is inconceivable because the atheist denies the existence of God. To the faithful Latter-day Saint, communication from God is fundamental to all he believes because God is the center and most glorious of all intelligences. The faithful member seeks divine guidance when he prays and when he sings with his congregation such hymns as "Guide Us, O Thou Great Jehovah." This seeking of divine guidance is the core of this lesson.

HOW DOES GOD REVEAL HIS WILL TO MAN?

Divine Revelation is a spiritual gift. The Prophet Joseph Smith in a revelation concerning his brother, Hyrum, said: "Deny not the spirit of revelation, nor the spirit of prophecy, for wo unto him that denieth these things;" (D&C 11:25.) A study of the Doctrine and Covenants by Roy W. Doxey[1] gives a summary of several methods by which Joseph Smith received revelations. These are listed with the sections citing the method as follows:

1. By an angel or angels—Section 2; 13; 27:1-4; 110.
2. By the Urim and Thummim—Sections 3; 6; 7; 11; 14; 15; 16; 17.
3. By the spirit of prophecy and revelation—Sections 1:64; 20.
4. By visions—Sections 76; 107:93.
5. By the "still small voice"—Section 85.
6. By a "voice"—Section 130: 12-13.

Joseph Smith described in some detail how to receive revelations. He said:

A person may profit by noticing the first intimation of the spirit of revelation; for instance, when you feel pure intelligence flowing into you, it may give you sudden strokes of ideas; so that by noticing it, you may find it fulfilled the same day or soon; (i.e.) those things that were presented unto your minds by the Spirit of God will come to pass; and thus by learning the Spirit of God and understanding it, you may grow into the principle of revelation, until you become perfect in Christ Jesus.[2]

James E. Talmage speaks of this kind of revelation as the "highest degree" because the words spoken ". . . are the words of God Himself; the mortal mouthpiece is but the trusted conveyer of these heavenly messages. With the authoritative 'Thus saith the Lord,' the revelator delivers the burden committed to his care."[3] He mentions ways by which the divine purpose is revealed to man: "through the dreams of sleep or in waking visions of the mind, by voices without visional appearance or by actual manifestations of the Holy Presence before the eye."[4] Elder Talmage adds:

---

[1]Doxey, Roy W., *Latter-day Saint Prophets and the Doctrine and Covenants*, Salt Lake City, Deseret Book Company, 1963. See pages 28 and 29.

[2]Smith, Joseph, *History of the Church*, Salt Lake City, The Church of Jesus Christ of Latter-day Saints, 1948, Vol. 3, p. 381.

[3]Talmage, James E., *Articles of Faith*, Salt Lake City, The Church of Jesus Christ of Latter-day Saints, 1957, pp. 229-230.

[4]*Ibid.*, p. 229.

Under the influence of inspiration, or its more potent manifestation, revelation, man's mind is enlightened and his energies are quickened to the accomplishment of wonders in the work of human progress; touched with a spark from the heavenly altar, the revelator preserves the sacred fire within his soul and imparts it to others as he may be instructed to do; he is the channel through which the will of God is conveyed.[5]

That divine revelation is of spiritual origin is made clear in Section 76 of the Doctrine and Covenants:

For thus saith the Lord—I, the Lord, am merciful and gracious unto those who fear me, and delight to honor those who serve me in righteousness and in truth unto the end. . . . And to them will I reveal all mysteries. . . . For by my Spirit will I enlighten them, and by my power will I make known unto them the secrets of my will—(D&C 76:5, 7, 10.)

WHO MAY RECEIVE REVELATIONS?

All men who will read the scriptures and hearken to the prophets of God will benefit and receive for themselves the revelations of God as transmitted by His spokesmen. For example, the Israelites were admonished to witness the hand of God and to observe certain ceremonies of the Passover: "And Moses said unto the people, Remember this day, in which ye came out from Egypt, out of the house of bondage; for by strength of hand the Lord brought you out from this place. . . ." (Exodus 13:3.)

Revelation of God can come to all men in the sense that something previously obscure is suddenly made clear and visible. The act of God in delivering the Israelites from the most powerful nation on earth reveals to all who will see that God is a Being of power, compassion, and saving grace. Thus can mankind everywhere receive revelation of God —by witnessing His glories, His creations, and His magnanimity to men regardless of wealth, station or race.

Revelations relating to the Church as a whole come through those who have been called to preside over the Church. Joseph Smith was designated as "Prophet, Seer, and Revelator." (D&C 124:125.) Similarly today the president of the Church is the one authorized to receive revelations for the Church as a whole. His associates in the high quorums of the Church are empowered to receive revelations pertaining to their high offices, as explained by the Prophet Joseph Smith:

[5]*Ibid.*, p. 229.

I (Joseph Smith) made a short address, and called upon the several quorums, and all the congregation of Saints, to acknowledge the Presidency as Prophets and Seers and uphold them by their prayers. . . . I then called upon the quorums and congregation of Saints to acknowledge the Twelve, who were present, as Prophets, Seers, Revelators, and special witnesses to all the nations of the earth holding the keys of the kingdom, to unlock it, or cause it to be done, among them, and uphold them by their prayers.[6]

Likewise are all others who have been called by authority and who are worthy of such gifts authorized to receive revelation pertaining to their own spheres of activity. President Joseph F. Smith testified to this as follows:

I believe that every individual in the Church has just as much right to enjoy the spirit of revelation and the understanding from God which that spirit of revelation gives him, for his own good, as the bishop has to enable him to preside over his ward. Every man has the privilege to exercise these gifts and these privileges in the conduct of his own affairs, in bringing up his children in the way they should go, and in the management of his farm, his flocks, his herds, and in the management of his business, if he has business of other kinds to do; it is his right to enjoy the spirit of revelation and of inspiration to do the right thing, to be wise and prudent, just, and good in everything that he does. I know that this is the thing that I would like the Latter-day Saints to know.[7]

TESTS OF DIVINE REVELATION

People are continually playing hunches, even in religious matters. In the Ancient Church and in the Restored Church there have been apostate groups who have claimed credence by revelation. The scriptures give us many tests of divinity and some are listed below.

Jesus gave two criteria which are applicable to many situations. He challenged all men to test His teachings. When the Jews

. . . marvelled, saying, How knoweth this man letters, having never learned? Jesus answered them, and said, My doctrine is not mine, but his that sent me. If any man will do his will, he

---

[6]Smith, Joseph, *History of the Church*, Salt Lake City, The Church of Jesus Christ of Latter-day Saints, 1948, Vol. 2, p. 417.

[7]Nibley, Preston, Compiler, *Inspirational Talks for Youth*, Salt Lake City, Deseret Book Company, 1941, p. 212.

shall know of the doctrine, whether it be of God, or whether I speak of myself. He that speaketh of himself seeketh his own glory: but he that seeketh his glory that sent him, the same is true, and no unrighteousness is in him. (John 7:15-18.)

The test here is twofold:

(1) testing the principle in practice and

(2) appraising the advocate as being self-seeking or sincerely God-seeking.

There are some who profess to have revelations, but actually they act on hunches. We have learned to apply several tests of credibility in such matters.

1. Is the person claiming revelation living a worthy life?

2. Is the subject matter in harmony with Christ's teachings?

3. Is the person acting within the dimensions of his calling and responsibility?

4. Is he mentally competent to distinguish right from wrong? (A person suffering from mental illness is not competent.)

5. Is time needed for the things presented to "come to pass"?

6. Are the matters presented in harmony with the revelation of those appointed to watch over the Church?

A further test of credibility relating to number four above is one that we observe regarding Joseph Smith. Many of his detractors accused him of hallucinations and similar mental aberrations. *But his family who knew him best knew him to be competent.* And the ultimate test—truth by performance and fulfillment—has proved beyond doubt the veracity of his claims.

Those who play hunches should know the meaning of the word "hunch." As defined by Webster a hunch is "a strong, intuitive impression that something will happen;—from the gambler's superstition that it brings luck to touch the hump of a hunchback." Those who play hunches are usually not spiritually minded at all. They rely on fragments of past experience and common superstition to guide them. Like gamblers, they often seek supernatural powers in an unholy pursuit.

As bearers of the Priesthood, we should follow the admonition of Moroni regarding revelation. He said:

. . . ponder it in your hearts. And when ye shall receive these things, I would exhort you that ye would ask God, the Eternal Father, in the name of Christ, if these things are not true; and if ye shall ask with a sincere heart, with real intent, having faith in Christ, he will manifest the truth of it unto you, by the power of the Holy Ghost. And by the power of the Holy

Ghost ye may know the truth of all things. . . . I would exhort you that ye deny not the power of God; for he worketh by power, according to the faith of the children of men, the same today and tomorrow, and forever. (Moroni 10:3-5, 7.)

HOW SHOULD WE SEEK DIVINE REVELATION?

To be creative in furthering God's kingdom among men is a challenge to every bearer of the Melchizedek Priesthood. To meet new and unique situations with imagination and a *desire* to find constructive answers calls for exercise of inborn talent, application of creative thinking, the seeking of divine guidance, and the gift of revelation.

Class members, at this point, may be asked to give scriptural references on how to seek divine guidance. Answers may be listed on the chalkboard.

Here are some points from the scriptures:

1. *Live worthily.* (Fear God and serve Him in righteousness. D&C 76:5-10.) (Avoid sin. Colossians 3:5-10.)

2. *Receive the Holy Ghost.* ("God shall give unto you knowledge by his Holy Spirit, yea, by the unspeakable gift of the Holy Ghost." D&C 121:26.)

3. *Be humble.* ("And whoso knocketh, to him will he open; and the wise, and the learned, and they that are rich, who are puffed up because of their learning, and their wisdom, and their riches—yea, they are they whom he despiseth; and save they shall cast these things away, and consider themselves fools before God, and come down in the depths of humility, he will not open unto them." II Nephi 9:42.)

4. *Ask in faith.* ("If any of you lack wisdom, let him ask of God . . . But let him ask in faith, nothing wavering. For he that wavereth is like a wave of the sea driven with the wind and tossed." James 1:5-6.)

5. *Study and think deeply.* (Jesus fasted forty days and forty nights "being full of the Holy Ghost . . . and led by the Spirit into the wilderness." Luke 4:1-2.) (". . . whatsoever things are true, honest, just, pure, lovely, of good report . . . think on these things." Philippians 4:8.) (". . . ponder it in your hearts." Moroni 10:4.) (". . . you must study it out in your mind. . . ." D&C 9:8.)

6. *Test promptings for truth.* (". . . ask me if it be right, and if it is right I will cause that your bosom shall burn within you. . . ." D&C 9:8.) (". . . he that asketh in Spirit shall receive in Spirit. . . . He that asketh in Spirit asketh according to the will of God. . . . all things must be done in the name of Christ . . . and unto the bishop of the church, and unto such as God shall appoint and ordain to watch over the church and to

be elders unto the church, are to have it given unto them to discern all those gifts lest there shall be any among you professing and yet be not of God." D&C 46:27-31.)

What Would Jesus Do?

E ven though Jesus was God, yet He sought revelation from His Father in Heaven in making decisions and in obtaining strength. On the occasion of selecting the Twelve Apostles, Jesus retired to a mountain to pray, ". . . and continued all night in prayer to God." (Luke 6:12.) In his greatest agony, wherein "he suffered the pain of all men," He prayed for strength to do his Father's will: "Father, all things *are* possible unto thee; take away this cup from me: nevertheless not what I will, but what thou wilt." (Mark 14:36.)

Using the Savior's example, define in your mind your most pressing problem. Then read the revelations of God as contained in the scriptures and teachings of the living prophets that apply to your problem. Pursue the steps outlined in the scriptures to receive personal guidance by divine revelation:

1. Live worthily
2. Receive the Holy Ghost
3. Be humble
4. Ask in faith
5. Study and think deeply on the problem
6. Test promptings for truth

Act on the truth as revealed to you, and you will know in your heart by the power of testimony whether or not it comes from God.

Read and ponder: D&C 42:14, 59-61; D&C 88: 63-65; Moroni 7:27-38.

SPECIAL INSTRUCTIONS TO THE TEACHER

1. Cite personal experiences or have quorum members cite faith-promoting experiences wherein revelation and the prompting of the

Holy Ghost were used in the areas of family or Priesthood stewardships.

2.   Emphasize the principle of keeping *all* of the commandments of God as being essential to receiving the Holy Ghost.

3.   Share the following quotation of President Marion C. Romney with quorum members. Challenge the brethren to follow this counsel in their personal problems and Priesthood stewardships.

INSTRUCTIONAL MATERIALS

IS019—Joseph Smith's First Vision (as an illustration of how God reveals His will to men in opening a dispensation).

MAKING DECISIONS CORRECTLY

by President Marion G. Romney

Now, we have the Holy Ghost. Every one of us who are members of the Church has had hands laid upon our heads, and we have been given, as far as ordinance can give it, the gift of the Holy Ghost. But, as I remember, when I was confirmed, the Holy Ghost was not directed to come to me; I was directed to "Receive the Holy Ghost." If I receive the Holy Ghost and follow his guidance, I will be among those who are protected and carried through these troubled times. And so will you, and so will every soul who lives under his direction.

Now, my brothers and sisters, we need to seek that Spirit. We need to realize that it is a real guide. The Lord has given us several tests by which we may know when we have that Spirit.

Now I tell you that you can *make every decision in your life cor-. rectly if you can learn to follow the guidance of the Holy Spirit.* This you can do if you will discipline yourself to yield your own feelings to the promptings of the Spirit. Study your problems and prayerfully make a decision. Then take that decision and say to him, in a simple, honest supplication, "Father, I want to make the right decision. I want to do the right thing. This is what I think I should do; let me know if it is the right course." Doing this, you can get the burning in your bosom, if your decision is right. If you do not get the burning, then change your decision and submit a new one. When you learn to walk by the Spirit, you never need to make a mistake. I know what it is to have this burning witness. I know also that there are other manifestations of guidance by the Spirit.

I know, for example, what Enos was talking about when he said, ". . . the voice of the Lord came into my mind again, . . ." He didn't say it came into his ear, but that it "came into my mind again, saying: . . ." He had been asking the Lord to bless his brethren, the Nephites, as everyone who gets the Spirit asks the Lord to bless his brethren . . . and his fellow men. ". . . the voice of the Lord came into my mind again, saying:"—and what the voice said is most important—"I will visit thy brethren according to their diligence in keeping my commandments." (See Enos 10.)

I must terminate these remarks. But I know what that voice is like, because *I have had it come into my mind and give me names when I have had to select stake presidents. There is nothing mysterious about it to people who learn to be guided by the Spirit. The voice of the Lord has come into my mind, in sentences, in answer to prayer.*

Now I know, brothers and sisters, that we can be guided by the Spirit. I counsel you to seek more diligently through earnest prayer the guidance of the Spirit. Learn to live your lives by the guidance of the Spirit. . . .

Oh, that's the way to pray to reach the Lord—all alone, where you are not fashioning prayers for the ears of any mortal person. In secret prayer you can kneel down and in the sincerity of your heart pour out your soul to God alone.

The path from man to God is prayer. Do as the Book of Mormon prophets advise: "Pray unto the Father with all the energy of heart." (Moroni 7:48.) The answer to such prayer is the guidance of the Holy Spirit. The key to happiness is to get the Spirit and keep it. The right to get it we were given when we were confirmed members of this Church. Walk by it back into the presence of God. So doing we will not need to be put to flight by our troubles. (Marion G. Romney, "Seek the Spirit," *Improvement Era*, 64:947-49 [Dec. 1961]. Italics added.)

Spiritual Gifts

LESSON FOLLOW-UP

Quorum members could be asked to relate how certain scriptural statements have helped them in solving problems in recent months.

LESSON OBJECTIVES

The Priesthood holder should feel motivated to seek his spiritual gifts "by the Spirit of God." (D&C 46:11.)

INTRODUCTION

Let us begin with a thrilling story of the power of God's Priesthood at work among men today. This account came out of the attack upon Kwajalein during World War II.

The men of the United States Marines were moving in to the beach. As they edged closer, the splatter of machine guns laid a death pattern on the men wading toward shore. Part of the account follows:

As I was a war correspondent, my boat was going in behind the first line of men, and we came upon these two wounded Marines in the water. One, from the stain of red around him, we could tell was wounded badly; the other, wounded too, was holding the other's head above water. We picked them up, amidst a hail of shots from shore, then pulled back toward safer retreat to render first aid. The one seemed too far gone to need much help, but the other refused aid until his wounded buddy was attended. But our help seemed insufficient, as we soon realized, and we announced our decision to his comrade. Then it happened.

This young man, the better of the two, bronzed by the tropical sun, . . . slowly got to his knees. His one arm was nearly gone, but with the other, he lifted the head of his unconscious pal into his lap, placed his good hand on the other's pale brow and uttered what to us seemed to be incredible words—words which to this moment are emblazoned in unforgettable letters across the doorway of my memory: "In the name of Jesus Christ, and by virtue of the Holy Priesthood which I hold, I command you to remain alive until the necessary help can be obtained to secure the preservation of your life."

Today, the three of us are here in Honolulu, and he is still alive. In fact, we walked down the beach together today, as we convalesce. He is the wonder of the medical unit, for—they say—he should be dead.[1]

How did this bearer of the Holy Priesthood know that he could be instrumental in saving his companion? By faith. In his heart burned the testimony of truth—"that which the Spirit testifies unto you even so I would that ye should do in all holiness of heart. . . ." (D&C 46:7.) There are many spiritual gifts, and each Priesthood bearer is capable of exercising those gifts with which he is endowed. This lesson is given to inspire us to exercise this power.

LESSON DEVELOPMENT

WHAT SPIRITUAL GIFTS EXIST IN THE CHURCH?

In a world of hard reality, we ofttimes forget that powers beyond our understanding lie within our grasp if we but exercise them in righteousness. The Lord has exhorted us to remember these powers and has given us a listing of some of them and has told us how to use them and why we have them. In a revelation through the Prophet Joseph Smith we are told:

> . . . I would that ye should always remember, and always retain in your minds what those gifts are, that are given unto the Church.
>
> For all have not every gift given unto them; for there are many gifts, and to every man is given a gift by the Spirit of God.
>
> To some is given one, and to some is given another, that all may be profited thereby.
>
> To some, it is given by the Holy Ghost to know that Jesus Christ is the Son of God, and that he was crucified for the sins of the world.

---

[1] See Tanner, Paul B., "Are Souls Perishable?" *The Instructor,* July, 1962, pp. 240-241.

To others it is given to believe on their words, that they also might have eternal life if they continue faithful.

. . . to some it is given by the Holy Ghost to know the differences of administration . . .

. . . to some to know the diversities of operations, whether they be of God . . .

. . . to some is given, by the Spirit of God, the word of wisdom . . .

. . . to another is given the word of knowledge . . .
. . . to some it is given to have faith to be healed.
. . . to others it is given to have faith to heal.
. . . to some is given the working of miracles;
. . . to others it is given to prophesy;
. . . to others the discerning of spirits.
. . . to some to speak with tongues;
. . . to another is given the interpretation of tongues.
. . . to the bishop of the church, and unto such as God shall appoint and ordain to watch over the church . . . to discern all those gifts lest there shall be any among you professing and yet be not of God.

. . . unto some it may be given to have all those gifts. . . . (D&C 46:10-27, 29.)

WHAT SIGNS SHALL FOLLOW THEM THAT BELIEVE?

We are cautioned by the Lord not to seek signs as such.

For verily I say unto you, they are given for the benefit of those who love me and keep all my commandments, and him that seeketh so to do; that all may be benefited that seek or that ask of me, that ask and not for a sign that they may consume it upon their lusts. (D&C 46:9.)

That signs shall follow baptism and reception of the Holy Ghost is made clear in this revelation:

And these signs shall follow them that believe—

In my name they shall do many wonderful works;
In my name they shall cast out devils;
In my name they shall heal the sick;
In my name they shall open the eyes of the blind, and unstop the ears of the deaf;

And the tongue of the dumb shall speak;

And if any man shall administer poison unto them it shall not hurt them;

And the poison of a serpent shall not have power to harm them.

But a commandment I give unto them, that they shall not boast themselves of these things, neither speak them before the world; for these things are given unto you for your profit and for salvation. (D&C 84: 65-73.)

ARE THE GIFTS OF THE SPIRIT WITH US TODAY?

Each member of the Melchizedek Priesthood should be able to bear testimony of the spiritual gifts that have blessed him. For example, the gift of healing is widespread throughout the Church, and protection from harm and evil has saved many lives and souls.

Class members at this point may be invited to briefly relate, if appropriate, how the power of the Priesthood has blessed their own lives or those of others they know through faith-building experiences.

SOME EXAMPLES OF SPIRITUAL GIFTS

Among recorded incidents of gifts, the following are only indicative of the rich abundance of such manifestations among faithful Latter-day Saints:

The following account is told by Clarence D. Taylor:[2]

It was called the most remarkable steamship iceberg collision on record in an 1891 issue of *Windsor Magazine*. Somehow the badly damaged *Arizona* managed to make it to Port St. John, Newfoundland, and land safely all its crew and passengers, after the ship had collided with an iceberg in the wake of an angry, storm-tossed sea.

Behind this story reposes an example of faith and the power of the Priesthood, for the Lord did provide for His servants in their time of need and blessed them with His authority to carry out the mission to which He had called them. Henry Aldous Dixon held such authority and used it during this incident.

He was a South African convert of 1856 and a man of great faith and humility. Elder Dixon and three other missionaries— Joseph Vickers, William H. Coray, and J. L. Jones—were aboard the *Arizona* bound for Great Britain. As the elders prepared for evening prayers, the ship's engines suddenly

---

[2]See *The Instructor,* January 1963, p. 3.

stopped and a great crunching noise of crumbling timbers and sheet metal rang through the cold, clear night.

Rushing on deck with all the other passengers, the missionaries beheld an immense, blue-white mass of ice on the forecastle deck in front of the bow of the vessel. The ship *Arizona*, travelling at full speed, had struck an iceberg. The force of the collision was so great as to cave in completely the ship's bow and to break off and pile up more than 20 tons of ice on top of the deck. Both anchors were broken; and the anchor chains, tested to hold 12 tons, were severed. The huge hole in the bow, 30-feet deep by 20-feet wide, extended below the water mark; and the break extended along the whole length of the keel. More than 4,000 gallons of water filled the front compartments; and several of the sailors were buried in the avalanche of ice when it settled on the forecastle decks, so that it took some time to dig them out.

With such a huge hole in the ship's bow, the front compartments filled with water, and with the weight of 20 tons of ice on the front decks, the sea had to be calm to enable the captain and crew to get the ship to the nearest port without sinking.

The four elders frequently knelt together and prayed for the safety of the ship and passengers. But this night tragedy was unusually special. It demanded great faith and the blessings of the Master. With righteous faith and in exercise of the Holy Priesthood, Elder Henry A. Dixon went alone on deck and there rebuked the wind and the waves and prayed for a calm sea.

Thirty-six hours later the ship limped into Port St. John. The prayers of the Elders had been answered; and the promise which Elder Dixon had given the passengers that no lives would be lost, that the ship would safely reach port, and that all would reach their destination in safety, had been fulfilled.

A most remarkable manifestation of tongues is related by Karl G. Maeser.[3] This is his account of the incident that occurred at the time of his baptism:

It was in October, 1855, that President (Franklin D.) Richards arrived. With Elder Budge acting as interpreter, he held with

---

[3]Pratt, Orson, *Masterful Discourses and Writings of Orson Pratt,* Salt Lake City, Bookcraft, Inc., p. 316.

us a few interviews, and we were ready for baptism. Accordingly on Sunday, October 14, 1855, myself, Edward Schoenfeldt, and Edward Martin were baptized. This was the first of such ordinances to be performed after the order of The Church of Jesus Christ of Latter-day Saints in that country. On October 19th, my wife, Anna, her sisters, Ottilie Schoenfeldt, and Camilla Meith, and their mother, Henrietta Meith, and their brother, Emil, were also initiated into the Church through baptism, making now eight souls in all. This service took place in the famous Elbe River, at a spot opposite the farthest linden trees in the so-called "Ostra Begerge."

On coming out of the water, I lifted both my hands to heaven and said, "Father, if what I have done just now is pleasing unto Thee, give me a testimony, and whatever Thou shouldst require of my hands I shall do, even to the laying down of my life for this cause."

There seemed to be no response to my fervent appeal, and we walked home together, President Richards and Elder Budge at the right and left of me, while the other men walked some distance behind us so as not to attract attention. Our conversation was on the subject of the authority of the Priesthood. Suddenly I stopped Elder Budge from interpreting the President's remarks to me, as I understood them perfectly. I replied to him in German, and again the interpretation was not necessary, as I was also understood by the President. Thus we kept on conversing until we arrived at the point of separation, when the manifestation as suddenly ceased as it had come. It did not appear to be strange at all, while it lasted, but as soon as it stopped, I asked Brother Budge what that all meant and received the answer that God had given me a testimony.

GIFTS OF THE SPIRIT CAN BE YOURS

To be worthy of spiritual gifts one must overcome evil and live righteously. In his epistle to the Galatians, Paul said: ". . . walk in the Spirit, and ye shall not fulfill the lust of the flesh. For the flesh lusteth against the Spirit, and the Spirit against the flesh: and these are contrary the one to the other. . . ." (Galatians 5:16-17.) Then Paul lists the works of the flesh as "adultery, fornication, uncleanness, lasciviousness, idolatry, witchcraft, hatred, variance, emulations, wrath, strife, seditions, heresies, envyings, murders, drunkenness, revilings, and such like." (Galatians 5:19-21.) Paul then calls all men to live by the Spirit, and he lists the fruits of the Spirit as "love, joy, peace, long-suffering, gentle-ness, goodness, faith, meekness, temperance, . . ." (Galatians 5:22, 23.) Paul realized the need for us to help one another and gave us the key to quorum activity. He said,

> If a man be overtaken in a fault, ye which are spiritual, restore such an one in the spirit of meekness; considering thyself, lest thou also be tempted. Bear ye one another's burdens, and so fulfill the law of Christ. (Galatians 6:1, 2.)

The key that unlocks the treasure of spiritual gifts is the key of clean living. By power of the Holy Priesthood, a *worthy* man can open the windows of heaven and bring showers of blessings upon those whom he loves. "To every man is given a gift by the spirit of God." (D&C 46: 11.) To exercise that gift, we are cautioned to observe two conditions: ". . . all things must be done in the name of Christ, whatsoever you do in the Spirit; and ye must give thanks unto God in the Spirit for whatso-ever blessings ye are blessed with." (D&C 46:31-32.)

APPLICATION

What Would Jesus Do?

W hen Jesus was upon this earth, He enjoyed the gifts of the Spirit. Jesus ". . . received grace for grace; and he received not of the fulness at first, but continued from grace to grace until *he received* a fulness." (D&C 93:12-13. Italics ours.) Through His faith in God, fasting and prayers, He was able to lay hold on all the gifts of the Spirit. He set the example for us. As Priesthood holders we are expected to seek spiritual gifts through the exercise of faith, prayer and diligence in magnifying our duties.

Ask yourself: How would the gifts of the Spirit aid me as a patriarch to my family? As a home teacher? As a steward in the Priesthood? Read and ponder D&C 46:7-26.

SPECIAL INSTRUCTIONS TO THE TEACHER

1. Emphasize the fact that the presence of the gifts of the Spirit is proof of the divinity of the Lord's work.

2. Bear testimony that the gifts of the Spirit are present in the Church today.

3. Challenge the brethren to diligently seek the gifts of the Spirit.

INSTRUCTIONAL MATERIALS

IPO10 (ISO10), Spiritual Gifts, would fit in well with the section of the lesson entitled, "What Signs Shall Follow Them That Believe?"

In Times of Crisis

LESSON FOLLOW-UP

One or several quorum members might be asked to witness examples where they have seen or enjoyed the gifts of the Spirit in operation.

LESSON OBJECTIVE

The Priesthood holder should feel motivated to use his Priesthood and faith to stabilize the family situation in times of crises, and to distinguish between little things and major catastrophies which cause discomfort and sorrow.

INTRODUCTION

A MAN WITH NEW PROBLEMS

John Orville Brown was the town's most respected and successful citizen. He had all that a man could ever desire. He was the president of his stake, father of ten children and had a very prosperous sheep ranch. He was a happy man, a man who had never experienced any severe crisis.

The first indication of any hardship or "set back" in his life occurred about a year ago. Several hundred head of his sheep were caught in a blizzard in an upper mountain pass. It was impossible for food to be dropped in to them by air. Within a matter of days they were dead. Since that time the difficulties and crises in his life have continued to mount.

Earlier this year, his two eldest boys were killed in an airplane crash. Then one of his youngest daughters contracted a rare disease which required special medical attention. Last month John himself had suffered a mild stroke that required prolonged hospitalization. He had seen his world collapse around him within a year's time. Because of his terrific medical expenses and other losses, he was faced with the loss of his ranch. Several of his children had grown bitter against the Church. One was on the verge of apostasy. His wife had even chastised him, suggesting that if he had spent more time at home instead of at his work and Church, much of their sorrow could have been avoided. Even several of his close friends and confidants had suggested to him that it was because of his lack of faith that he was experiencing this trial. In the face of all that had transpired, all John could ask himself was: "Why—Why me, Lord?"

LESSON DEVELOPMENT

The quorum might discuss the following:

1.   In light of such devotion and faith in the Gospel as illustrated in the above experience, how do we reconcile such a tragedy?

2.   How could you use your Priesthood to solve some of the crises raised in this situation?

3.   What growth and development could come out of such an experience?

The foregoing story is fictitious in its modern setting but analogous to the experience of Job. The quality that endears the Christian today to the ancient prophet is his unchanging and constant devotion to his Father in spite of his almost unbearable load. In the face of his prolonged trial we read one faithful utterance after another:

. . . the Lord gave, and the Lord hath taken away; blessed be the name of the Lord.

In all this Job sinned not, nor charged God foolishly. (Job 1:21-22.)

. . . while my breath is in me, and the spirit of God is in my nostrils;

My lips shall not speak wickedness, nor my tongue utter deceit.

God forbid that I should justify you: till I die I will not remove mine integrity from me. (Job 27:3-5.)

To understand better the "why" of crises in our lives, the quorum might consider the following statements and scriptures.

THE PURPOSE OF ADVERSITY

The over-all purpose of trial and adversity was explained by Lehi to his son, Jacob:

For it must needs be, that there is an opposition in all things. If not so, my first-born in the wilderness, righteousness could not be brought to pass, neither wickedness, neither holiness nor misery, neither good nor bad. . . . (II Nephi 2:11.)

In the light of Lehi's statement, what prupose would a crisis have?

Some have considered Job's experience as fictitious, but the Lord revealed to Joseph Smith that Job's adversity was as much a reality as Joseph's trial while in the Liberty Jail. After making a fervent appeal to the Lord for redress, Joseph was given the following encouragement that all his adversity had a purpose:

My son, peace be unto thy soul; thine adversity and thine afflictions shall be but a small moment;

And then, if thou endure it well, God shall exalt thee on high; thou shalt triumph over all thy foes. . . .

Thou art not yet as Job; thy friends do not contend against thee, neither charge thee with transgression, as they did Job.

And they who do charge thee with transgression, their hope shall be blasted, and their prospects shall melt away as the hoar frost melteth before the burning rays of the rising sun; . . . . (D&C 121:7, 8, 10, 11.)

Note: Several of the greatest revelations to the Church came out of Joseph's trial while in Liberty Jail.

One of the difficulties we have in understanding "why" is that we impose upon God the limitations of our mortality. Of this, Sterling W. Sill has said:

It is a serious mistake to judge God within the narrow limits of our own understanding and abilities. God has created worlds without number and is able to hold them all in perfect control. But even the greatest worlds are not the most prized of God's creations. The welfare of His children is far more important, and He has said that the greatest of all His gifts is the eternal life that He bestows upon us.[1]

It should be understood that trials and adversity do not always come to us as a test of our faith or originate from the adversary. Much of our tribulation is caused from our folly in the use of our agency. But

---

[1]Still, Sterling W., *The Upward Reach*, Salt Lake City, Bookcraft, Inc., 1962, p. 338.

regardless of the source of the trial, all adversity can give us experience and can be used for our ultimate good.

The quorum teacher might have a brother who has experienced some sorrow through a recent trial report briefly on the effect it had upon him and his family.

THE CAUSES OF OUR SORROW

With adversity in its proper perspective, the quorum might consider some of the most common causes of unhappiness. These might be listed on the chalkboard.

CAUSES OF MAN'S UNHAPPINESS

1. Family discord.
2. Financial difficulty.
3. (List other causes as suggested by the quorum.)
4.
5.
6. (etc.)

After the foregoing list has been completed, the class might discuss the following questions:

1. Which problems might be controlled by man? Which ones are beyond his control?

2. What special resources do we have as Priesthood bearers that can help us solve our problems?

During the 1965 April Conference of the Church, Elder Eldred G. Smith gave us the following suggestions:

I remember an experience I had when a good sister who wanted a special blessing came to my office. When I asked her why she wanted a special blessing, she refused to tell me. I learned from her that her husband was a member of the Church and held the Melchizedek Priesthood, so I spent considerable time trying to teach her the principle of Priesthood order, where the father in the home should bless the members of the family, . . .

Sometime later she returned to my office. . . .

She said the reason she refused to tell me why she wanted a blessing was that she wanted the blessing because there wasn't the proper relationship between her and her husband, . . .

Then she added, "That was one of the finest things that ever happened." She said she went home, she prayed about it, she thought about it, and then finally she mustered enough courage to ask her husband for the blessing. Of course it shocked him, but she was patient; she let him think it over a bit, ponder about it, and pray about it; and finally he gave a blessing. Then she added, "There has never been such a fine relationship in our home in all our lives as we have had since he gave me that blessing."[2]

THE PLACE OF FAITH IN TIMES OF SORROW

Another principal cause of unhappiness is worry. Where doubt exists, there is no place for faith to face a problem or crisis.

One Priesthood holder, a professor on a prominent university campus who does quite well financially by writing books and giving lectures in addition to his teaching responsibilities, said: "Look at me. I've had nothing but good fortune. I'm just waiting for my day of trial to come." When asked, however, to take a Priesthood assignment picking cherries, he replied, "I'd like to, but I can't find the time in my schedule." Is this brother experiencing any trial now? How might faith be exercised in meeting some of the challenges in this brother's life?

The lesson that must be learned in man's "second estate" is the same that Christ illustrated through His trial in Gethsemane, that "by descending below all things," He gained power and strength to "rise above all things," even death!

APPLICATION

What Would Jesus Do?

J esus provided us with our greatest example on how to overcome adversities and crises. In His darkest hour, Gethesmane, where He "suffered both body and spirit," He called upon His Heavenly Father in faith for strength to do our Father's will. Thus He "finished (His) preparations unto the children of men." (See D&C 19:18-19.)

As you face problems, crises, or adversities, instead of worrying about them or buckling under the weight, use your faith in Jesus

[2]Smith, Eldred G., "Family Unity through a Father's Blessing," *The Improvement Era*, June 1965, p. 534.

Christ for strength. If it is a family difficulty, sit down together, talk it over and pray about it in faith.

Single elders frequently face crises in their lives such as the anxieties attendant to their school work, or boy-girl problems. Seeking help through the Priesthood and the exercising of one's faith in such problems has been beneficial to many in the Church.

As a quorum, do you know of any brother who is experiencing trial and hardship? What might you do as a quorum to assist him?

SPECIAL INSTRUCTIONS TO THE TEACHER

1. Have quorum members provide positive examples from their own lives or recall someone they know well who has utilized his priesthood in meeting and overcoming adversity.

2. Bear testimony and give emphasis to the application "What Would Jesus Do?

INSTRUCTIONAL MATERIALS

Make use of chalkboard to list such things as *Causes of Man's Unhappiness.*

Pictures from daily newspapers of some tragedies that are common to families in our society might be shown.

Your Personal Standards

LESSON FOLLOW-UP

Discuss the benefits of a Priesthood holder possessing the gifts of the Spirit in his home. In his Priesthood assignments.

LESSON OBJECTIVE

The Priesthood holder should feel motivated so to act that his highest values are made known by his deeds.

INTRODUCTION

Let us first state that—

We Believe

. . . in worshiping Almighty God according to the dictates of our own conscience . . .

. . . in obeying, honoring, and sustaining the law . . .

. . . in being honest, true, chaste, benevolent, virtuous, and in doing good to all men . . .[1]

How well does the following description fit what we do?

Here in America we have reached the high tide of mediocrity, the era of the great goof-off, the age of the half-done job. The land from coast to coast has been enjoying a stampede away from responsibility. It is populated with laundry men who won't iron shirts, with waiters who won't serve, with carpenters who will come around someday maybe, with executives whose mind is on the golf course, with teachers who demand a single salary schedule so that achievement cannot be rewarded, nor poor work punished, with students who take cinch courses because the hard ones make you think, with spiritual delinquents of all kinds who have triumphantly determined to enjoy what was known until the present crises as "the new leisure."[2]

[1]From the "Articles of Faith," Articles 11, 12, 13.
[2]From an address by Charles H. Brower, President of Batten, Barton, Durstine and Osborne, Inc., at National Sales Executives Convention, May 20, 1958, published in *Speeches and Articles* by BBDOers, Gen. 1202.

QUESTIONS TO PONDER

Class members could be invited to discuss briefly these questions:

What dictates do we receive today from our conscience regarding personal standards?

Are we honoring the *spirit* of the law or just its letter?

Are we making *honest decisions*, telling the *whole truth*, being *chaste in thought* as well as deed, being *benevolent in attitude* as well as money, practicing *virtue in business dealings*, and doing *good to all men*, or only to those from whom we expect favors?

These questions penetrate our personal ideas of what we value most highly in life. They march right over the dead husks of our hollow words and challenge our actions. The basic question of personal standards is not what we profess, but what we do about what we profess.

LESSON DEVELOPMENT

WHAT DOES HYPOCRISY MEAN?

Jesus condemned the hypocrisy of the Scribes and Pharisees.

In all literature there is no more eloquent denunciation than his attack upon those "who sit in Moses' seat," the law givers, the learned men, the religious leaders, and the intellectual aristocracy of his times. He said, ". . . whatsoever they bid you observe, that observe and do; but do not ye after their works: for they say, and do not." (Matthew 23:2-3.) Then He listed their hypocrisies:

They bind heavy burdens on men's shoulders, but they themselves will not lift a finger to move them.

They do their work to be seen of men.

They make themselves conspicuous by their clothes.

They love the uppermost rooms at feasts and the chief seats in synagogues.

They ask to be called Rabbi—when there is only one Rabbi, even Christ (and all ye are brethren.)

They devour widows' houses.

For a pretense they make long prayers.

They compass sea and land to make one proselyte, and when he is made, they make him twofold more of a child of hell than themselves.

109

They pay tithe of mint and anise and cummin, and have omitted the weightier maters of the law: judgment, mercy, and faith.

They strain at a gnat and swallow a camel.

They make clean the outside of the cup and of the platter, but within they are full of extortion and excess.

They are like whited sepulchres, which indeed appear beautiful outward, but are within full of dead men's bones. (Summarized from Matthew 23:4-23.)

MEANING OF HYPOCRISY

Jesus forgave sinners. He healed the lame and the blind, but the practices of the hypocrites He condemned. Inasmuch as personal standards and behavior involve our sense of integrity and our ability to be honest with ourselves, it is well to know just what we mean by honesty as contrasted with hypocrisy.

The word *hypocrisy* is derived from the Greek. It meant to be an actor—to wear a mask and play a role different from one's true personality. We now attach a stigma upon the word by implying an intent to deceive. Not only does a hypocrite put on an outward show which is different from his inner feeling and belief, but he assumes a virtue he does not possess and pretends to be something that he is not. It is the pretense and the misleading assumption of virtue that we resent. And it is this deceit which Christ condemned.

ARE WE ALL HYPOCRITES?

It all depends—as we like to say. We like to appear well, we recognize flaws in our personality, and we try to conceal them. We take assignments for which we are inadequately equipped or prepared, and we use various means to avoid public embarrassment. These are the kinds of rationalizations that we use to excuse our pretenses and our assumptions of more virtue than we actually possess. We sometimes try to wear a halo even though the fit is poor.

Are we all hypocrites? Probably we must answer the question with a sheepish "yes"—at least we may be hypocrites to some degree. But we can take measures to improve ourselves and minimize our pretenses. We can discover the gap between our words and our deeds, and we can work to close that gap. We can study our own value systems and give serious thought to their inconsistencies.

WHAT ARE "VALUE SYSTEMS"?

The term "value system" is used in this lesson to indicate that our beliefs on any principle come in clusters—parts of which we acquire at different levels of our maturity.

For example, our value systems may involve such an area as "loyalty." A boy may learn his first values of loyalty from his childhood gang where there were secret passwords and signs to identify the "in-group." A mature man may cling to these same concepts of loyalty and never progress beyond them. When such a person is elected to a political office later in life, or accepts some other responsibility where he is called to serve *all* the people, this value system needs to be upgraded or he may become nothing more than a political boss. Points of conflict between different segments of such a value system become evident when "mature" men behave as schoolboys regarding such matters as initiation rites, political campaigns and wearing regalia.

As Priesthood bearers we are constantly challenged to bring to the surface our buried value systems, to examine them for inconsistencies with our mature understandings, to repent, and to purify them with our growing wisdom. This really means that we should apply to our attitudes and actions our larger grasp of Christ's teachings and the promptings of the Holy Spirit.

Some of the value systems we need to examine critically are Truth, Tolerance, Neighborliness, Forgiveness, Beauty, Loyalty, Recreation, Progress, Success, and the like. We should always remember that Christ taught that we must follow good teaching and not bad example even though both may come from the same person.

WHAT IS YOUR VALUE SYSTEM OF HONESTY?

We believe in being honest. Throughout the Church we have displayed posters that implore each to "be honest with yourself." We teach honesty in our classes. Yet, each of us has his own value system of honesty, and one part does not always agree with another. Let us examine a few examples and discuss the values that conflict:

The well-meaning mother. A little boy reaches into the drawer, finds some money, takes it to the store and buys candy. The mother discovers his theft and teaches him that to steal money is wrong. It is dishonest. He did not earn the money, and it is not his to spend. She takes him to the store, he returns the candy, he takes the money back, puts it in the drawer, and together they pray for forgiveness. The boy has learned the meaning of honesty—or has he? He has learned that stealing money is wrong, and he has learned something about restitution and humility. These are good lessons, as far as they go. Do they go far enough?

The same boy comes home and announces that he has been asked to give a 2½ minute talk on "I Believe in Being Honest." The mother becomes very excited at the prospect of her boy appearing before the whole Sunday School. She buys him a new suit of clothes and impresses upon him how important it is to appear well. Then she asks him what he is going to say, to which he answers, "I don't know." "Well," says the mother, "I can soon fix that." And she proceeds to write out a speech which the boy memorizes. On the next Sunday he stands before the Sunday School and gives the speech. Friends crowd around afterward and tell him what a fine talk he has given and congratulate the mother on having such a bright boy. The mother feels good because she has taught her boy the value of preparation. She has taught him how to succeed. She has taught him some important words in his religious education. But has she taught him to be honest? She may have missed the opportunity completely.

The boy grows up to be a business executive, and he is asked to give an important address. He uses the exact words of others, but he gives no credit in his address. Is he being honest?

Among scholars there is a code of honesty which requires them to give bibliographical references to identify all direct quotations. The mother may never have experienced the value system of the scholars. But perhaps someone could help her to help her child learn *all* the values of a well prepared 2½ minute talk: that a speaker is more convincing if he thinks through ideas, expresses them in his own words, testifies only to those things which *he* knows or has experienced, and gives credit to whomever he quotes whether it be a writer of the scriptures or his own mother. Then he would learn to be honest in oral expression and not merely say, "I believe in being honest."

Class members might be invited to tell some ways in which we could improve on our personal honesty.

WHAT IS YOUR VALUE SYSTEM?

As Priesthood bearers, let us turn a soul-searching light upon ourselves. Do we have one value system of religion and another one of business practice? Some of our great literature has done much to suggest ways of bringing these two systems together. Among the greatest is *The Christmas Carol* of Charles Dickens. As you look at yourself in your business or employment mirror, whom do you see? Do you see

Scrooge before Marley's ghost? If so, perhaps, the immortal words of the repentant businessman should be yours.

"But you were always a good man of business, Jacob," faltered Scrooge, who now began to apply this to himself.

"Business!" cried the Ghost, wringing its hands again.

"Mankind was my business: charity, mercy, forbearance, and benevolence were, all, my business. The dealings of my trade were but a drop of water in the comprehensive ocean of my business!"

Where do you stand on the "purpose of business?" Is there any relationship between the fate of ancient Carthage and the observation of Polybius, the Greek historian, who said, "At Carthage, nothing which results in profit is regarded disgraceful." Is is disgraceful in our society to prey on the weakness of men for the purpose of making a profit? Should it be?

"What would you do?" This question was asked of 1,700 business executives by the Reverend Raymond C. Baumhart, S. J., doctoral candidate at Harvard University. The cases presented were like this:

Suppose you are president of a company in a very competitive industry. Your competitor, you learn, has made an important discovery. If you had the opportunity to hire one of his employees who knew the process, would you do it?[3]

When asked, "What would I do?" forty-eight percent said they would probably hire him. Fifty-two percent said they probably would not hire him. When asked "What would the average executive do?" the answers said seventy percent would probably hire him.

APPLICATION

What Would Jesus Do?

T he Savior provides us with an example of perfect integrity. He always acted in a manner consistent with the standards of His Heavenly Father's Gospel. He taught by the example he lived. So should it be with all those who bear His Priesthood.

[3]This study was reported in "How Ethical Are Businessmen?" in *Harvard Business Review,* July-August, 1961.

In light of the personal standards illustrated in this lesson, compare your actual performance with your belief. Are you satisfied with each? Are the two consistent with each other? Do you see opportunities to close the gap between your belief and your actions? Can you make promises to yourself and others and keep them?

Read and ponder 2 Nephi 31:13, 19-20; D&C 1:38; D&C 136:4, 20.

SPECIAL INSTRUCTIONS TO THE TEACHER

Divide the quorum into groups of four or five. Give each group a copy of the following: (You may desire to adapt it to fit your quorum.)

The elders' quorum presidency telephoned thirty elders to find two men to work on a landscaping project at the ward meetinghouse. Of the twenty-eight men who responded negatively, nearly all said something like "Oh, I would really like to help, but . . ." followed by an excuse.

Some of the men had responded honestly, some had not. What would be some criteria for determining which of these elders were honest and which were not? (List your responses.)

After the groups have had a few minutes to list their ideas, allow each group to report to the combined quorum.

Request that each member of the quorum evaluate himself as you ask the following questions:

1. Have you ever responded similarly to the way the twenty-eight men in the example did?
2. Were you honest?
3. How might your response be altered if you really were interested in doing what Jesus would do?

Every Man Is a Teacher

LESSON FOLLOW-UP

Quorum members could be asked to comment on this question: Have you been instrumental in any way in raising the ethical standards in your business or profession or place of employment? What about the promises you made to yourself?

LESSON OBJECTIVE

The Priesthood holder should feel motivated to become a more effective teacher through his example and the Spirit of the Lord.

INTRODUCTION

When a child says, "Show me, and then I can learn for myself," he is saying: "Please don't preach to me; just let me follow your example." In this lesson we hope that every bearer of the Priesthood will consider himself an engineer of learning experiences rather than a teacher who is only a preacher. This idea of helping people learn calls for a creative approach to teaching, and it calls for a shift from the traditional idea that a teacher is somehow like a fountain that spouts and that learners are like thirsty pilgrims dying for a drink. Rather, it pictures the teacher as an enthusiastic mountain climber who says to the boys absorbed in playing marbles: "Look up there, fellows—from the top of that peak you can see something so beautiful it will take your breath away. Come follow me; I'll help you pack, and I can show you the way. But YOU will have to do the climbing. Then YOU can feel the thrill of reaching the top of the world." He who would ignite another must himself first glow. It is this teaching power that we hope to capture in this lesson.

LESSON DEVELOPMENT

Let us begin by reading together this hymn which is sung by Sunday School teachers throughout the Church:

HELP ME TEACH WITH INSPIRATION

Help me teach with inspiration, Grant this blessing, Lord, I
pray;
Help me lift a child's ambition To a higher, nobler way.
Mold my will to do Thy bidding, Open Thou mine eyes to see;
Free my soul with Truth eternal, Leave Thy Comforter with
me.
Help me reach a child in darkness, Help me lead him through
the night;
Help me come prepared to guide him, With Thy lamp of wis-
dom's light.
Let my vision of tomorrow, See the man this child will be;
Living by a good example, Living nearer, Lord, to Thee.
Fill my mind with understanding, Tune my voice to echo
Thine;
Touch my hand with gentle friendship, Warm my heart with
love divine.
Help me find Thy lambs who wander, Help me bring them to
Thy keep;
Teach me, Lord, to be a shepherd; Jesus, help me feed Thy
sheep.[1]

—Lorin F. Wheelwright

JESUS INSPIRES US TO BE BETTER TEACHERS

The greatest teacher of all time is Jesus Christ. Even those who
reject His divinity acknowledge Him as a great teacher. Why was He
great? Let us examine His life and learn from His methods. We can
catch only a glimpse in so short a time, but we can apply His example
to ourselves.

Jesus prepared Himself spiritually. The earliest account of Him as
a boy places Him in the temple talking with learned men, asking questions, and engaging Himself in spiritual matters which He described
as His "Father's business." Later He made peace with Himself during a
forty-day fast. He came to grips with His purpose in life and made the
spiritual decision of whom He would serve—God, not Satan. He went
to holy places to study the scriptures, and His knowledge was so profound that He quoted them at will throughout His ministry and often
confounded the Scribes and Pharisees. He continually sought divine

---

[1]Copyright 1958 by Pioneer Music Press, Salt Lake City. Used by permission.

116

guidance and proclaimed that He was inspired of His Father and that His doctrine was of God, not Himself. He looked into the hearts of men to find the hunger of their souls. His chief concern was for their enlightenment, their growth, and their salvation as children of God.

HE HELPED MEN SEE WHAT THEY COULD BECOME

He said, "I am come unto this world that they which see not might see . . ." (John 9:39.) Jesus understood that a person must be ready to learn before he can be taught. He studied the responses of those whom he addressed. When He found readiness he struck while the "iron was hot" and drove His lessons home. When He found an attitude of indifference, He challenged it. He found Simon called Peter and his brother Andrew casting a net and said: "Follow me, and I will make you fishers of men. And they straightway left their nets, and followed Him." (Matthew 4:17-20.) An able teacher plants the seed of greatness in his pupil and cultivates that seed with patience until it comes to fruition. He never lets him lose sight of what he might become.

JESUS MADE FRIENDS OF HIS DISCIPLES

Jesus walked and talked with His disciples. He ate with them and listened to them. He asked favors of them and responded to their suggestions. He shared His inner life with them and trusted them. He said, "Ye are my friends if ye do whatsoever I command you. Henceforth, I call you not servants . . . But I have called you friends." (John 15:14-15.) His kindness was seen daily by those who followed Him.

His sense of universal love overwhelmed those who were accustomed to the status symbols of His time. To Jesus, a hated tax collector could be just as worthy of friendship and concern as could a Nicodemus, who was afraid to be seen in public with such a controversial figure. Jesus made a friend of the woman at the well; then He taught her and she brought her friends to Him. This was His method.

JESUS DEFIED CLOSED MINDS

Jesus disliked the practices of those with eyes that would see not or ears that would hear not. He knew that a closed mind is like a clenched fist: it can strike hard but you can put nothing in it. He compared nonreceptivity to stony ground where one has not roots "in himself." Such a person, He said, could be easily offended. He explained in His parable of the sower why some people have closed minds: they are like fields filled with thorns; they hear the word, but "the care of this world, and

117

the deceitfulness of riches choke the word." (Matthew 13:22.) We must personify what we expect our students to be—seekers after truth.

HE PRACTICED WHAT HE PREACHED

He walked among men doing good, His deeds went before Him and aroused the people to come to see and hear this man. He condemned the hypocrites' false pretenses. He called all men to free themselves from the shackles of petty tyrannies, and He practiced His freedom before the world. He preached that the Sabbath was made for man, not man for the Sabbath. He said: "If ye continue in my word, then are ye my disciples indeed; and ye shall know the truth, and the truth shall make you free." (John 8:31-32.) To free one's soul, He said, one must become a child of God, believe with the faith of a child, and live to please a loving Father. Jesus taught us that deeds are the best sermons.

JESUS DRAMATIZED HIS LESSONS

We hear much about teaching facilities, visual and auditory aids, and the necessity of a controlled environment. These are refinements of our civilization and attempts to improve learning. But we must remember that the greatest Teacher of all used the resources at hand to dramatize His eternal truths; He *used* them, and used them well. He knew that people needed tangible evidence to believe the intangible.

He picked a lily from the field and showed it to illustrate how God provides. He tok a coin to challenge the political spies and asked, "Whose picture is it?" If they could see Caesar and render ribute to him, could they not see God and render tribute to Him? What could be more dramatic than a mob hurling stones? Yet, He made of the stone the eternal symbol of vengeance and He made every man look within himself to see if he were worthy to hurl it at another. He walked the last mile and met death on a cross between thieves and made vivid in men's minds the truth that saving the souls of mankind justifies the ultimate sacrifice. He was no coward. He made the truth dramatically impressive. He wanted His lessons to be remembered.

We may not be able to be as effective, but at least we can go far beyond the mere telling. We can involve our learners in actions beyond the word. We can make our truths come alive by giving them live settings and vivid portrayal.

HE OFTEN SPOKE IN PARABLES

To speak in parables is a challenge to the creative teacher. Can *you* tell a story that is fascinating in itself and doubly instructive because of its second meaning? Jesus did. Where did He get His parables? Did He go to the library of teaching materials when He was preparing His sermons and borrow them? Yes! But His "library" was mankind. He observed with clear vision what people around Him said and did. He noticed the way they worked, the objects upon which they placed great value, and He observed their human relationships. Then He constructed His stories, using those things which people already knew and upon which they based their own value systems. But He used them in a profound way. He endowed ordinary objects with spiritual significance. His teachings live because they provoke thought in our minds. We become part of the process. We cannot be lazy of mind in the presence of Christ's parables. If we are, we miss the point.

For those who would become great teachers, Jesus challenges us to be inventive—to be observant and to use our own imaginations. He says in effect, "Don't let your story be dull! Make it a living symbol that has meaning to man!" Be a teacher of creative imagination, like Jesus, whose mind worked constantly to enrich the pastures where God's lambs might feed, and grow, and become strong in the fold.

To teach as Jesus taught we must give wings to our words and let our message soar. This is how He taught with inspiration.

APPLY THE PRINCIPLES OF JESUS

To clarify how a bearer of the Priesthood might apply the example of Jesus to himself, let us examine a case and discuss our approaches to its solution.

The boy who chooses poor companions. John is a vigorous youth of eleven and he is making decisions that can shape his whole future. Here is his father's view of him:

> I come home tired from work and expect to find the lawn cut. I have told John repeatedly that he should tend to his duties and forget those kids up the street. Tonight I found it still uncut and getting so long that with one good storm it will be hay before we can mow it. I am tired of trying to get that boy to do his work. He seems to evade me and run off with those kids all the time. I scold him and his mother scolds him and we are just getting nowhere.

119

Here is what the mother says of the boy and his problems with his father and the lawn chore.

John is a good boy and his father is a good man. I love them both, but they just don't get together. John has found boys up the street who have a car and lots of spending money and seem to have nothing to do but fool around, and they like John and take him everywhere. The older boys smoke, and I suspect that they tell lots of stories that I would never hear. John thinks they are manly and that they live exciting lives. He is not very respectful to his father, and I can't do anything with him.

Here is what the elders quorum president says about John and his father:

This family has been only partially active. The mother goes to Relief Society, and the father is an elder who served a mission, but he seems to be completely absorbed in his business and has little time for his family or his Church. The boy worries me. I think his companions are having a bad influence upon him. I have asked the home teachers to work with the father to begin solving this problem.

SOME POINTS TO PONDER

Class members might be asked to comment on these questions:

Whose responsibility is it to guide this boy?

What can the home teacher do in working with the father?

What can the father do to prepare himself spiritually to help his son?

How can the father or mother give this boy experiences that will enable him to see what he might become?

What can the father do to be a friend to his boy?

What can the father do to show the boy how to choose good companions?

Is there any way this father can dramatize the importance of making a wise choice of friends?

How can this father talk with his son to inspire him? Are there any methods he can use to help him speak the boy's language?

WHAT IS OUR SOURCE OF GOSPEL TRUTH?

Not only must we follow Jesus in the methods He used as a teacher, but we are specifically directed to follow Him in content.

And we are commanded to follow Him in spirit. This revelation is pertinent:

> And again, the elders, priests and teachers of this church shall teach the principles of my gospel, which are in the Bible and the Book of Mormon, in the which is the fulness of the gospel.
>
> And they shall observe the covenants and church articles to do them, and these shall be their teachings, as they shall be directed by the Spirit.
>
> And the Spirit shall be given unto you by the prayer of faith; and if ye receive not the Spirit ye shall not teach. (D&C 42:12-14.)

The Lord commanded that teachers not only use the scriptures but He also declared: ". . . seek ye out of the best books words of wisdom; seek learning, even by study and also by faith." (D&C 90:15.)

This great stress on learning has inspired Latter-day Saints to build schools, to send their children to college, and to conduct vigorous programs of continuing education. The principal activity of most classwork in the quorums and the auxiliaries is teaching and learning the Gospel. The Church is also stressing the teaching of the Gospel in the home, and some lessons in this manual are devoted to this program.

WHAT CAN YOU DO TO INSPIRE OTHERS?

As bearers of the Priesthood we are instructed to teach the Gospel to others. We can and should follow the example of Jesus to make our teaching conform to truth and to use such teaching methods that our learners never forget our lessons.

It is the living sermon which is most convincing and at this point every Priesthood bearer can be a professional. You can personify the virtues you believe and can extend your influence far beyond classrooms by BEING a man of principles. You can also focus your example so that some young people—such as your own son or daughter—will see your light and follow it.

However, a good example *alone* is not enough. A good example is necessary if we get people to pay attention to our teachings. No one gets a testimony *only* because he sees a good example. He gets a testimony because he is taught the truth. But he pays attention to the teaching because of the example.

What Would Jesus Do?

This lesson centers on the example of what the Savior did as the Master Teacher when He walked among men. From His example, what can you do to become more effective as a teacher to those whom you serve? Do you study the Gospel on a regular basis so that you understand it? Do you live the example of what you know? Do you earnestly seek His spirit so that your teaching bears the stamp of testimony and the power of God?

Take some steps this week to become more effective as a teacher of righteousness, particularly in your home.

Read and ponder: D&C 42:12-14; D&C 90:15; D&C 43:16, John 13:1-16; Alma 39:11, D&C 88:74-80.

SPECIAL INSTRUCTIONS TO THE TEACHER

1. Ask class members to suggest the qualities that made Jesus the Master Teacher:

   Jesus the Master Teacher

   1.
   2.
   3.
   4.
   5.

2. Discuss the ways Priesthood holders can use His method to become more effective teachers.

3. Emphasize D&C 42:14.

Section

4

Your Priesthood Calling Is Magnified Through Love

Power Through Love

Quorum members could be asked to report briefly on what they did in the past week to become more effective in their teaching.

LESSON OBJECTIVE

The Priesthood holder should feel motivated to influence others by the power of love in the use of his Priesthood.

INTRODUCTION

Each bearer of the Melchizedek Priesthood has made a covenant with God. He has promised to live righteously and obey all of God's commandments to the best of his ability. In return, Christ has covenanted with him that "all that my father hath shall be given unto him." (D&C 84:38.) "And this is according to the oath and covenant which belongeth to the priesthood. Therefore, all those who receive the priesthood, receive this oath and covenant of my Father, which he cannot break, neither can it be moved." (D&C 84:39, 40.) This language has the ring of irrevocable law. It binds man and God together. What maintains the power of the Priesthood? The answer, in a large measure, is the substance of this lesson.

LESSON DEVELOPMENT

AN OLD BATTLE

The battle between *force* and *love* is as old as the war in heaven. It is fought daily on this earth and will probably remain the battleground of ideas, governments, societies, and conscience for some time to come. *As we face the pressure of daily life, the problem is to know how to win with love when force seems so simple.* Napoleon said of Jesus:

You are amazed at the conquests of Alexander. But here is a conqueror who appropriates to his own advantage, who incorporates with himself not a nation but the human race. Alexander, Caesar, Charlemagne and myself founded empires; but upon which did we rest the creations of our genius? Upon *force*. Jesus alone founded his empire upon love; and at this hour millions of men would die for him.[1]

When Joseph Smith cried out in Liberty Jail for relief from his oppressors he said, "O Lord God Almighty . . . let thine anger be kindled against our enemies." (D&C 121:4-5.) To this the Lord gave eloquent reply. He said:

> My son, peace be unto thy soul; thine adversity and thine afflictions shall be but a small moment . . . those who cry transgressions do it because they are the servants of sin, and are the children of disobedience themselves. . . . Wo unto them; . . . they themselves shall be despised by those that flattered them. They shall not have right to the priesthood, nor their posterity after them from generation to generation. (D&C 121:7, 17, 19, 20, 21.)

HOW CAN WE WIN WITH LOVE?

The great revelation on Priesthood contained in the 121st Section of the Doctrine and Covenants tells us "that the rights of the Priesthood are inseparably connected with the powers of heaven and the powers of heaven cannot be controlled nor handled only upon the principles of righteousness." (D&C 121:36.) Then comes the injunction to avoid unrighteous dominion. And the way to do this is spelled out in clear incisive language:

> No power or influence can or ought to be maintained by virtue of the Priesthood, only by persuasion, by long-suffering, by gentleness and meekness, and by love unfeigned;

> By kindness, and pure knowledge, which shall greatly enlarge the soul without hypocrisy, and without guile—

> Reproving betimes with sharpness, when moved upon by the Holy Ghost; and then *showing forth afterwards an increase of love toward him whom thou hast reproved, lest he esteem thee to be his enemy;*

> That he may know *that thy faithfulness is stronger than the words of death.* (D&C 121:41-44. Italics ours.)

---

[1]*Wisdom Magazine*, December 1956.

By kindness, and pure knowledge, which shall greatly enlarge the soul without hypocrisy, and without guile—

Reproving betimes with sharpness, when moved upon by the Holy Ghost; and then *showing forth afterwards an increase of love toward him whom thou hast reproved, lest he esteem thee to be his enemy;*

That he may know *that thy faithfulness is stronger than the cords of death.* (D&C 121:41-44. Italics ours.)

WHAT DESTROYS PRIESTHOOD POWER?

In this same revelation, we learn why many are called but few are chosen. Here is a list of sins that the Lord warns against:

1. to set our hearts on the things of this world,
2. to aspire to the honors of men,
3. to cover our sins,
4. to gratify our pride,
5. to gratify our vain ambition,
6. to exercise control, dominion, or compulsion in any degree of unrigheousness upon the souls of men.

. . . behold, the heavens withdraw themselves; the Spirit of the Lord is grieved; and when it is withdrawn, Amen to the priesthood or the authority of that man. (D&C 121:37.)

WHAT IS THE PROMISE FOR KEEPING THE COVENANT?

To those who pursue the path of love and shun the lures of force, the Lord makes a great promise. He says:

The Holy Ghost shall be thy *constant* companion, and thy scepter an *unchanging scepter of righteousness and truth;* and thy dominion shall be an *everlasting dominion,* and without compulsory means it shall flow unto thee forever and ever. (D&C 121:46. Italics ours.)

Class members at this point might be asked to give examples of men exercising great power through a spirit of love.

ORSON PRATT TELLS OF THE PRIESTHOOD'S POWER

Orson Pratt dwelt on this exalted concept of the Priesthood. He painted a picture of Priesthood power that serves as a beacon to all who seek guidance toward godliness. Keeping in mind the basic idea of this lesson, that the power of the Priesthood, in a large degree, is maintained by love, try to grasp the dimensions of that power:

The Priesthood of God is the great supreme, legal authority that governs the inhabitants of all redeemed and glorified worlds. In it is included all power to create worlds, to ordain fixed and permanent laws for the regulation of the materials in all their varied operations, whether acting as particles, as masses, as worlds, or as clusters of worlds. It is that power that formed the minerals, the vegetables, and the animals in all their infinite varieties which exist upon our globe. It is that authority that reveals laws for the government of intelligent beings—that rewards the obedient and punishes the disobedient—that ordains principalities, powers and kingdoms to carry out its *righteous* administrations throughout all dominions.[2]

WHY DO MEN TURN TO COMPULSION?

What idea is it that gets into men and creates a desire for oppression? In the revelation cited above, the Lord said, "We have learned by sad experience that it is the nature and disposition of almost all men, as soon as they get a little authority, as they suppose, they will immediately begin to exercise unrighteous dominion." (D&C 121:39.) Not only is this true in religious institutions but in all others.

The case of the business tyrant.—At a Priesthood meeting one of the brethren made comments that revealed a deep unrest concerning his work. Another brother approached him after the class and inquired further concerning his anxieties. This, in substance was the unburdening of soul that followed:

I work for a man who holds a responsible church position. To most people he is a righteous and honorable person. And in the coarser measures of uprightness I suppose he would get a passing grade. But as an employee I would flunk him. Here is what he does:

He blames his subordinates for everything that goes wrong. He takes personal credit for anything that goes right. He will not talk to us except to reprimand us. We are afraid to go to him for fear he will jump down our throats if we disclose

---

[2]Pratt, Orson, *Masterful Discourses and Writings of Orson Pratt*, Salt Lake City, Bookcraft, Inc., 1962, p. 316.

anything that is irregular. He does not seem to be concerned at all with how we feel about our work. His only concern is that we work hard and long and that we don't bother him.

I have been with this company for more than fifteen years, and I hold a responsible position. I hate my job, and hate my boss, and I am just counting the days until I can retire. In the meantime I'm keeping my mouth shut to avoid any excuse for his firing me before I can collect on the retirement. And believe me I've earned retirement working for that guy!

Assuming that this report is accurate, why would any man make his employees feel so resentful? From a purely selfish interest, the employer would gain much from good feelings that he now loses in half-hearted effort. Perhaps there are clues to the problem that all holders of the Priesthood might explore. Assuming each of us were the employer, how would we discover this sad state of affairs? Here are practices of more enlightened managers:

1. They learn the fine art of listening—to catch the feelings of others as well as ideas. (Is not this the seeking of knowledge?)

2. They learn to appreciate good performance and express it to those who do the work. (Is not this an expression of kindness?)

3. They are patient with those who make errors. (Is not this an expression of being long-suffering?)

4. They find remedies rather than faults and deal with problems rather than accusations. (Is not this an expression of gentleness?)

5. They seek out those who need orientation and convince them with sound reasoning how to correct errors. (Is not this the use of persuasion?)

6. When they correct a man in his error, they assure him that it is the error they dislike, not the man. (Is not this the showing of love to avoid making an enemy?)

HELPING A MAN TO SEE LOVE'S POWER

From the above description, what would you do as this employer's brother in the Church and as an employee of this man to help him overcome his weakness? The class might explore these approaches and try to arrive at a course of action which conforms to those principles which sustain Priesthood power:

1. Would you accuse him before others?

2. Would you avoid him altogether and do nothing?

3.   Would you start a rumor among Church members that so-and-so is a hypocrite?

4.   Would you investigate the facts and determine if your appraisal is shared by anyone else?

5.   Would you try to find a mutual friend who could drop a timely hint—so your employer could discover his problem for himself?

6.   Would you give him a good book on human relations?

7.   Would you exercise faith in prayer that he might find a way to communicate with his employees?

8.   Would you search the words of Christ to throw light on this kind of problem?

9.   What other ideas might you explore?

OLIVER COWDERY'S CASE

One of the classic cases in Church history involving the growth of hurt feelings into excommunication is the story of Oliver Cowdery. Space will not permit a full review of this case, but the essential facts are these:

Oliver Cowdery was a member of the First Presidency and an intimate friend of the Prophet Joseph Smith.

He was one of the three witnesses to the Book of Mormon and shared revelations, visions, and ordinations with the prophet.

He became involved in a dispute with the presiding brethren at Far West, Missouri, over the disposition of his property. He wanted to sell out; the brethren wanted him to keep the land as an indication of faith in building the central stake of Zion.

He sold his land and accused the presiding brethren of being "hot-headed, power-seeking, ignorant men."

He said, "I will not be influenced, governed, or controlled in my temporal interest by any ecclesiastical authority or pretended revelation whatever, contrary to my own judgment."

He said he was being tried illegally by an unauthorized court of the Church.

Formal accusations against him consisted of nine charges, including slander against Joseph Smith, pursuing filthy lucre, insulting a high council member, and treating the Church with contempt by not attending meetings.

The Church dropped the charges relating to property and

excommunicated him on the other charges. However, he failed to appear in his own defense and withdrew from membership.

He left the Church in 1838. In 1848 he spoke before the Kanesville Conference, bore his inspired testimony and said, "I wish to come humbly and be one in your midst. I seek no station. I only wish to be identified with you. . . . I wish to become a member."

He was baptized and died two years later. David Whitmer testified "Oliver died the happiest man I ever saw."[3]

It is impossible to judge the merits of Oliver Cowdery's case and the validity of the cross accusations without all the facts. But of one thing we can be sure: the atmosphere of Far West was filled with hurt pride, love of the things of this world, and compulsion; lacking was the basic power of the Priesthood: persuasion, long-suffering, gentleness and meekness, love unfeigned, kindness and pure knowledge. The pain and disappointment suffered by all those involved is only hinted in the documental records, but eye-witness accounts bore testimony to the bitterness that ensued. Yet, the saving grace of this unhappy event is the final chapter in which Oliver was accepted back into the fold of the Church and was received with "an increase of love toward him." It is notable also that he never denied his testimony of the restoration, and that he could say on his death bed, "Now I lay me down for the last time; I am going to my Saviour."[4]

POINTS TO PONDER

Class members could be invited to discuss these questions:

When dissension arises between brethren, how can an increase of hurt feelings be avoided?

What are the principles of the Priesthood that should govern?

How is the basic idea of this lesson to be applied—"The power of the Priesthood is maintained, in a large degree, by love"?

---

[3]Gunn, Stanley R., *Oliver Cowdery*, Salt Lake City, Bookcraft, Inc., 1962, chapters 10 and 12.
[4]Ibid., p. 209.

What Would Jesus Do?

O ne of the best ways to let love motivate your actions is to ask yourself continually, "What would Jesus do?" Would you accept the challenge to do that for a full week? The following are examples of situations that might prompt you to ask, "What would Jesus do?"

1. Another driver takes advantage of you on the highway.
2. Your children fail to understand the importance of reverence in a Church meeting.
3. Your employer blames you for something you didn't do.
4. The head of a family you home teach tells you you're not welcome any more.
5. Your neighbor is unkind to one of your children.

Read and Ponder: Moroni 7:46-48; D&C 121:37, 41-44.

SPECIAL INSTRUCTIONS TO THE TEACHER

Relate or have quorum members relate illustrations of how Priesthood holders were able to influence others wth their Priesthood through the power of love.

As I Have Loved You

LESSON FOLLOW-UP

There could be a short discussion on the following:

Describe how someone who has reproved you has then shown afterwards "an increase of love."

Have you had a situation where you were able to show "an increase of love" toward one you may have reproved?

LESSON OBJECTIVE

The Priesthood holder should feel motivated to learn to love as the Savior loves.

INTRODUCTION

Words have only the meaning which we assign to them. Thus, with a word such as "love," different people have different understandings as to what the word means.

The class instructor could ask some members of the class to indicate what they think it means to love someone.

In John 15:9 the following words of the Savior are recorded: "As the Father hath loved me, so have I loved you: . . ." Class members could be asked to indicate specific ways in which He, the Savior, does love us. Perhaps each person who is asked to respond might indicate *one* way in which He loves us. These might be listed on the blackboard.

LESSON DEVELOPMENT

He *has a righteous kind of love for Himself.* Concerning His youth we are told that He ". . . increased in wisdom and stature, and in favour with God and man." (Luke 2:52.) From the Doctrine and Covenants we read: "And he received not of the fulness at first, but continued from grace to grace, until He received a fulness." (D&C 93:13.) We know from the scriptures that He spent considerable time alone in prayer

133

and meditation. He also fasted. Is it not correct to assume that He contemplated during these times about the meaning of His life, the principles which should govern it, and how He might present these principles in the most effective way to others?

Let each class member answer the following questions to himself:

1.   During the past year have I read one of the Standard Works of the Church?

2.   Have I developed a system for regularly studying the meaning of a principle of the Gospel as presented in the Scriptures?

3.   Does our family hold a family home evening regularly? (Here is an opportunity for family members to help one another understand the principles of the Gospel.)

4.   Have I made a "personal commitment" to myself, the Savior, and my Heavenly Father to try to live the principles of the Gospel in all phases of my life?

Any individual who can answer "yes" to these questions will find himself "increasing in wisdom and stature, and in favour with" our Heavenly Father and with his brothers and sisters. He will become what newspaper columnist Sidney Harris has called an "actor," in the following story.

DO YOU ACT OR REACT?

I walked with my friend, a Quaker, to the newstand the other night and he bought a paper, thanking the newsie politely. The newsie didn't even acknowledge it.

"A sullen fellow, isn't he?" I commented.

"Oh, he's that way every night," shrugged my friend.

"Then why do you continue to be so polite to him?" I asked.

Before reading further about this incident you might ask some class members to comment with regard to what each of them would have done had he been so rudely treated. Then continue with the incident.

"Why not?" inquired my friend. "Why should I let *him* decide how I'm going to act?"

As I thought about this incident later, it occurred to me that the important word was "act." My friend *acts* toward people; most of us *react* toward them. He has a sense of inner balance which is lacking in most of us; he knows who he is, what he stands for, how he should behave. He refuses to return incivility for incivility, because then he would no longer be in command of his own conduct.

JESUS LOVES HIS FATHER

He has an everlasting faith, trust, and love for His Heavenly Father and our Heavenly Father.

The Savior was repeatedly praying to our Heavenly Father. Consider one of His recorded prayers (for example, the one found in John, chapter 17), and note the kinds of things for which He prayed. ". . . Holy Father, keep through thine own name those whom thou hast given me, that they may be one, as we are." (verse 11) "I pray not that thou shouldest take them out of the world, but that thou shouldest keep them from the evil." (verse 15.) When we pray:

1. Do we tend to ask for specific things, such as a physical object, and then expect the Lord to give it to us?

2. Do we ask for the kind of things for which the Savior prayed that we might be "one" with others, that we might be able to keep the commandments of our Heavenly Father in spite of the temptations of this world?

The class instructor might have someone read the following prayer on the Sacrament:

O God, the Eternal Father, we ask thee in the name of thy Son, Jesus Christ, to bless and sanctify this bread to the souls of all those who partake of it, that they may eat in remembrance of the body of thy Son, and witness unto thee, O God, the Eternal Father, that they are willing to take upon them the name of thy Son, and always remember him and keep his commandments which he has given them; that they may always have his Spirit to be with them. Amen. (D&C 20:77.)

What does it mean to take upon oneself the name of the Savior? In answering the question, with regard to the behavior of a Priesthood holder in his family, he might answer to himself the following questions:

1. Did I earnestly try to make clear to my children before they were baptized the importance of the covenant they were about to make with their Heavenly Father?

2. Throughout the period of their growing up, did I take advantage of "teaching moments" to clarify the meaning of the principle of the Gospel?

3. In our family do we regularly study the meaning of the basic principles of the Gospel as contained in the instructions given by the Lord in the sixty-eighth section of the Doctrine and Covenants?

DEVELOP A PERSONAL RELATIONSHIP

The Savior had a personal relationship with our Heavenly Father. We, as holders of His Priesthood, can have the same kind of relationship, not only to our Heavenly Father, but to the Savior as well. One of the members of the Church expressed his personal feeling toward the Savior as follows:

I REMEMBER[1]

It was a ministry to the beaten, bewildered people of Judah. When they were sick, He healed them; when they wept, He comforted them; when they were hungry, He fed them; when others forgot, He remembered. He was a lonely man seeking the lonely; a man of sorrows and acquainted with grief—yet His sorrows were those of others and His grief not of His own making.

The humble loved Him, but many among the influential despised Him. Sadducees and Pharisees called Him a glutton, a wine-bibber, a friend of harlots. Such epithets left Him trembling in spirit. Once, while the city slept, He walked alone through Jerusalem's empty streets and out the eastern gate to the garden. There, above the moon-drenched city, He cried out, "O Jerusalem, Jerusalem, thou that killest the prophets, and stonest them which are sent unto thee, how often would I have gathered thy children together, even as a hen gathereth her chickens under her wings, and ye would not!" (Matthew 23:37.)

It began on a Thursday night in April. Jesus had returned to the city for the last time after a farewell supper with those who knew and loved Him best; He had led them to Gethsemane. There, in the garden, Jesus laid bare His very soul in such anguish as only a God could endure. Others may think of Calvary as His place of atonement, but I think of Gethsemane, too.

In the morning, following His arrest, Jesus was brought before the high priest and the Jewish Sanhedrin for trial. He listened to the lies of false witnesses, felt the slap of hands upon His face, and heard their sentence of death for claiming to be the Son of God. He said nothing. Nor did He speak a defense be-

---

[1]Story by Rodney Turner.

fore the Roman governor, Pontius Pilate. Even the fury of His own people shouting, "Crucify Him, Crucify Him" failed to break His silence. The ministry of words was over; only the ministry of blood remained.

As the sun reached its zenith at noon, the whipped, bleeding body of Jesus was being nailed to a cross like those He may have seen in Sepphoris as a child many years before. The hours dragged by in an agony of mockery and tears.

Mary stood by the cross. The sky grew dark. It was three o'clock . . . and Jesus, with a mask of inexpressible weariness upon His face, lifted His eyes to His Father's eyes and whispered, "Father, into thy hands I commend my spirit." (Luke 23:46.)

How do you remember Him?

HE RESPECTED ALL HUMAN BEINGS
He had a respect for all human beings, each one.

"There cometh a woman of Samaria to draw water: Jesus saith unto her, Give me to drink. . . . Then saith the woman of Samaria unto him, How is it that thou, being a Jew, asketh drink of me, which am a woman of Samaria?" (John 4:7, 9.) But He gave her water which "shall be . . . a well of water springing up into everlasting life." (John 4:14.) To Him, she was a child of our Heavenly Father, a human being, His sister. He wanted her to know the same joy that He Himself knows and to find salvation and exaltation in His Kingdom.

Each of us can have this same respect, this same concern, this same love for one another, in our families and in every other group. We may differ in age, in experience, in wisdom, and in intelligence, but each of us is a child of the same Father in heaven. Consider the consequences of the way that the fathers in the following two incidents treated their children:

A GIRL WHO WAS RESCUED

It is rather difficult for me, a girl, to draw a line or designate explicitly where normal citizenship behavior ends and juvenile delinquency begins. Long before I began to commit crimes against society, I was fully aware of my intense feelings of hostility and disregard for the legal code and moral restrictions of our society. . . . As far as I can see, the disharmony between my father and me had a great deal to do with my apparent lack of conscience.

My childhood years were ones of great anxiety in which I had feelings of disconent whenever I was at home. The display of love was almost nonexistent between my father and me, for many times I had experienced traumatic situations at his hands. The first instance of remembrance occurred when I was only five years of age. After finding a sack full of kittens near a river, I gave all but one away, keeping a small crippled one for myself. A few months later, after I had nursed it to a point of complete recovery, my father informed me that we were moving and the kitten had to be put away. He proceeded to destroy the kitten before my eyes. In this instance, as in others that followed, I ran off and hid myself, cursing my father and vowing to pay him back someday.

Her opportunity came shortly thereafter, when she became a member of a juvenile gang and participated in all kinds of crime, including dope smuggling. After two years she became "hooked" by the dope herself.

Life no longer was important, and twice I attempted suicide, but I was discovered by my friends and saved in time. I decided then that I would just die slowly by increasing overdoses of heroin.

Fortunately she was saved. Although she was not a member of any church, she one day attended a meeting of The Church of Jesus Christ of Latter-day Saints.

Two people showed me a great deal of interest—one a teacher for the young women and one a very lovely young girl a year older than myself. They saw that something was wrong with me and for weeks attempted to get me out to more meetings. Finally, I attended Sunday School one morning. During the meeting I suddenly felt the pangs of withdrawal, and I had to get up and leave. These interested people followed me, cornered me and inquired as to what was wrong and wondered if they might be able to help. I began to shake and tremble. My head was pounding and I broke down. Falling to my knees, I poured out my situation, as I was too weak to care about anything.

Soon after this, I had much spiritual help and found that I had a desire to live after all. So, for the following two years I decreased my intake of dope and silently and prayerfully went through withdrawal. Doctors said I couldn't do it without medical help, but I did it and without my family ever knowing until I was almost cured.

All connections had been broken with my former companions, and this beautiful girl that helped me through it all by love, prayers, and tenderness, also motivated me to attend college. So, at eighteen years of age I began a new life full of meaning, happiness, and purpose.

A FATHER WHO LOVED HIS SON

Throughout my life as I grew up as a boy, my father and I had many serious arguments. One day, when I was seventeen, we had a particularly violent one. I said to him, "This is the straw that breaks the camel's back. I'm leaving, and I will never return." So saying, I went to the house and packed a bag. My mother begged me to stay, but I was too mad and upset to listen. I left her crying at the doorway.

As I left the yard and was about to pass through the gate, I heard my father call to me.

"Frank," he said, "I know that a large share of the blame for your leaving rests with me. For this I am deeply sorry. But I want you to know that if you should ever wish to return to our home, you'll always be welcome. And I'll try to be a better father to you. Finally, I want you to know that I'll always love you."

I said nothing, but went to the bus station and bought a ticket to a hundred miles from nowhere. But as I sat in the bus watching the miles go by I began to think about the words of my father. I began to realize how much maturity, how much goodness, how much love it had required for him to do what he had done. He had apologized. He had invited me back and he left the words ringing in my ears: "I love you."

It was then that I realized that the next move was up to me. I knew that the only way I could ever find peace with myself was to demonstrate to him the same kind of maturity, goodness and love that he had demonstrated toward me.

I got off the bus. I bought a return ticket to my home and went back. I arrived just shortly before midnight. I entered the house and turned on the light. There in our rocking chair sat my father, his head in his hands. As he looked up and saw me, he rose from the chair and we rushed into each other's arms.

That was the beginning of a new relationship between my father and me. Those last years that I was home were among the happiest of my life. I shall be forever grateful to him that in a moment of crisis he was able to put first things first.

What Would Jesus Do?

J esus exemplified the two great commandments, "Thou shalt love the Lord thy God with all thy heart, and with all thy soul, and with all thy mind," and "Thou shalt love thy neighbor as thyself." (Matthew 22:37, 39.)

As His representative, you have the opportunity to lead your family to greater love for our Heavenly Father and His Son, Jesus Christ. You can do this by directing their lives to the principles contained in the standard works. Take a principle and concentrate on living it in your home for a period of time.

Secondly, you have the opportunity to use love in your relationships with your wife and children. Ask yourself the ways in which you can more effectively show your expression of love to them.

Read and ponder: John 15:12-15; D&C 84:63, 77; Matthew 22:37-40.

SPECIAL INSTRUCTIONS TO THE TEACHER

1.   You may want to use a picture of Jesus washing the feet of His apostles in teaching the section of the lesson entitled, "I Remember."

2.   Assign members of the quorum to read or tell the stories in the lesson.

INSTRUCTIONAL MATERIALS

Meetinghouse library picture:
OP125—Jesus Washing Feet

A Time and Place

LESSON FOLLOW-UP

1. Let two or three quorum members indicate one way in which the Savior demonstrated His love for others.

2. Ask quorum members to indicate whether or not they found any major way in which they can emphasize love for other family members.

LESSON OBJECTIVE

The Priesthood holder should feel motivated to carefully consider how he uses his time so that he can give proper time to things that are most important.

INTRODUCTION

And the boys grew: and Esau was a cunning hunter, a man of the field; and Jacob was a plain man, dwelling in tents. . . .

And Jacob sod pottage: and Esau came from the field, and he was faint:

And Esau said to Jacob, Feed me, I pray thee, with that same red pottage; for I am faint: therefore was his name called Edom.

And Jacob said, Sell me this day thy birthright.

And Esau said, Behold, I am at the point to die: and what profit shall this birthright do to me?

And Jacob said, Swear to me this day; and he sware unto him: and he sold his birthright unto Jacob.

Then Jacob gave Esau bread and pottage of lentiles; and he did eat and drink, and rose up, and went his way: Thus Esau despised his birthright.

(Genesis 25:27, 29-34.)

WILL YOU LOVE ME AT SEVENTY-FIVE?

Shaunna was a beautiful, intelligent, seventeen-year-old girl. Her parents loved her very much, and throughout her lifetime they had tried to teach her to want the Lord's kind of marriage. "The Savior wants you to find someone," they said, "whom you can love with your whole soul and who can love you in the same way. He should be a man whom you love with the 'breath, smiles, tears' of all your life, as Elizabeth Barrett Browning indicated. With such a person you may achieve a kind of 'paired unity' so that you are one in spirit, one in purpose, and one in your respect for each other. If you choose such a man and both of you live worthily, you will be able to have your marriage solemnized in the temple of the Lord."

Parents often wonder how well they have taught their children. How well will their children perform in the acid test of experience? Shaunna's first real test came when she was still seventeen.

She was flattered when Jay asked her to go to the Junior Prom. You see this prom was not a high school prom; it was the university extravaganza. Jay was several years older than Shaunna, and he possessed many characteristics that appealed to her—intelligence, poise, and an apparent consideration for others. She had to admit to herself that she was emotionally and physically attracted to him.

The dance itself was everything she had hoped it would be. But after it was all over and they had ridden around for a while, Jay stopped his new convertible and turned off the key and Shaunna found herself close beside him. She soon learned that his intentions were not just to talk with her. Her moment of trial had come. But she was prepared for it because she had thought it through many times before. What would she do when faced with such a crisis?

She told Jay about many things she admired in him. She also told him about the kind of marriage and family life she wanted to achieve. Then she asked him, "If we were both seventy-five, would you ask me to go out with you?" It took Jay a little while to understand what she meant, but he finally did, and the crisis was over. She had wanted him to understand that there was more to dating and courting than physical attraction. If they were seventy-five, would her actions during her life have made her an acceptable and desirable companion?

142

NO TIME FOR HIS SON

Ed worked hard and was successful—in his occupation, that is. He had accumulated a considerable fortune and, as a result of his wealth, had great power and influence in the community.

But his occupational success had had its price. He was married to his business and had left most of the rearing of his children to his wife. "I'm sorry," he had often said when his son asked him for some of his time, "I've got to go to a meeting, but we'll do it on some other occasion." However, there always seemed to be another meeting, and the "other occasion" never came.

Ed was shocked and upset when the police arrested his son for a serious crime. "I have given him everything," he told the officers. He had given his son many material things, but he had not given him *real consideration as a human being*. Ed had not taught his son to accept responsibility. In many ways, he had not shown his son by the way he acted that he really loved him.

WHAT ARE YOUR GOALS?

Each legitimate goal and activity in life has its own time and place. One of the important things each individual should do is to take the time to think seriously, prayerfully, and thoroughly about the *main* goals of his life. Let class members indicate four or five *major* objectives that each of them has for his life here upon earth. The following principles may help in clarifying what is meant by "the time and the place."

1. At no time should one lose sight of the purposes of this life as defined by the Savior. He said that we should seek for *eternal* life, salvation, and exaltation and that in order to attain them we must understand, accept, and live the principles He gave to us. These principles must become the hub of the wheel, the main motif of the symphony, the central beacon which guides our lives. Many people unconsciously accept the values of the society in which they live. They never really seriously question them to see if they are desirable values. Had Esau gone through this process of careful contemplation, reflection, fasting, and prayer, he would never have sold his birthright. He did get some satisfaction from the food Jacob gave to him, but the pottage was a cheap glass imitation rather than the real diamond. The real diamond was his birthright. "But lay up for yourselves treasures in heaven, where neither moth nor rust doth corrupt, and where thieves do not break through nor steal." (Matthew 6:20.)

IT PAYS TO THINK AHEAD

The right time for physical intimacy between a man and a woman is when they are married. Then it becomes a symbol of their love for each other—spiritually and intellectually as well as physically. They become partners in creation with their Heavenly Father in giving His children a chance to come to this earth and fulfill the measure of their creation. When confronted with the same temptations which seventeen-year-old Shaunna had, an individual must remember that this situation is not the time nor the place for such intimacy.

2. It was said of the Savior, "He suffered temptations but gave no heed unto them." (D&C 20:22.) In order to be prepared for temptations and to attain the same maturity which He had, we must think through *beforehand* what we will do when we are confronted with a temptation. At the time of the temptation, emotional stress and social pressure may prevent us from thinking clearly and from being in tune with the Holy Ghost.

One time a group of Church workers was making a trip to attend a convention for one of the auxiliaries of the Church. During part of their journey they traveled through a canyon on a very narrow road. While they were riding along the road, someone asked what could be done to minimize the effects of sliding off the road down the canyon. Two or three suggestions were given.

A week later they were making a similar trip to attend another convention. Suddenly a member of the party saw that the driver had gone to sleep and that the car was heading toward the embankment. The driver immediately awakened and did a masterful job of keeping the car upright until it came to a stop. Several members of the group were bruised and shaken up, but no one was seriously hurt. When asked how he had been able to handle the situation so successfully after awakening, the driver replied, "I remembered the things we discussed a week ago, and they really helped me."

When we are alone—thinking, praying, reading, and fasting—we are much more able to arrive at the right decisions. Some refer to this as "The Art of Contemplation," and make it a regular part of their lives.

3. (Before discussing the next point, ask class members if they have sometimes found themselves letting their family role suffer when they are confronted with the demands of several roles in their lives. If this has been the case, why is it? Certainly they love their wife and children. Perhaps some will say that they are forced to do so by the demands of their occupational role, for example. But is this really so, or are there other factors at work?)

BALANCE IS IMPORTANT

It is possible to play several different roles in our life, but we must keep each role in mind and give it its just due. We play many different roles, such as a family role, a Church role, the role of citizen and an occupational role. Occupational success is important and desirable, but nothing is more important than our children or our wife. We do our basic teaching of our children each day of our lives *by our total behavior.* Teaching is not merely "telling" something to children; it is much more than that. We might ask ourselves the following questions: "Am I striving to help my children achieve the same objectives their Heavenly Father wants them to achieve?" "Can I be patient when they are impatient, responsible when they are irresponsible?" "Do I let them know, in one way or another, that I really love them and that I am really concerned about them?" Sometimes a man does have to attend important meetings. But on such occasions he should let his children know that he is also concerned about them; and they should realize that when he can, he will give them a *significant,* meaningful, and important part of his life. He does have time—important time—for them.

In this connection, fathers must keep in mind the "timing" principle. When a person has several roles to play, each of which is important, he should never neglect any of them, and if at one time he must give more effort and energy to one of them, he should make it up to the other roles later on. One man promised his wife and children, "When I am with you, I will really be *with you.*" By this statement he meant that he would give of himself to them in meaningful ways and not neglect them.

APPLICATION

What Would Jesus Do?

I f we seek first the kingdom of God and His righteousness, as Jesus instructed in the Sermon on the Mount, we will place first things first. What priorities would Jesus make? Who are the most important people, and what are the most important things in our lives? Time is the substance of which life is made. How should time segments be apportioned for an active Priesthood holder?

Only as you take the time to meditate seriously on this matter will you be able to give proper time to things that are most important.

Read and ponder: Ecclesiastes 3:1-2; Alma 34: 32-34; Jacob 2:18-19; Matthew 6.

SPECIAL INSTRUCTIONS TO THE TEACHER

1. Ask what stress Jesus gave to our taking sufficient time and effort for matters of importance in our lives. Cite specific examples.

2. Make a list of various roles Priesthood members in your group perform. Write the list on the chalkboard as they are given. Attempt to classify them in the order of their importance.

3. Allow an active Priesthood holder who seems to plan his time well and who gives adequate consideration to his flamily to tell what he has done that helps him to fulfill his roles.

4. Challenge each Priesthood member to analyze the roles for which he is responsible and think through the amount of time and effort he should give to each role. Suggest he develop a specific plan so that each role receives the appropriate attention it deserves.

Christlike Love

Ask quorum members to:
1. Give a good example of doing things at the right time of life.
2. Discuss how conflicts can be resolved with the various roles for which one is responsible in life.

LESSON OBJECTIVE

The Priesthood holder should feel motivated to more fully understand and practice what it means to love as Jesus taught of love.

LESSON DEVELOPMENT

Now the sons of Mosiah were numbered among the unbelievers; and also one of the sons of Alma was numbered among them, he being called Alma, after his father; nevertheless, he became a very wicked and an idolatrous man. And he was a man of many words, and did speak much flattery to the people; therefore he led many of the people to do after the manner of his iniquities.

. . . as they were going about rebelling against God, behold, the angel of the Lord appeared unto them;

. . . saying: Alma, arise and stand forth, for why persecutest thou the church of God?

. . . Behold, the Lord hath heard the prayers of his people, and also the prayers of his servant, Alma, who is thy father; for he has prayed with much faith concerning thee that thou mightest be brought to the knowledge of the truth; therefore, for this purpose have I come to convince thee of the power and authority of God, that the prayers of his servants might be answered according to their faith. (Mosiah 27:8, 11, 13-14.)

A certain man had two sons:

And the younger of them said to his father, Father, give me the portion of goods that falleth to me. And he divided unto them his living.

And not many days after the younger son gathered all together, and took his journey into a far country, and there wasted his substance with riotous living.

And when he had spent all, there arose a mighty famine in that land; and he began to be in want.

And he went and joined himself to a citizen of that country; and he sent him into his fields to feed swine.

And he would fain have filled his belly with husks that the swine did eat: and no man gave unto him.

And when he came to himself, he said, How many hired servants of my father's have bread enough and to spare, and I perish with hunger!

I will arise and go to my father, and will say unto him, Father, I have sinned against heaven, and before thee,

And am no more worthy to be called thy son: make me as one of thy hired servants.

And he arose, and came to his father. But when he was yet a great way off, his father saw him, and had compassion, and ran, and fell on his neck, and kissed him.

And the son said unto him, Father, I have sinned against heaven, and in thy sight, and am no more worthy to be called thy son.

But the father said to his servants, Bring forth the best robe, and put it on him; and put a ring on his hand, and shoes on his feet:

And bring hither the fatted calf, and kill it; and let us eat, and be merry:

For this my son was dead, and is alive again; he was lost, and is found. . . . (Luke 15:11-24. Italics ours.)

Class members might indicate what they think these two incidents, as reported in the scriptures, have to do with the title of this lesson: "Christlike Love." What does this kind of love involve?

The following question may also help us to understand the objective of this lesson: Assuming that parents consciously want to have children, what motives impel them to want these children?

WHY DID WE COME TO EARTH?

What goals does our Heavenly Father want us to achieve while we are upon the earth? According to the scriptures, some of the goals are that:

1. He wants us to acquire a physical body. The spirit and the body constitute the soul of man. (D&C 88:15.) He wants us to learn to manage our emotions rather than be enslaved by them. (Romans 8:6, 7.)

2. He wants us to acquire the kind of power that comes from the right type of knowledge or from wisdom. (D&C 6:7.)

3. He is concerned that we participate in certain "saving" ordinances such as baptism and temple marriage. (D&C 33:11; 132:7.)

4. He wants us to experience lasting joy. (John 15:11.)

5. He is vitally concerned that we give devotion to all of His teachings so that we might become more and more like Him and become worthy to live in His presence eternally. (D&C 11:30; 76:50-70.)

To love a person the way our Heavenly Father and the Savior love us is to be committed to do everything we can to help him become a son or daughter of Christ.

> And now, because of the covenant which ye have made ye shall be called the children of Christ, his sons, and his daughters; for behold, this day he hath spiritually begotten you; for ye say that your hearts are changed through faith on his name; therefore, ye are born of him and have become his sons and his daughters. (Mosiah 5:7.)

We will be sensitive to the individual's hopes, aspirations, and problems and the circumstances which surround his life. We must try to put ourselves in the other person's position and think how we would feel if we were in his place. We would need to learn to think of the other individual literally as a brother or a sister. Everyone on this earth *is* a child of the same Father in heaven.

WE MUST BE "BORN AGAIN"

To experience this kind of love for another requires that we be "born again" and receive the influence of the Holy Ghost in our life. Its influence and the influence of the Priesthood generally are exercised as follows:

. . . only by persuasion, by long-suffering, by gentleness and meekness, and by love unfeigned;

By kindness, and pure knowledge, which shall greatly enlarge the soul without hypocrisy, and without guile—

Reproving betimes with sharpness, when moved upon by the Holy Ghost; and then showing forth afterwards an increase of love toward him whom thou hast reproved, lest he esteem thee to be his enemy;

That he may know that thy faithfulness is stronger than the cords of death. (D&C 121:41-44.)

Class members might give examples of an un-Christlike kind of behavior that the world may call love.

SOME PEOPLE LOVE CONDITIONALLY

Many individuals do not appear to love others in a truly Christlike way, but in more of a selfish way.

Recently a man and his wife, both of whom are in their forties and the parents of six children, came to a marriage counselor. The woman told the counselor that her husband had recently told her he no longer loved her. The counselor asked the husband if this were correct, and he replied that it was. When asked why he had made the statement, the husband replied that his wife no longer satisfied some of his basic needs; she was no longer physically attractive.

Again, a parent may find it easy to accept a gifted child or a child who achieves according to the parent's desires. At the same time, such a parent may make a child who is not so gifted but who tries to do the best he can with his abilities feel inferior because he does not match the achievements of the gifted child.

These individuals are committed to the eternal welfare of other people only as those people do what *they want done* the way they want it done. What they are really saying, whether they realize it or not, is that they will accept another person only if that person meets certain expectations. But unconditional love requires a different attitude. The elder Alma continued to pray for his son, Alma, even though his son was making many mistakes. The father of the prodigal son had the true vision of love when he said, "It was meet that we should make merry, and be glad; *for this thy brother was dead, and is alive again; and was lost, and is found.*" (Luke 15:32. Italics ours.)

(Note the difference in the attitude of the father in the parable and the attitude of the prodigal son's brother. See Luke 15:25-30.)

SORROWFUL BUT NOT RESENTFUL

Christlike love causes a person to be sorrowful over the sins of a brother or sister and at the same time to be forgiving and not resentful or judgmental. (D&C 64:7-10.) Such love inspires a person to be kind when another is unkind and patient when another is impatient. Jesus taught, "Love your enemies, bless them that curse you, do good to them that hate you, and pray for them which despitefully use you, and persecute you; that ye may be the children of your Father which is in heaven: for he maketh his sun to rise on the evil and on the good, and sendeth rain on the just and on the unjust." (Matthew 5:44-45.)

It does not mean that we say to the sinner, "I agree with your sinful behavior." It does mean that we continually try to make the meaning of the great principles taught by the Savior clear to him *that he might know the same joy that we ourselves have known*. Conversely, to be made aware of our mistakes may be painful, but the pain may turn into gratitude if we know that another person is making us aware of them, not to get even or depreciate us as a human being, but because he loves us and wants to help us. We learn in Hebrews: "for whom the Lord loveth, he chasteneth. . . ." (Hebrews 12:6.)

The joys of loving in the sense described in this lesson are many. In the first place, when another person really understands that we are interested in him, he will often be motivated to overcome his immature behavior. Furthermore he will often return the same kind of love to us: "Give love and love to your heart will flow."

Class members might think of a time when they made a mistake and were sorry for it. If it involved another person, did you worry about what action that person would take towards you? If that person did forgive you, how did it make you feel?

Or think of someone who gave freely to you in some way, not with the thought in mind of having you do something in return for him, but simply because he loved you. Did you find that this action made you want to do some loving act for him?

CHRISTLIKE LOVE GROWS

Secondly, we must remember that in loving one person unselfishly we may be helping many others to understand this kind of love, because the person whose life has been touched by us will touch many others in the same way.

Finally, there comes a kind of divine influence into a person's life when he tries, as the elder Alma did, to help another person understand the love of our Heavenly Father. In the story of *The Other Wise Man* by Henry Van Dyke, Artaban gave unselfishly to his fellow human beings throughout his life. Consequently, the Savior told him that in truly loving his fellow human beings—his brothers and sisters—he had also loved Him, the Savior, in the most mature way. ". . . Verily I say unto you, Inasmuch as ye have done it unto one of the least of these my brethren, ye have done it unto me." (Matthew 25:40.)

APPLICATION

What Would Jesus Do?

J esus demonstrated love in His encounter with the woman taken in adultery (John 8:3-11), the woman who desired forgiveness (Luke 7:36-50), and the lawyer who attempted to trap Him (Luke 10:25-37). Study these situations in the life of our Savior and see how His example can be a guide to us in our daily relationships.

Should a bearer of the Holy Priesthood out of the abundance of his heart frequently express his love and devotion to his wife and children? Should they have any doubt as to his willingness to offer Christlike love? Would Jesus have each Priesthood holder also consciously try to practice *empathy*—the placing of oneself in the position of another person and trying to understand his feelings, his needs, his problems, his hopes and his aspirations?

This week make a conscious attempt to use this kind of love in your everyday association with your family members.

Read and ponder: John 8:3-11; Luke 7:36-50; Luke 10:25-37.

SPECIAL INSTRUCTIONS TO THE TEACHER

1. Use case studies where Christlike love could be applied and allow class members to respond as to what they would do in the given situations. Then have them decide what Jesus would have them do. As examples:

   a. Robert had been very active in the Church from a very young age. He had frequently shown enthusiasm about going on a mission. You are proud of him and look forward to his representing the family in the mission field. Today he announces to the family that he has joined the Air Force and will be leaving for training camp in three days.

b. Jane is to be married in the temple in two weeks. The announcements and invitations for the reception have been mailed to hundreds of relatives and friends. Tearfully, Jane confides that she and Phillip are not worthy to enter the temple.

c. You are looking forward with great anticipation to the accomplishments of your newborn son. As time goes on, you come to realize that he is a mentally retarded child.

2. Discuss what was involved on the part of Alma the elder and the father of the prodigal son to exercise Christlike love. How can we put into practice the examples portrayed in these two stories?

3. Why is it necessary that we keep in mind our Heavenly Father's feeling and desire for each of His children as we make decisions as to our behavior with our own children?

4. List some of the elements that are essential if we are to practice showing Christlike love.

5. Bear your testimony regarding the love we receive from our Heavenly Father and our Savior and of the need for us to follow this example.

INSTRUCTIONAL MATERIALS

Meetinghouse library pictures:
IQ031-IS031—The Purpose of Life

The Sensitive Line

1. Invite quorum members to give examples of Christlike love that they have personally experienced or know about.

2. To love someone in a Christlike way does not mean we approve of all of his behavior. It *does* mean that we try to help him to become more like the Savior and our Heavenly Father. (Discuss.)

LESSON OBJECTIVE

The Priesthood holder should feel motivated to love other people, especially his own family, the way the Savior loves him.

INTRODUCTION

PATIENCE WITH A SON

Randy was an active little boy. One of the truly bright moments of the day for Randy's father was when he entered his home each night after spending a challenging ten hours at the office. "Daddy!" Randy would shout as he ran to his father. Then his father would throw Randy up into the air or give him a ride on his back. Sometimes Randy would put his arms around his father and whisper in his ear, "I love you, Daddy." On one occasion when he told his dad how much he loved him, tears came to his father's eyes and Randy asked, "Why are you crying, Daddy?" But Randy's question was difficult for his father to answer.

Once Randy tried to put a nail into an electric light socket. His father saw him just in time and took the nail away. With anger and fierce resentment in his voice Randy shouted, "I hate you!" His father felt deep pain when he heard these words; but he said to himself, "Randy is only a child, and I must be patient with him. I must not make him the victim of my hurt feelings. I should not try to get even with him."

Acting upon these motives the father took Randy upon his knee and explained to him as well as he could how much he loved him. He tried to tell Randy that the reason he had not permitted him to put the nail into the light socket was that he knew Randy might be hurt. The father did not succeed very well, but he tried to explain what electricity can do if it is not properly controlled. Finally he said to Randy, "There will probably be many times when you will not like what I do. You can always say, 'I don't like what you did,' but never say 'I hate you.' I love you and I always shall."

Several days later Randy came to his father. With a mischievous smile on his face he said, "I don't *like* you, Daddy. I *love* you, and I'll never say 'I hate you' again." And he never did.

(It might now be appropriate to ask the class members to indicate what would have happened to the relationship between Randy and his father if his father had treated Randy the same way Randy treated him when he said, "I hate you." Perhaps Randy would have felt that they were now "even." But because his father demonstrated a greater maturity, in the final analysis Randy could only feel good inside if he treated his father with the same love and kindness with which he himself had been treated.)

LESSON DEVELOPMENT

Members of the class might now be given the opportunity to give examples of crossing the "sensitive line." The following two cases will illustrate the type of examples which might be given.

AN UNGUARDED MOMENT

Mary wanted to be a "homemaker" rather than just a "housekeeper." She saw two great opportunities in her role: (1) to help her husband in every way possible, and (2) to be an influence in the lives of her children in assisting them to "walk uprightly before the Lord."

She tried, therefore, to maintain a reasonable balance between order and relaxation. She trained her children to put things away but permitted them to enjoy themselves, realizing that a happy atmosphere as well as orderliness would be important for the success of her home.

When her husband came home at night, he usually found her dressed neatly, and regardless of what she was doing, she always found time to come to the door and greet him affectionately.

The evenings he spent at home with her were always enjoyable. She was genuinely interested in what he had done during the day, and he found himself able to reveal his innermost feelings to her concerning his disappointments, defeats, hopes, and successes. He told her once that one of the principal reasons he was able to approach each day with a feeling of confidence was that their relationship with one another was so good. Her love, expressed in many ways, gave him security, courage, and poise. One of the best compliments he ever gave to her was to tell her, "I love to come home."

Usually he controlled his emotions very well, but one day after a particularly bitter disappointment at the office, he found himself irritable and nervous as he entered their home. Dinner was to be a few minutes late, and the children were extra hungry. The quarreling and crying of the two youngest ones irritated him further, and he sent them to their room.

"Don't be hard on the children, dear," his wife said. "They're just hungry." Later, embarrassed, he apologized, and his wife readily forgave him; but for a while things were not quite the same between them, and his children did not make him a part of their lives as they once had done.

ONE WORD WAS MISSING

Tom was a journalist. His newspaper had given him the assignment of traveling to several cities to report some important civic projects, and he decided to take his wife and seventeen-year-old son with him. He wanted to develop a more meaningful relationship with them, especially with his son.

One hot day they decided to eat their lunch in a public park. As they were eating, Tom said to his son, "Pass the salt." His son made no move to comply. Raising his voice slightly he again said, "Pass the salt." Again his son ignored the request. Now thoroughly irritated, he raised his voice still more. "What's the matter with you? I said, 'Pass the salt.'"

The son got up and left the table. Tom followed him, and as he caught up with him he saw there were tears in the boy's eyes. "I don't understand it," said his father. "What's wrong?"

It was some time before his son answered. Finally he said, "Dad, ever since I can remember, we've had a kind of inferior-superior relationship. I don't think you have meant it to be that way, but the impression you give is that you think of yourself as being superior to me. Please don't misunderstand me. I know you have more knowledge than I; your experience is much greater than mine and you have more wisdom. But, Dad, I'm a person, too.

"I notice that when we have company for dinner you never say, 'Pass the salt.' You always say, '*Please* pass the salt.' That *please* means a lot to me, Dad; it's a symbol of respect."

This incident was a great learning experience for the journalist, and it eventually changed his whole relationship with his son. Five years later when the son married, he said to his father, "Dad you have changed your attitudes and actions toward me. You've shown real respect during the last five years, and I only hope I can treat any son I might have in the same way you have treated me." The father never forgot these words.

COURTESY AT HOME TOO

The world outside our homes is often complex and difficult. Most individuals, realizing that their success is dependent upon how they treat others, lean over backwards in order to be courteous and considerate of them. They do not say, "I hate you," to their associates. Generally, they do not shout at those who do not agree with them. They say "please" when they make a request.

But when these same individuals come home at night, they sometimes "take out" on other family members the feelings of irritation, injustice, or resentment they have experienced in their associations with those outside the home. It need not be this way.

What are some *legitimate* ways of releasing unpleasant but rather normal tensions that build up in the regular course of living? (Class members might be asked to indicate some of the ways that they have discovered for releasing these tensions. The teacher could list some of the responses on the chalkboard.) If the following have not been listed they might be added:

1. Some individuals who primarily engage in mental activities in their occupations adopt a physical activity such as playing golf or tennis or cultivating a garden.

2. Many people develop a real appreciation for beautiful music, literature, or paintings. For example, they find fulfillment as well as relaxation not only in listening to music but also in learning to play a musical instrument, not with the thought of becoming a professional, but of finding a way to express deep feelings.

3. Many fathers and mothers plan family activities at the close of the day, such as going into the mountains to fish, going on a picnic together, and so on.

Whatever activity we select, we should be sure that it is not enslaving, but rather that it represents a change from what we have done for a considerable period during the day. After we have engaged in the activity, we should find renewed desire to continue with our regular duties.

JESUS AND THE "SENSITIVE LINE"

It may take each of us some time to understand fully the meaning of the "sensitive line." But actually it stems from the two great commandments given by the Savior: ". . . Thou shalt love the Lord thy God with all thy heart, and with all thy soul, and with all thy mind. . . . And the second is like unto it, Thou shalt love thy neighbor as thyself." (Matthew 22:37, 39.) We would never think of speaking disrespectfully to our Heavenly Father or the Savior. Similarly, we should not speak disrespectfully to our husband or wife, our children, or anyone else with whom we come in contact. All of us are children of our Heavenly Father.

If we do not cross the "sensitive line" in our homes, the Holy Ghost will be able to dwell with us, bringing the attributes of ". . . faith, virtue, knowledge, temperance, patience, brotherly kindness, godliness, charity, humility, diligence." (D&C 4:6.)

APPLICATION

What Would Jesus Do?

I n our relationships with our wife and children, when we find ourselves tempted to raise our voice or do something that would mean crossing the "sensitive line," let us ask ourselves, "Would the Savior behave that way?" Have I spoken crossly to my wife and children this last week? What atmosphere of love and unity could I create in my home this week by speaking softly and treating my family with greater kindness, respect and understanding?

Ponder: Matthew 7:12; Matthew 25:31-40.

SPECIAL INSTRUCTIONS TO THE TEACHER

1. Quorum members might be asked to relate several of the

stories in the lesson or other personal experiences that illustrate the principle of love and respect.

2. Discuss what it means to cross over the "sensitive line." Illustrate this with stories.

3. Discuss the ways in which the Priesthood holder can keep this side of the "sensitive line" by asking himself, "What Would Jesus Do?"

Section

You Are the Patriarch in Your Home

Patriarch in Your Own Home

LESSON FOLLOW-UP

(1) What do class members understand by the "sensitive line"? (2) Have class members indicate some ways in which one crosses the "sensitive line." (3) What factors will help to maintain a relationship which will eliminate crossing the "sensitive line"? (Emphasize that when one respects and loves another person, he does become sensitive to the feelings of that person.)

(This discussion should not exceed five minutes.)

LESSON OBJECTIVE

The Priesthood holder should feel motivated to give serious consideration to his responsibilities as a patriarch of his home so that he will be prepared to make proper use of the powers and privileges of the Priesthood in his family unit.

INTRODUCTION

Class members might be invited to comment on the significance of the following oft-quoted statements by President David O. McKay:

1. No other success can compensate for failure in the home.[1]
2. I picture heaven to be a continuation of the ideal home.[2]

LESSON DEVELOPMENT

Speaking in the general Priesthood session of the April, 1964, General Conference of the Church, Presiding Bishop John H. Vandenberg said: "Someone has said: 'There is no need of searching out your genealogy if you do not know where your children were last night.' "

[1]*Conference Report,* April, 1964, p. 5.
[2]*The Improvement Era,* October, 1948, p. 618.

Why is it true?

Bishop Vandenberg said further: "There is no calling in this Church that supersedes that of being a father. No assignment in the Church should ever be considered as an excuse to neglect the home. The home is a basic unit of the Church."

THE FATHER'S ROLE

Numerous sociologists, educators and churchmen are becoming alarmed over the diminishing role fathers generally in our society are playing in the home. Studies show and writers have pointed out that the influence of the father in the home has dropped off alarmingly. Responsibilities he used to assume are left to the mother to carry out or more often than not are not being carried out at all. Could this be one of the reasons for the tremendous growth in juvenile delinquency today in many countries?

Latter-day Saint fathers should all understand the importance of the family and accept the responsibility that has been given by the Lord to Priesthood bearers in this regard.

THE PATRIARCHAL ORDER

Simply stated as regards to families, the patriarchal order includes the fact that the Father is the presiding authority in the home.

Dr. John A. Widtsoe has written:

The home, composed of father, mother and children, is the unit of all society. The human family is but the total of individual families or homes. The home is the ultimate unit of the Church. In the end as in the beginning the home will be the unit of progress and government. . . .

The position which men occupy in the family, and especially those who hold the Melchizedek Priesthood, is one of first importance and should be clearly recognized and maintained in the order and with the authority which God conferred upon man in placing him at the head of his household.

There is no higher authority in matters relating to the family organization, and especially when that organization is presided over by one holding the higher Priesthood, than that of the father. . . . The patriarchal order is of divine origin, and will continue throughout time and eternity. There is then a particular reason why men, women, and children should understand this order and this authority in the household of the people of God, and seek to make it what God intended it to be, a qualification and preparation for the highest exaltation for his children. In the home the presiding authority is always vested in the father and in all home affairs and family matters there is no other authority paramount.[3]

EVERY FAMILY A KINGDOM

Each family in the Church is really a kingdom or government within itself. The father, by virtue of the sealing blessings of eternal marriage, is the head of that government. This is what constitutes patriarchal office in the family. Originally it was the only government on the earth and was passed down from Adam to his descendants. Eventually, as society became more complex, the manner of governing the peoples of the earth had to change, but as far as the Church is concerned the same order exists within the families as God set it up originally with Father Adam. And this same order will exend into the eternities.

Dr. John A. Widtsoe has emphasized this by saying, "The government of heaven is by family. It is patriarchal. . . ."[4]

When we begin to comprehend the meaning of this doctrine we can see the great challenge and responsibility that rests upon the shoulders of a father in a Latter-day Saint home. He is the head of an eternal family. He is the patriarch. He can make out of a home what he will. He can be a dictator, make a slave out of his wife, and servants out of his children, and rule with a heavy hand, or he can preside over a home with love, wisdom, gentleness, understanding, patience, and cooperation.

MANY ARE CALLED, FEW ARE CHOSEN

Class members at this point could be asked to comment on these verses from the 121st section of the Doctrine & Covenants as to how they apply to a father in the home:

Behold, there are many called, but few are chosen. And why are they not chosen?

Because their hearts are set so much upon the things of this

[3]Widtsoe, John A., *Priesthood and Church Government*, Salt Lake City, Deseret Book Co., Revised Edition, 1954, pp. 80-81.

[4]Widtsoe, John A., *Evidences and Reconciliations*, Salt Lake City, Bookcraft, Inc., Vol. II, p. 100.

world, and aspire to the honors of men, that they do not learn this one lesson—

That the rights of the Priesthood are inseparably connected with the powers of heaven, and that the powers of heaven cannot be controlled nor handled only upon the principles of righteousness.

That they may be conferred upon us, it is true; but when we undertake to cover our sins, or to gratify our pride, our vain ambition, or to exercise control or dominion or compulsion upon the souls of the children of men, in any degree of unrighteousness, behold, the heavens withdraw themselves; the Spirit of the Lord is grieved; and when it is withdrawn, Amen to the Priesthood or the authority of that man. . . .

No power or influence can or ought to be maintained by virtue of the Priesthood, only by persuasion, by long-suffering, by gentleness, and meekness, and by love unfeigned;

By kindness, and pure knowledge, which shall greatly enlarge the soul without hypocrisy, and without guile—Reproving betimes with sharpness, when moved upon by the Holy Ghost; and then showing forth afterwards an increase of love toward him whom thou hast reproved, lest he esteem thee to be his enemy;

That he may know that thy faithfulness is stronger than the cords of death. (D&C 121:34-37, 41-44.)

PRIESTHOOD MEMBERS CANNOT SHIRK DUTIES

Holders of the Priesthood should not shirk their duties as fathers, no matter what else they do in the Church, and expect the blessings that are promised for the faithful. The father holds in his hands the eternal happiness and the salvation of the members of his family.

Some of the saddest stories in the Church involve fathers who have become disgruntled or disaffected because of some minor matters, and their resultant actions have taken their families out of the Church. The foolish actions or the neglect of one man, in a few generations can lead to the loss of hundreds of people to the Church, with the chance that they will be lost throughout the eternities.

On the other hand, families have been blessed for generations because an inactive father changed his ways and became a faithful member of the Church and brought Church standards into his home.

(The class leader might invite class members to cite examples of the above in their own families as well as in other families they know.)

CHALLENGES TO PRIESTHOOD HOLDERS

Discuss the following propositions:

As patriarch or the head of the family in Zion, I will make proper use of the powers and principles of the Priesthood by:

1. Living an exemplary life and striving to keep all of the commandments of God.

2. Accepting responsibility of being truly the presiding authority in my home.

3. Making my home, as the Lord has instructed, "a house of prayer, a house of fasting, a house of faith, a house of learning, a house of glory, a house of order, a house of God." (D&C 88:119.)

4. Living for and receiving revelation and inspiration for the blessing and guidance of my family.

5. Creating a home atmosphere where a spirit of love, understanding, cooperation, helpfulness, and sympathy abound, where children will feel free to express themselves and talk over their problems, their hopes, and their ambitions. (When children have questions or problems they should not be obliged to go to their bishop or their seminary teacher to talk about them. Relationships between children and their parents should be such that they will go to their parents first when they need someone to talk to.)

6. Making my wife a queen and partner in my home by showing her all of the love and consideration I possibly can at all times and in all things.

7. Naming and giving a father's blessing to my children (upon invitation from the bishop).

8. Confirming my children members of the Church (upon invitation from the bishop).

9. Conferring the Aaronic Priesthood upon my sons and ordaining them to offices in the Aaronic Priesthood (under the direction of the bishop).

10. Conferring the Melchizedek Priesthood upon my sons and ordaining them elders in the Church (under the direction of the stake authorities).

11. Kneeling in family prayer regularly.

12. Giving family members an opportunity to take turns at blessing the food.

13. Directing home worship service, including the holding of regular family home evenings.

14. Giving special patriarchal blessings to my wife and children. Have you ever given your wife or children a patriarchal blessing?

Speaking on this subject President Joseph Fielding Smith has said:

Fathers can give patriarchal blessings: A faithful father who holds the Melchizedek Priesthood may bless his own children, and that would be a patriarchal (father's) blessing. Such a blessing could be recorded in the family records, but it would not be preserved in the archives of the Church. Every father who is true to his Priesthood is a patriarch over his own house. In addition, children may receive a blessing by an ordained patriarch. A father blessing his own child could, if he received the inspiration to do so, declare the lineage of the child.[5]

Fathers should give blessings to their children at such times as when a son or daughter goes into the mission field, when a child goes to college, when a child gets married, or when any member of the family needs guidance in an important calling or responsibility or decision.

15. Preparing my sons to be ready to accept their patriarchal responsibility after they are married in the temple, and preparing my daughters to become wives of worthy Priesthood bearers who will sustain and uphold them as patriarchs in their families.

16. Putting into practice the principles of the fast and the ordinance of anointing with consecrated oil members of the family who are sick, and pronouncing a blessing upon their heads.

17. Giving guidance to all members of the family in standards set up by the Church regarding such matters as dress, dancing, dating, and general conduct.

A CELESTIAL LAW

The patriarchal order in the family is a celestial law. If we expect to live it in the celestial kingdom then we must learn to live it here. If we cannot learn to live the law here, in this life, we cannot expect to gain the blessings of exaltation in the celestial kingdom.

The happiest homes in the Church, yes, in the world, are those in which the father makes proper use of the powers and the sacred privileges of the Priesthood.

---

[5]McConkie, Bruce R., Compiler, *Doctrines of Salvation:* Sermons and Writings of Joseph Smith, Bookcraft, Salt Lake City, 1956; Vol. III, p. 172.

What Would Jesus Do?

J esus has given very specific counsel to fathers concerning their responsibility. To the members of the First Presidency He said, "Set in order your own home." (See D&C 93:40, 43, 44-50.) To set a home "in order" means to "bring up your children in light and truth" (verse 40); to cause one's family to "repent and forsake some things" (verse 48); to "pray always" (verse 49); and to "see that they are more diligent and concerned at home" (verse 50).

Review the seventeen "Challenges to Priesthood Holders" during the coming week concerning your responsibility as a Patriarch in your home. Ask yourself: which of these responsibilities need I give attention to in order to put my home in order? Look for opportunity to discuss these matters with your companion and other members of your family. Seek the help of the Holy Ghost so that you will be strengthened in areas where you may be failing.

Read and ponder: Abraham 1:2; D&C 86:9-11; Genesis 48; D&C 76; 56; D&C 88:21-32.

SPECIAL INSTRUCTIONS TO THE TEACHER

1. Concentrate the lesson discussion on the seventeen things a father should be doing. Use illustrations of these things to make it heart-warming.

2. Challenge fathers to give serious and prayerful consideration to these items in an effort to put their homes in order.

INSTRUCTIONAL MATERIALS

Meetinghouse library pictures dealing with fathers:
OP055, OP167, OP173, OP204, OQ017, OQ020, OQ263, OQ269, OQ262, OQ275

Do You Really Love Her?

LESSON FOLLOW-UP

It is suggested that one or more quorum members be given the opportunity to report on what success they have had in putting any of last week's seventeen suggestion statements into operation.

(This discussion should not exceed five minutes.)

LESSON OBJECTIVES

The Priesthood holder should be motivated to (1) understand the kind of relationship that is desirable to have with one's wife and (2) carefully look at his relationship with his wife.

INTRODUCTION

Isaiah said: "Come now, let us reason together. . . ." (Isaiah 1:18.)

Class members might comment on how these wise words could apply in these husband-wife situations: planning family finances; discussing discipline of their children; arranging social engagements; planning a family vacation; assigning jobs in the home.

LOVE YOUR WIFE

"Wives, submit yourselves unto your own husbands, as unto the Lord. For the husband is the head of the wife, even as Christ is the head of the Church: and he is the Saviour of the body. Therefore as the church is subject unto Christ, so let the wives be to their own husbands in every thing. *Husbands, love your wives, even as Christ also loved the church, and gave Himself for it;* That He might sanctify and cleanse it with the washing of water by the word, That He might present it to Himself a glorious church, not having spot, or wrinkle, or any such thing; but that it should be holy and without blemish. *So ought men to love their wives as their own bodies. He that loveth his wife loveth himself.* For no man ever yet hated his own flesh; but nourisheth and cherisheth it, even as the Lord the church: For we are members of His body, of His flesh, and of His bones. For this cause shall a man leave his father and mother, and shall be joined unto his wife, and they two shall be one flesh." (Ephesians 5:22-31. Italics ours.) Remember, *"neither is the man without the woman, neither the woman without the man, in the Lord."* (I Corinthians 11:11. Italics ours.)

LESSON DEVELOPMENT

MARRIAGE ORDAINED OF GOD

Marriage is a partnership ordained of God in which a man and a woman enter into a contractual relationship to love and sustain one another. When marriage is solemnized as He ordained, it is through the Holy Priesthood and sealed by His power. Thus God becomes a member of the marriage partnership.

In several places the prophets remind us that a man shall leave his father and mother and cleave unto his wife and they shall be one flesh. If they are to succeed in becoming truly one they must subordinate selfish interests and desires and with their companion, under the influence of the Lord, unitedly seek common noble objectives.

The principal objective of the marriage union is to become partners with God in the creation of an eternal family. All of the principles of the Gospel, either directly or indirectly, relate to this objective. Through the ordinances the Lord has revealed, He has provided men an opportunity to accept His invitation to become sons and daughters in His family. Although all mankind are literally His spirit children, only those who choose to accept the Gospel and receive its ordinances and be faithful to its covenants will be part of His family in the patriarchal order in the Celestial Kingdom.

THE FATHER LEADS THE WAY

The presidency in the patriarchal order rests with the Priesthood; therefore, it is the right and responsibility of the husband to preside. President Joseph F. Smith said: "There is no higher authority in matters relating to the family organization, and especially when that organization is presided over by one holding the higher Priesthood, than that of the father. The authority is time honored, and among the people of God in all dispensations it has been highly respected and often emphasized by the teachings of the prophets who were inspired of God.

The patriarchal order is of divine origin and will continue throughout time and eternity."[1]

It is the husband's responsibility to provide leadership for his wife. In the perspective of the Gospel, "leadership" does not mean the right to dictate, command, and order. On the contrary, it means to guide, protect, point the way, set the example, make secure, inspire, and create a desire to sustain and follow. Literally, the husband is to lead the way.

As partners with God in building a family, the husband and wife should pray to Him regularly, expressing the gratitude of their hearts for that partnership and the privilege of being able to approach Him, and they should acknowledge Him in all things and seek His constant guidance and influence in directing the affairs of the family. The husband should preside, offering the prayer or blessing when appropriate, and asking his wife and children to do so when proper.

Furthermore, the husband should lead out by example—and encouragement where necessary—in attending meetings, keeping family records, doing genealogical research, visiting the temple regularly (where possible by location), in sustaining the authorities, in telling others about the message of the restoration, and in all other righteous things.

PARTNERSHIP BRINGS STRENGTH

As already mentioned, although the husband is the highest authority in the home and has the right to preside, his role is that of leader and not commander. A wise leader and president always seeks counsel from those who are in a position to contribute good counsel. Inasmuch as the husband and wife constitute a partnership, the husband should seek the counsel of his wife as his companion. If a family is to be built, it is they, together with the Spirit of the Lord, who will build it. The husband does not do this alone, although he does hold the Priesthood.

They should not only counsel together, pray together, study together, but they should also plan together and work together. As mortals they both have their imperfections and inadequacies and both make their mistakes. However, they should both be sufficiently humble, as well as interested in their own progress and that of the family, to accept suggestions from the other. This will probably result in personal and family improvement.

---

[1]Smith, Joseph F., *Gospel Doctrine* (Fifth Edition), Salt Lake City, Deseret Book Company, 1939, pp. 286-287.

FIDELITY IS LOVE'S NOBLEST OFFSPRING

President David O. McKay has declared: "Love is the highest attribute of the human soul, and fidelity is love's noblest offspring."[2] Most, if not all, of the virtues are the natural fruit of genuine love.

President McKay has given inspired counsel regarding the physical dimension of the love relationship between a man and his wife. He said: "Let us instruct young people who come to us to know that a woman should be queen of her own body. The marriage covenant does not give the man the right to enslave her or to abuse her or to use her merely for the gratification of his passion. Your marriage ceremony does not give you that right.

"Second, let them remember that gentleness and consideration after the ceremony are just as appropriate and necessary and beautiful as gentleness and consideration before the wedding.

"Third, let us realize that manhood is not undermined by the practising of continence, notwithstanding what some psychiatrists claim. Chastity is the crown of beautiful womanhood, and self-control is the source of true manhood, if you will know it, not indulgence. Sexual indulgence whets the passion and creates morbid desire.

"Let us teach our young men to enter into matrimony with the idea that each will be just as courteous and considerate of a wife after the ceremony as during courtship."[3]

In a related vein President McKay gives a clear warning to those men who might be tempted to forsake their wives for another. He says: "As teachers, we are to let the people know, and warn these men— and this is not imagination—who, after having lived with their wives and brought into this world four or five children, get tired of them and seek a divorce, that they are on the road to hell. It is unfair to a woman to leave her that way, merely because the man happens to fall in love with some younger woman and feels that the wife is not so beautiful and attractive as she used to be. Warn him! Nothing but unhappiness for him and injustice to those children can result."[4]

One of the characteristics of genuine love is unselfishness. A husband must be willing—not only willing, but eager—to freely give of himself for his wife. He must not become so involved in matters of a more or less strictly personal interest that he neglects her. He must

---

[2]McKay, David O., *Gospel Ideals*, Salt Lake City, Deseret News Press, 1953, p. 489.

[3]*Ibid.*, pp. 471-472.

[4]*Ibid.*, p. 473.

realize that she has some interests that may be her own as an individual and she should not only be allowed but encouraged to do those things commensurate with their worth toward her personal development. But although each must have some individual interests, the husband must never lose sight of the underlying and fundamental objective of building a unit of our Father's eternal family.

FORGIVENESS BRINGS PEACE

Certainly one of the divine attributes which is necessary to the husband who would be worthy of the place he holds as head of a family is that of being forgiving. In the teachings of the Savior there is no principle—with the possible exception of love—which was taught more frequently and given more emphasis than forgiveness. There is no place in the marriage relationship for holding grudges. Forgiving others of their imperfections and misdeeds, wittingly or unwittingly done, is not only essential to one's receiving forgiveness from his Heavenly Father, but is necessary if he is to have peace in his own soul here. The husband who would be unforgiving creates for himself misery which cankers his own soul. Forgiveness, on the otherhand, brings peace and tranquility to both forgiver and forgiven.

"LITTLE THINGS" ARE IMPORTANT

A husband worthy of the name should be thoughtful, kind, and courteous. He should strive to know and cultivate an interest in doing the "little things" for her.

(The teacher might here ask class members to describe some of the "little things" a man might do to make his wife—and himself—happier.)

A husband who would honestly love his wife must also respect her. President Joseph F. Smith said: "Parents, in the first place, whether they do it or not, should love and respect each other, and treat each other with respectful decorum and kindly regard, all the time. The husband should treat his wife with the utmost courtesy and respect. The husband should never insult her; he should never speak slightingly of her, but should always hold her in the highest esteem in the home, in the presence of their children."[5]

President David O. McKay, with another dimension of respect in mind, said: ". . . preserve the privacies of your house, marriage state, and heart, from father, mother, brother, sister, aunt and from all the

---

[5]Smith, *op. cit.*, p. 282.

world. You two, with God's help, build your own quiet world. Every third or fourth one you draw into it with you will form a party and stand between you two. That should never be. Promise this to each other. Remember the vow at each temptation. You will find your account in it. Your souls will grow, as it were, to each other, and at last will become as one. Ah, if many a pair had, on their marriage day, known the secret, how many a marriage were happier than, alas, they are!"[6]

One manifestation of respect, as well as of love and simple human dignity—or the lack of them—which a husband reveals in his relationship with his wife is the language he uses. In this regard, President McKay has said: "I cannot imagine a man's being cruel to a woman. I cannot imagine her so conducting herself as to merit such treatment. Perhaps there are women in the world who exasperate their husbands, but no man is justified in resorting to physical force or in exploding his feelings in profanity. There are men, undoubtedly, in the world who are thus beastly, but no man who holds the Priesthood of God should so debase himself."[7]

One final attribute which must be mentioned is that of expressing gratitude. (The teacher here might invite class members to describe some of the specific, different ways in which a husband could say "thank you" to his wife.)

The husband should be constantly conscious of this word of the Lord regarding the authority of the Priesthood in all of his relationships to his wife: "the rights of the Priesthood are inseparably connected with the powers of heaven, and . . . the powers of heaven cannot be controlled nor handled only upon the principles of righteousness. . . .

"No power or influence can or ought to be maintained by virtue of the priesthood, only by persuasion, by long-suffering, by gentleness and meekness, and by love unfeigned;

"By kindness, and pure knowledge, which shall greatly enlarge the soul without hypocrisy, and without guile—" (D&C 121:36, 41-43.)

---

[6]McKay, *op. cit.*, p. 472.
[7]*Ibid.*, p. 476.

What Would Jesus Do?

Consider how your actions might be different in relation to how you regard and treat your wife if you seriously applied the Savior's counsel in D&C 121:36, 41-43.

You might wish to analyze the kind of a husband you are by considering the following application of the principles in D&C 121.

WHAT IS YOUR SCORE?

	Yes	No
1. At least once a week do I volunteer to assist my wife, or even take over with one of her chores, such as doing the dishes, preparing a meal, putting the small children to bed, waxing the kitchen floor, or putting up the lunches for school?	——	——
2. At least once a month do I invite my wife out for a "date" to go someplace where *she* wants to go?	——	——
3. Occasionally do I bring home a little surprise remembrance for her and express appreciation for all that she does for me?	——	——
4. Do my wife and I (and the rest of the family) pray together every day?	——	——
5. When delayed at my employment, do I always call my wife to so advise her?	——	——
6. Do my wife and I ever read together such literature as the scriptures, a good book or magazine article?	——	——
7. Do I always remember the important anniversaries: her birthday, our wedding day, Mother's Day and others?	——	——
8. Do I regularly show her little courtesies such as opening the car door for her and assisting her with her chair at the dinner table?	——	——
9. Do I make it a practice of never embarrassing her before the children or others?	——	——

10. Do I invite her counsel on all major decisions regarding family fianances? _____ _____
What is your score?
Read and ponder: I Corinthians 13:1-13; Moroni 7:20, 44-48; Ephesians 5:25-33.

---

1. Point out some of the positive qualities about men in the quorum in relation to how they love and respect their wife. To do this you may want to contact several wives and have them relate the good things their husbands do for them.

2. Use examples of how great leaders in the Church treat their wives.

3. Have each Priesthood holder take the application quiz. Challenge them to do something about the "no" areas.

Is Your Wife a Partner?

Selective class members might be asked to report what they did in a positive way to improve the "no" areas in the check list taken last week.

LESSON OBJECTIVES

The Priesthood holder should be motivated to focus on some ways that he can genuinely show respect for his wife and dedicate himself more completely to his responsibility of helping her fulfill her potential (1) as a daughter of our Heavenly Father and (2) as a partner and counselor to him—both now and in eternity.

INTRODUCTION

A PRIESTHOOD LEADER'S EXPERIENCE

Charles K. is a counselor in his elders quorum presidency. He is a full tithepayer, keeps the standards of the Church, is active in all his assignments, and is also quite a successful businessman. As a counselor in the presidency, he is "indispensable" according to his elders quorum president.

Coming home from Priesthood meeting one Sunday, he found that his wife and children were still not ready for Sunday School. As he walked into the house, he was greeted by his two youngest children still in their underclothes.

"Hi, Daddy," they said.

"Aren't you kids ready yet?" Charles yelled. Looking around for his wife he found her combing their oldest daughter's hair. "What's wrong?" he snapped, "Aren't you ready yet?"

"No, I'm not ready yet," replied his wife, Linda. "You wouldn't be ready either if you had had my problems this morning."

178

"It seems to me that your whole problem is that you're never organized," said Charles. "You stay in bed too long and when you finally do get up you're never organized. Then we're always late for church—it never fails."

"If you'd come home and help instead of standing there and griping, we might be able to make it on time," retorted Linda.

"If I ran my business the way you run this home, we'd have been broke long ago."

Linda's eyes were now blazing with anger. "If I ran the home like your business is run—" She couldn't finish because tears filled her eyes. Exasperated, she finally blurted out, "I've had it! I've just had it! All you have done lately is complain about things you don't see done or lecture on things you think should be more important to me. You never notice the nice things I do. Did you ever stop to consider the kind of morning I've had? No, you didn't notice how clean the kids are—especially after they spilled shoe dye all over themselves. You just complain because things aren't going the way you want them to. Do you ever notice when we *are* on time for church? Ever since you've been in the elders quorum presidency you think you have the only job in the Church. You make me feel that none of my jobs is important. I haven't been able to feel good about doing my Primary work or anything else in the Church because you complain about the time involved or the cost of baby sitters. I don't know why you feel your time is so much more important than mine."

At this point Linda was cut off by Charles. "All right, all right, Linda. I'm sorry. You've made your point now. You don't need to nag all the time."

"When you complain you think it's constructive criticism," she said. "When I complain you call it nagging. Charlie, if that's all the Priesthood does for you, what's the value of it?"

Charles didn't say any more as he hustled the children out to the car. Finally Linda joined her husband and family. As they walked in the church together, they were greeted by the Sunday School president. "Made it," said Charles.

"If all the families in the Church were like yours, Charlie, we wouldn't have any worries," the president replied.

"If he only knew," Linda thought as she sat down. "If he only knew."

LESSON DEVELOPMENT

1. Even though Charles felt it was justified, what effect would

this criticism have upon Linda's attitude and self-confidence? (Nearly everything we do is to protect, maintain, and then, if possible, enhance our self-concept. Therefore, whenever a person is criticized he immediately defends his self-concept by striking back or by cutting off communication. It should also be remembered that there is value in Linda's knowing Charles' true feeling if he does not humiliate her.)

2. In what way could Charles convey his feeling and concern for being on time without bringing about antagonism?

3. Why do some Priesthood bearers feel that their role is more important than that of their wife?

4. Even though the attitude that he is more important than his wife is wrong, if Charles has felt this way what could he do to emphasize the importance of his wife's position in the family?

5. In what way is Linda, or any other woman, equal to her husband though he is a Priesthood bearer? What are some specific things a husband can do to help his wife develop her full potential?

6. Discuss the responsibilities of the wife and mother as they relate to the Priesthood in the home.

PRESIDENT MCKAY'S WORDS ON A MOTHER'S ROLE

In speaking of the role of mothers and its importance, President David O. McKay has said:

Motherhood is the greatest potential influence either for good or ill in human life. The mother's image is the first that stamps itself on the unwritten page of the young child's mind. It is her caress that first awakens a sense of security, her kiss the first realization of affection, her sympathy and tenderness, the first assurance that there is love in the world. True, there comes a time when father takes his place as exemplar and hero of the growing boy, and in the latter's budding ambition to develop manly traits, he outwardly seems to turn from the more gentle and tender virtues engendered by his mother. Yet that everdirecting and restraining influence implanted during the first years of his childhood lingers with him and permeates his thoughts and memory as distinctively as characteristic perfume clings to each particular flower. . . . The ability and willingness properly to rear children, the gift of love and eagerness, yes, longing to express it in soul development, make motherhood the noblest office or calling in the world. It is the greatest of all professions, the most beautiful of all arts. . . .[1]

---

[1]McKay, David O., *Treasures of Life*, Salt Lake City, Deseret Book Company, 1962, pp. 39-41.

HOW MUCH TIME FOR YOUR FAMILY?

In harmony with the emphasis that President McKay places upon the importance of motherhood and the time she invests in the home, the Priesthood bearer needs to analyze the time he allocates to his family. (It is suggested that the following diagram be placed on the chalkboard to help quorum members evaluate the amount of time they invest in family responsibilities. Use the schedule of one of the class members as an illustration. Black out eight hours for sleep and complete the diagram as it would be on a typical day.)

THE 24-HOUR DAY IN OUR HOME

How much time do you as a husband dedicate each day to the personal development of your family—your most precious possession? How can a busy man better use his time to develop good family relationships? (It's not necessarily the amount of time but rather the quality of time spent that counts.) Family relations are strengthened when the husband will schedule a definite period of time for personal growth and development in the lives of each member. For example:

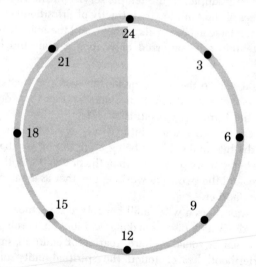

a. Take time to understand the responsibility and role of your partner. (One couple found it very profitable in developing better family relationships to take ten minutes before going to sleep each night to analyze how each of them might have helped in making the family a closer unit that day.)

b.   Take time to talk with your children about their interests, problems, and goals. (One father set up a program wherein he scheduled half an hour per week for each child to counsel and help him with his particular interests.)

c.   Develop some common hobbies and interests in which all the family can participate and enjoy. (Music, gardening, crafts, sports, outings, etc.)

LEADERSHIP IN THE HOME IS A PARTNERSHIP

As a wife sees her husband devote more of his time to developing better family relations, she will more fully appreciate the value of the Priesthood in the home.

> The Priesthood is for the benefit of all members of the Church. Men have no greater claim than women upon the blessings that issue from the Priesthood and accompany its possession. . . . the man holds the Priesthood, performs the priestly duties of the Church, but his wife enjoys with him every other privilege derived from the possession of the Priesthood. This is made clear, as an example, in the temple service of the Church. The ordinances of the temple are distinctly of Priesthood character, yet women have access to all of them, and the highest blessings of the temple are conferred only upon a man and his wife jointly.[2]

We might add to the above quote the words of the Apostle Paul: ". . . neither is the man without the woman, neither the woman without the man, in the Lord." (I Corinthians 11:11.)

With these thoughts in mind it becomes evident that it is improper to speak of the husband's role as being more important than the wife's or the wife's being more important than the husband's. Both are of a different nature, and the two roles working together as a partnership complement one another.

In what ways does a wife fulfill her role as a partner and counselor to her husband? (Briefly discuss making decisions concerning a vocation, finances, spiritual or social welfare, rearing of children, etc.)'

One Priesthood bearer found the spiritual unity of his family greatly improved when he counseled with his wife concerning all activities and expenditures relating to the Church. When he desired to pay $500.00 for the construction of a new chapel, the Priesthood bearer

---

[2]Widtsoe, John A., *Priesthood and Church Government*, Salt Lake City, Deseret Book Company, Revised Edition, 1954, p. 83.

found, after counseling with his wife, that she was willing to sacrifice with him some needed home furnishings in order that they might make their church contributions.

In viewing the type of relationship a Priesthood holder should have with his wife, how appropriate are these words of counsel from the Lord:

> We have learned by sad experience that it is the nature and disposition of almost all men, as soon as they get a little authority, as they suppose, they will immediately begin to exercise unrighteous dominion.

> Hence many are called, but few are chosen.

> No power or influence can or ought to be maintained by virtue of the priesthood, only by persuasion, by long-suffering, by gentleness and meekness, and by love unfeigned;

> By kindness, and pure knowledge, which shall greatly enlarge the soul without hypocrisy, and without guile—(D&C 121: 39-42.)

APPLICATION

What Would Jesus Do?

One of the keys to what the Savior would do is to have His Spirit with us so that we can discern His will. During the week, allow some time for prayerful meditation on the question, "How can I cultivate a relationship with my wife that will invite the spirit of the Lord in our home?

Here are several suggestions:

1. You might read with your wife the case study of Charles and Linda. You might ask your wife what you could do to help build her confidence and effectiveness in making decisions regarding spiritual affairs in the home.

2. During the coming week you might make a conscious effort to be more understanding of your wife's point of view, and to look for specific areas where she is making a unique contribution to the family and compliment her on these contributions. Priesthood holders who are unmarried and living at home might make a more conscious effort to be considerate of their mothers and express their love to

them throughout the week for all that their mothers have done for them.

3. You can sit down with your children and show them ways that all of the family members can compliment their mother and assist her in the many responsibilities in the home. You could make it a point to stress the importance of the mother in the home, and then have the children tell how their mother has done something special for them during the past week. Read Matthew 12:25.

SPECIAL INSTRUCTIONS TO THE TEACHER

1. Discuss the case study of Charles and the questions which follow.

2. Empahsize the partnership concept as it applies to husband-wife relationships.

3. Obtain ideas from quorum members on how they have genuinely tried to (1) help their wives fulfill their potential as daughters of our Heavenly Father and (2) how they have attempted to make them partners in their relationship.

INSTRUCTIONAL MATERIAL

VVMP—1458 16 mm film *Are You Listening?* available at the regional meetinghouse library.

Affectionately Yours

LESSON FOLLOW-UP

The following questions will help us evaluate the extent of our efforts this past week in helping our wives to develop confidence as a partner and counselor to us. (Class instructors should use discretion in their discussion so as to avoid embarrassment to class members.)

1.   What did you do specifically to be more understanding of your wife and her point of view? In what way did this affect your relationship with your wife and possibly your children? (The teacher might call upon a quorum member to relate an experience on how this was accomplished.)

2.   What have you done as a husband and a father to build a positive image of your wife in the eyes of your children? (For an unmarried Priesthood bearer, what have you done to enhance the image of your mother?)

(This discussion should not exceed five minutes.)

LESSON OBJECTIVES

Priesthood holders should feel motivated to improve the spiritual climate of the home by (1) understanding his wife's needs so that she will be sufficiently secure to develop more her creative and spiritual potential, (2) seeking for ways in which he might express his love and affection to her so that she will feel appreciated as a partner and (3) maintaining continually within the home an atmosphere of courtship.

INTRODUCTION

The following letter typifies a problem all too frequently experienced by married couples:

My dearest wife,

I'm writing this letter to you, dear, because I don't think I

185

could say these things to you face to face. I'm only sorry that we didn't get this worked out before I had to leave on my business trip. I guess this is one of our main problems—there doesn't seem to be any communication between us as there used to be. Perhaps I should take the blame for this because of being so involved in my work that I haven't had time for the choicest possession I have—my family.

It seems trite to say "I love you" after all those things we said to each other last night. I've thought a lot about the things you said—my long hours at work, and when I am home I'm too tired to give attention to you or the kids—my doing the things I most like to do instead of what you desire to do—my inappreciation for your efforts as a wife and mother—the fact we don't do the things we used to do together. Well, it hit home, honey, and I guess it's true. I know we have grown apart but it's hard to put my finger on why. The only thing I know is that when you told me that I didn't love you any more nothing could be further from the truth. So trite as it may seem, I want to tell you, "I love you."

I've been thinking today about our temple marriage. Remember how happy we were that day? What's happened since then, dear? Where have we missed out? We used to be able to talk things out—to express our feelings out of love rather than anger like last night. I want you to know that I too want our relationship to be as before—but I don't understand what you want. Things can work out between us—I know that. But I'll need your help. Won't you help me?

Affectionately yours,
Your loving husband

LESSON DEVELOPMENT

Because of your friendship with the husband in the above situation, suppose that his wife came to you with this letter. How would you counsel her?

1. What apparently is this brother doing that doesn't convince his wife that she is loved any more?

2. What causes the breakdown in communication between a husband and wife after it has been such a vital part of their relationship in the beginning?

UNDERSTANDING A WIFE'S NEEDS

To ascertain the specific steps that a Priesthood bearer might take in improving the spiritual climate of his home, we might consider the development of one's total personality. It is suggested that the following diagram be placed on the chalkboard for quorum members to observe during the ensuing discussion:

As the diagram suggests and as was demonstrated by the Savior's life, complete development of one's personality is dependent upon the satisfaction of *all* of man's basic needs rather than the satisfaction of a particular need. Frequently, a Priesthood bearer will feel that he has met all the needs of his wife when he has provided adequate physical comfort for her, failing to remember that real happiness is dependent upon her emotional, creative, and spiritual needs also being fulfilled.

For example: One brother, after providing a $50,000 home with all its furnishings for his wife was not able to understand why she still remained unsatisfied. He complained, "I just can't understand it. Here I gave her the best of everything and she still isn't satisfied." Discuss some of the reasons for her dissatisfaction in light of the foregoing diagram.

It has been found that three areas of major difficulty in husband-wife relations, from the husband's point of view, are (1) a concern over the wife's personal grooming, (2) her housekeeping abilities, (3) the way she disciplines and cares for the children. The teacher might focus on a discussion in one of these areas. For example: one Priesthood bearer expressed a desire for his wife to pay more attention to personal grooming. What could he do specifically to assist her to be more conscious of her physical appearance, keeping in mind that frequently a person is not willing to develop himself creatively or spiritually until he feels emotionally secure?

SOME WAYS OF COMMUNICATING

Several ways in which the Priesthood bearer might help his wife to attain security in their relationship have been suggested by President Hugh B. Brown:

> Couples should realize that if their marriage is to succeed they must, with eternal vigilance, keep their love growing by nourishing and cultivating it constantly.
>
> Daily investments in mutual compliments pay wonderful dividends in family solidarity, understanding, and success. There is no woman but who likes to have her husband tell her he loves her, wishes to be with her, how to him she is the best-dressed woman in town, how he likes her hairdo and even her kitchen apron. Complimenting her on her appearance, her cooking, and housekeeping will prove to be a wonderful tonic to her sometimes wilting spirit. . . .
>
> It is not only what we do that tends to break up our marriages, but what we fail to do. There is an old proverb that says, "What he was saying to her was drowned out by what he did not do." The husband lying on the couch in the front room, may shout to his wife in the kitchen and say, "Honey, I love you," but it would be much more convincing if he would express it by taking a dish towel or a broom to help a bit. Sometimes a man says to his wife, "I love you," but his conduct says more loudly, "I love me."[1]

It is well that the Priesthood bearer take the time to evaluate the extent to which he is providing this atmosphere. At this point the teacher may have each brother take a few minutes to evaluate personally his growth in this particular area by using the rating scale on page 189 (a copy should be provided for each class member):

---

[1]Brown, Hugh B., *You and Your Marriage*, Salt Lake City, Bookcraft, Inc., 1960, pp. 97-99.

MY SPIRITUAL I.Q.

		Not yet!	I'll do it Someday	I'll do it Now	I am trying	I am doing fine
1.	FAITH (James 2:26.) — I am actively putting into practice the teachings of the prophets of the Church such as home teaching, family home evening, etc.	....		....	....	....
2.	VIRTUE (Doctrine & Covenants 121: 45.) — I am striving continually to control any undesirable thoughts that would have produced unrighteous action.	....	....	....	....	....
3.	KNOWLEDGE (Doctrine & Covenants 88: 118.) — During this past week, I have read out of the Standard Works to my family.	....	....	....	....	....
4.	TEMPERANCE (Doctrine & Covenants 59: 16-20.) — I am able to control my eating habits and exercise restraint in things not fit for my body.	....			....	....
5.	PATIENCE (Matthew 5: 38-42.) — When provoked in a family situation, I am able to forbear against retaliating by words or actions.	....	....		....	....
6.	GODLINESS (Doctrine & Covenants 84: 20.) — In the exercise of my Priesthood I worthily partake of the ordinances, and worthily use this privilege.	....	....	....	....	....
7.	BROTHERLY KINDNESS (Doctrine & Covenants 38: 24.) — I treat the members of my family as I myself desire to be treated.		....	....	....	....
8.	CHARITY (Moroni 7:47.) — Love for Jesus Christ prevails in our home through our prayers and manner of speaking to one another.	....	....	....	....	....

189

EXPRESSING LOVE AND APPRECIATION

What are some of the specific things a Priesthood bearer might do to show his wife that he appreciates her and is cognizant of her needs as well as his own?

1. Constantly evaluate the wife's needs and determine what you might do to help meet these needs. One very busy brother, who, in addition to a demanding occupation, has a responsible church position, sets aside one of his evenings so that he might take his wife to a social function of her liking. Another brother who is a school teacher has coordinated his schedule so that he can take care of the children while his wife takes a class in school of her interest.

2. The wife needs to be accepted as a person of equal worth to her husband. Moreover, the wife needs to constantly know her worth. Subtle inferences and critical remarks about her appearance or way of doing things have the effect of causing her to defend her established ways, inhibiting free communication. A person cannot experience creative or spiritual development in a threatened atmosphere or climate where she must constantly justify her actions. On the other hand when the wife is acclaimed for her virtues, she can more freely develop her skills which will in turn become family assets.

MAINTAINING AN ATMOSPHERE OF COURTSHIP

Added to the foregoing suggestions is the counsel of President David O. McKay regarding the essentiality of continued courtship in marriage:

Next to loyalty as contributive to a happy home, I should like to urge continued courtship, and apply this to grown people. Too many couples have come to the altar of marriage looking upon the marriage ceremony as the end of courtship instead of the beginning of an eternal courtship. Let us not forget that during the burdens of home life—and they come—that tender words of appreciation, courteous acts are even more appreciated than during those sweet days and months of courtship. It is after the ceremony and during the trials that daily arise in the home that a word of "thank you," or "pardon me," "if you please" on the part of husband or wife contributes to that love which brought you to the altar. It is well to keep in mind that love can be starved to death as literally as the body that receives no sustenance. Love feeds upon kindness and courtesy. It is significant that the first sentence of what is now known throughout the Christian world as the Psalm of Love, is, "Love suffereth long, and is kind." The wedding ring gives no man the right to be cruel or inconsiderate. . . .[2]

In the development of the total personality it will be remembered that completeness is attained only as one develops the spiritual side of his nature. (Refer back to chart.) With this in mind, when does a person feel best motivated to express kindness and consideration to another? In the letter read at the beginning of the lesson why do you think that the brother referred to his temple experience as one of his happiest days? The Priesthood bearer could ask himself: "What is the connection between maintaining an atmosphere of courtship within my home and having the Spirit of the Lord present?" In determining the steps essential to retaining this Spirit, quorum members may be reminded again of the counsel of the Lord in the Doctrine and Covenants:

1. "Let thy bowels also be *full of charity* toward all men, AND TO THE HOUSEHOLD OF FAITH, . . .

2. "Let *virtue* garnish thy thoughts unceasingly;

3. "Then shall thy confidence wax strong in the presence of God; and the doctrine of the Priesthood shall distil upon thy soul as the dews from heaven. THE HOLY GHOST SHALL BE THY CONSTANT COMPANION, . . ." (D&C 121:45-46.)

From this counsel it can be seen that to have the Spirit of the Lord in one's life (this would also include the home) continuous love and virtue are necessary if the Priesthood bearer is to attain a spiritual communication as idealized and exemplified by President David O. McKay.

APPLICATION

What Would Jesus Do?

Y ou have probably noticed that the most frequently reiterated passage of scripture in this manual is D&C 121:34-45. This is so because it is the commandment of the Savior to all Priesthood holders on the principles that should govern their relationships with others. In order that you might demonstrate to your wife that she is truly loved and appreciated, you should:

1. Evaluate your worthiness to have the companionship of the

[2]McKay, David O., "Harmony in the Home," *Improvement Era*, June, 1956, p. 396.

Holy Ghost. You may find a need to rededicate yourself to the principles of righteousness that will in turn renew a spiritual love in your heart for your wife.

2.   Make a list of all the qualities that attracted you to your wife when you first married her. You could then discuss with her some of her needs and expectations in marriage and to what extent she feels these needs and expectations are being met through your relationship. You should set the stage for this discussion and allow plenty of time for a frank discussion in the spirit of love. From this discussion you can then best determine the role you have in your specific situation to help your wife feel greater self-fulfillment.

3.   Seek for opportunities to court your wife as you did before marriage. You could seek to find ways to express your appreciation to her when she least expects it. Such tokens of appreciation might consist of arranging for a babysitter and taking her out for the evening, and/or bringing her something thoughtful or special.

Read and ponder: I Peter 3:7; D&C 121:34-35.

SPECIAL INSTRUCTIONS TO THE TEACHER

1.   Emphasize that the key to maintaining a close spiritual relationship with one's wife is to maintain a spiritual relationship with the Lord. It is inconsistent for a man to say that he loves the Lord but not his wife.

2.   If the rating scale "My Spiritual I.Q." is used in your lesson presentation, care should be taken to protect the confidential nature of each man's personal self-evaluation. A very meaningful application of this lesson might be to challenge each member to conscientiously strive to improve in the area of his greatest need as shown by himself on his spiritual I.Q. rating scale. Copies of this scale should be prepared by the teacher to be distributed at the appropriate time during the lesson presentation. Sufficient time for contemplation in completing the evaluation should be allowed.

3.   Discuss ways in which an atmosphere of courtship might be maintained in the home.

Disagreements Can Be Resolved

It is suggested that the class instructor call upon one or two quorum members to report briefly their success in the following two areas:

1.   How did you specifically determine some of your wife's needs during this past week, and were you able to demonstrate consideration in helping her meet these needs? (Be careful in relating incidents, do not betray confidence or cause embarrassment.)

2.   How did you attempt to relive a courtship experience with your wife during the past week? What was the result of your efforts?

(This discussion should not exceed five minutes.)

LESSON OBJECTIVE

The Priesthood holder should be motivated to resolve disagreements through love, understanding, listening and discussion.

INTRODUCTION

THE SECOND MILE OF THEIR MARRIAGE

They were a young married couple. During the first months of their marriage they had experienced great joy. Being married was a new adventure. But now, quite naturally, certain problems in their relationships were beginning to emerge.

There was the question of finances, for example. They had not discussed money matters before their marriage, but now they found they had differences of opinion with regard to whether he should just give her a certain amount of money for specific purposes. He felt that since he presided in the home it was his responsibility to decide the things for which they would spend their money. She thought that they should discuss the things for which they wanted to make financial expenditures, reach an agreement, and then have a joint checking account.

193

They were also finding some difficulty in their relationships with their "in-laws." It hurt the wife when one day her husband said to her, "This is not the way my mother used to bake pies. Why don't you drop by some day and let her show you how to do it?" Although she had not said anything at the time, she found herself developing some resentment toward his mother. She realized that such feelings were wrong, but she also felt that he had been wrong in comparing her cooking with his mother's cooking.

There were other trouble spots. He was still going to school, so he felt it necessary to spend most of his evenings studying. She liked to talk to him and wanted to go out and participate in several organizations, but she did not wish to do so by herself. He kept reiterating to her how important it was that he take full advantage of his educational opportunities and that later they would do many things together. She could see that he had a valid argument, but nevertheless she felt some resentment over the whole situation. And she was not sure that the whole trouble existed because of the requirements of his schooling. Not wishing to create tension in their relationship over and above that which already existed, she remained silent and kept her feelings to herself. In her reflective moments, however, she found herself wishing that there were some way that her tension might be diminished. "Is it possible to eliminate some of the tension," she asked herself, "or should I accept it as a normal part of living?" (At this point class members could be invited to react to her question.)

LESSON DEVELOPMENT

Every individual who comes into the world is, in some ways, a distinctive personality. But he also possesses characteristics—common to all human beings—which permit people to understand one another more easily. The personality differences we have often contribute to our conflicts with other people. The teachings of the Savior emphasize the love that individuals should have for one another. We should respect one another and should help one another achieve the goals indicated by our Heavenly Father—lasting joy, salvation, and exaltation. We should continually strive to become more like Him. Before answering the question of how conflicts can be resolved and how we can help one another, let us consider another factor.

SOME REASONS PEOPLE ARE DIFFERENT

Not only are the personalities of individuals different in some ways, but also people live in different circumstances. Parents, for example, are older than their children. They have had many experiences which their children have not had. Therefore, they see things from a different point of view. Similarly, men are different from women in a number of ways. They have different responsibilities, for instance. If the oldest child in a family is in his teens, he lives under conditions which vary considerably from those of a newborn baby. A husband who comes home at night, tired and frustrated, may tend to view things from a perspective that seems strange to his wife if she has had a relaxing day. On the other hand a wife and mother who has a number of small children may be nervously exhausted by the end of the day, whereas her husband may have had a relatively pleasant day. Still another way in which people may differ is in the amount of knowledge they have.

How can members of the family direct their energies constructively so that they *complement* and help one another rather than conflict with one another and only accentuate their problems?

(Let class members consider the disagreements between the husband and wife mentioned at the beginning of the lesson and see what they would do to try to resolve them.) Following are some suggestions which may be useful:

SOME DIFFERENCES CANNOT BE REMOVED

The above discussion has emphasized that some differences among individuals are normal, and some of them cannot be changed. For example, a gifted child with great intellectual ability might find it rather easy to get A's in school while another child with very limited ability in this area might have difficulties in school, although he might be talented in other ways. Many times individuals either consciously or unconsciously try to force others to conform in ways which are impossible for the others. The motto or slogan of Alcoholics Anonymous offers a helpful suggestion to us all: "God give me the serenity to accept the things I cannot change, the courage to change the things I can, and the wisdom to know the difference."

SOME TIMES ARE BETTER THAN OTHERS

Generally, when people are tired or hungry, or for some reason have depressing problems urgently confronting them, they are not in the best position to resolve their differences. One couple has made it a rule in their home to take up a family problem that concerns them as parents only when they are alone, when they can relax, and when they do not have some other physical, emotional, or intellectual problem which might tend to produce a negative attitude. One wife never takes up a major problem with her husband until she has fed him a good meal, including his favorite dishes. Another couple discusses any differences only after they have listened to some beautiful music or participated in an activity they both enjoy.

KNOWLEDGE HELPS SOLVE PROBLEMS

Many times disagreements among individuals exist because of the differences in the extent of their knowledge. Individuals might make it a habit to ask one another, "Why do you think or feel this way?" and then honestly listen to the answer given. They might thus gain new insights which would help them to see the difficulty from another point of view. Perhaps the knowledge of both persons involved is insufficient or inaccurate. A young son recently told his father that a given scripture was found in a certain book in the Bible. His father insisted it was found elsewhere. An older daughter listened to their rather heated discussion and said, "Why don't we look it up?" When they did they discovered both of them were wrong. The Lord has instructed us to ". . . treasure up in your minds continually the words of life, . . ." (D&C 84: 85.) The more extensive and accurate one's knowledge, the easier it is to make wise decisions.

ATTITUDES ARE IMPORTANT

The attitude that people have toward one another often determines what they are willing to hear. A marriage counselor recently had a couple in his office who had such difficulties in their marriage that they were seriously considering a divorce. He asked each of them to try to define the problem. The woman's explanation was very emotional. After she had finished, the counselor asked the man to describe the problem from his point of view. The husband had hardly completed the first sentence when the woman violently objected to what he had said. In fact, she objected in the same way to everything that he said. The counselor finally had to ask her to leave so that he could hear the statement of her husband. It became clear to the counselor that one of the problems—although surely not the only problem in this relationship—stemmed from the fact that this woman never really listened to her husband. She interpreted his actions and feelings in terms of her own feelings and jealousies. She was looking at him through colored glasses. Until she saw him through the glass of objectivity and respect, the problems in their relationship would never be solved.

GO MORE THAN ONE EXTRA MILE

The love taught and exemplified by the Savior would indicate that we ought to go more than one extra mile in trying to understand a fellow human being. A young man was dating a girl who seemed to have all the characteristics of the girl he wanted to marry. From everything he was able to observe she was sincerely devoted to the principles of the Gospel. Therefore, he was terribly shocked when she told him one day of a mistake that she had once made. She also told him that she had repented. His first reaction, however, was that he simply could not marry her because he would have to live with the memory of her mistake. But he did acquire the maturity to forgive her, not just in a routine sort of way by merely saying he forgave her, but with his whole soul, genuinely feeling the forgiveness and never mentioning the incident again. Such forgiveness motivated her to go many extra miles to demonstrate her love and appreciation for him.

A husband ought to make allowance for the fact that sometimes his wife is nervously exhausted at the end of a day and not expect everything in the house to be in the same precise order as it is when she is not so tired. Likewise, a wife ought to be so sensitive to her husband's feelings that she will know when he has not had the success in his occupation that he would like to have had. At these times she should give him assurance of the many successful experiences he has had. She should be patient and help him to relax.

Parents should understand their children so well that when a young child says he has a pain in his stomach and does not want to go to school, they realize that what he may be saying is that he is having difficulty with the teacher or with other children.

An older child who is doing well in school should have patience with the younger child and not say to him, "Oh, you ought to be able to do that. It's so simple." Rather, he might say, "Would you like me to show you how it is done?"

ESTABLISHING THE TERMS OF OUR RELATIONSHIP

One of the most useful things that members of a family can do is to take the time to discuss thoroughly the terms of their relationships. It would be well to bring out in such a discussion the following ideas:

1. We do love each other. Therefore no experience that we might have, no problem we face, and no trial that we might be asked to experience will ever cause us to question our love for one another. We need to remember always that our love "is stronger than the cords of death." (See D&C 121:41-46.)

2. We may disagree for various reasons, but let us discuss our disagreements with a desire to discover the truth and then make whatever adjustments seem to be necessary. If our motive is to achieve the best possible family relationship, we should be willing to admit our mistakes and we should be compassionate when others err.

3. Our behavior should be such that the Holy Ghost can manifest His influence in our lives. That influence can be of great significance in our actions and in our relations with one another.

The Savior has told us, ". . . I say unto you, be one; and if ye are not one ye are not mine." (D&C 38:27.) Perhaps the suggestions given in this lesson will help each family achieve such oneness.

APPLICATION

What Would Jesus Do?

The Savior has said, "Thou shalt live together in love." (D&C 42:45.) As head of the family are you doing all you can in the spirit of love and understanding to resolve disagreements? Do you use the methods that the Savior used of persuasion, longsuffering and kindness?

Try honestly listening with understanding to your wife this week. Select the appropriate time to discuss a problem or situation that you may need to resolve. Then seek together the Holy Spirit to cause your union to "be one."

Read and ponder: 3 Nephi 11:29-30; 3 Nephi 12:23-24; D&C 64:8-11; D&C 42:22, 45.

SPECIAL INSTRUCTIONS TO THE TEACHER

You may want to encourage the members of the quorum to express themselves regarding past experiences involving disagreement, and how they resolved the disagreement. Encourage examples of where the disagreement was resolved through love, understanding and prayer.

Eternity Together Begins Now

LESSON FOLLOW-UP

Ask quorum members to indicate some suggestions that they have found that help resolve differences.

LESSON OBJECTIVES

The Priesthood holder should feel motivated to (1) develop common goals and interests with his wife and (2) build for the future together by planning both temporally and spiritually.

INTRODUCTION

The following dialogue between a bishop and one of his ward members illustrates the challenge that many Latter-day Saint couples face in building their eternal relationship together:

Bishop: "Well, Sister Murray, what can I do for you?"

Sister: "Bishop, it's about my husband and me . . . I don't know quite where to begin. It's not that we're not getting along—It's just that, well . . . ever since the children came along we never do the things we used to. After taking care of the kids all day, I just want to get away for awhile. We used to go out to a symphony or a movie once in a while, but now we never go anywhere."

Bishop: "I understand, Sister Murray. This is one of the common challenges that every couple face in their marriage. How long have you and Larry been married?"

Sister: "Five years next month. I don't want you to get the idea that our marriage is on the rocks, but I am worried about our marriage, bishop. When Larry gets home he's always too tired to do anything with us. He tells me he wants to relax. Well, after four years of this, I'm getting tired, too. Sometimes I wonder if I'll be able to hold up."

The foregoing conversation illustrates two typical conflicting needs —the husband who has a need for rest after work, and the wife who has a need for a diversion activity. There is frequently a desire by the husband who recognizes his wife's need to take her to activities that they enjoyed before their marriage, but because of children in the home, he feels that they are not free to go as they please. Because this is a common situation in many Latter-day Saint homes, the teacher and the quorum members might discuss together some practical steps that could be taken in satisfying the needs of both the husband and the wife.

DEVELOPING COMMON GOALS, INTERESTS AND HOBBIES

Development of common goals, interests, and/or hobbies is high on the list for those who have achieved a successful companionship in their marriage. The teacher could place the following topics on the chalkboard and then ask class members what goals, interests and hobbies each member and his wife had in common prior to his marriage? Through discussion each class member may complete on a sheet of paper the following list of common goals, interests, and hobbies which he and his wife had before they were married:

Goals	Interests	Hobbies
1.	1.	1.
2.	2.	2.
3.	3.	3.
4.	4.	4.
5.	5.	5.

After this list is completed to the satisfaction of the quorum members, the teacher could provide a sheet of paper to each quorum member. Each brother might then be asked to divide the sheet into two parts as illustrated below. On the left side of the sheet he could list: Personal Goals, Interests, and Hobbies. On the right side of the paper he should label this: Wife's Goals, Interests and Hobbies. (The unmarried Priesthood bearer might consider some of the goals, interests, and hobbies that he wants in his prospective wife and that would correspond with his goals, interests and hobbies.)

Using the list already completed on the board as reference, the teacher could then ask each brother to fill out both sides of the paper. After each brother has completed this exercise, the teacher might ask him to now mark with a plus each of the goals, interests, and hobbies that correspond with the wife's goals, interests, and hobbies; then mark with a minus each of the goals, interests, and hobbies that do not correspond. A zero may be used to designate a goal, an interest, or a hobby that the Priesthood bearer knows his wife has but is unable to specify what it is. For example, he might know that the wife meets each Tuesday night with a women's organization, but has never bothered to find out her interest in the organization. The quorum member could then be asked to add up all the pluses, minuses, and zeros.

Personal Goals, Interests, Hobbies		Wife's Goals, Interests, Hobbies
Interests:		Interests:
1. Outdoor activities	( )	1. Home beautification
2.	( )	2.
3.	( )	3.
4.	( )	4.
5.	( )	5.
Hobbies:		Hobbies:
1. Planting garden	( )	1. Swimming
2.	( )	2.
3.	( )	3.
4.	( )	4.
5.	( )	5.
Goals:		Goals:
1. Family activity	( )	1. Keeping attractive
2.	( )	2.
3.	( )	3.
4.	( )	4.
5.	( )	5.

Total ( )

Evaluation:

       7—10 pluses—Very good.

       5—7   pluses—Fair.

       0—5   pluses—Must do better.

BRINGING YOUR INTERESTS TOGETHER

It should be noted that although a couple's interests or hobbies are different this doesn't necessarily mean that they are not companionable. One wife of a Priesthood bearer knits for a hobby, while her husband, who enjoys reading as a hobby, reads aloud to her. In another couple's case, the husband enjoys fishing, the wife painting. They have achieved a successful companionship by the husband having his wife accompany him on his fishing trips, and while he stream fishes, she does her painting.

The important quality in achieving companionship in marriage is the willingness to understand each others' interests and share in these together. Many couples have combined hobbies together such as golf, gardening, home decoration, bird watching, and rock hunting. Others share mutual interests together such as music, reading, friends, dances, and movies. One couple who share mutual friends arrange to get together often to play wholesome games. Both couples have small families. When the couple in either family desire to go out together, an effective arrangement has been made for the other couple to babysit for them.

PLANNING FOR FINANCIAL SECURITY

In addition to developing common goals, interests, and hobbies together, another characteristic of a happy, successful home is the mutual effort of the husband and wife to live within their means regardless of their economic bracket.

President Heber J. Grant has said:

If there is one thing that will bring peace and contentment into the human heart, and into the family, it is to live within our means. And if there is any one thing that is grinding and discouraging and disheartening, it is to have debts and obligations that one cannot meet.[1]

Successful living within one's means calls for the joint planning of a budget by both husband and wife. Elder Hugh B. Brown has written:

The husband who refuses to take the wife into his confidence on money matters, on income, expenditures, and investments, and who makes her beg for every cent of money she spends, should not be surprised if his wife eventually asserts her independence, claims her rights as a human being and as a partner, and refuses longer to be treated as a little child. A man should be frugal but

---

[1]Grant, Heber J., *Relief Society Magazine*, Vol. 19, p. 302. Quote taken from address delivered by Ezra T. Benson, Brigham Young University, "Debt—An Increasing Threat," Salt Lake City: Deseret Book Co., 1962, p. 19.

not penurious. Wives are entitled to dignity and consideration and not merely to penny-pinching indulgence. . . .

Every husband should know how impossible it is for a
wife to budget and spend wisely from the joint income if
she is not allowed to know how much she has to spend.
The wife who is taken into the confidence of the husband
on money matters will usually resist the temptation to be
extravagant or to gamble on the future by buying needless
things because they are cheap or can be obtained with
little or no down payment. The income of the average
family, meager though it may be, can be made to cover
necessary expenses. Also the wise husband will provide his
wife with a monthly allowance for personal needs, and
this item in the budget should not be audited.[2]

Frequently, the complaint is heard by families that "we can't
follow a budget." At this point, it would be well to discuss how
the quorum member can live successfully within a budget by
planning jointly with his wife their economic expenditures and
needs. This may be done through (1) discussion, (2) special report
by a qualified quorum member who successfully follows a simple
and workable budget. (Pre-arrange to give him three to five minutes. The teacher should select between this report and one which
might be given under the consideration of wills, etc.)

A second reason for planning the family finances jointly is to
prepare the wife to assume the "general manager's" job in the
event that the husband should be removed from the scene.

It might be well for the teacher to have a brief report by a
lawyer or quorum member on the advisability and preparation of
wills. (Limit report to three to five minutes. A commercialized
program should be avoided.)

BUILDING A SPIRITUAL FOUNDATION

Without an understanding of the relationship between providing for one's material security and planning for one's spiritual
well-being, the members of the Church will frequently use an
economic objection as the excuse for not living a spiritual principle. Several examples are as follows:

---

[2]Brown, Hugh B., *You and Your Marriage*, Salt Lake City: Bookcraft,
Inc., 1960, pp. 158-159.

SPIRITUAL PRINCIPLE	ECONOMIC OBJECTION
1. Tithing	"We can hardly make ends meet as it is, let alone donate 10% to the Church."
2. Fast Offering	"We don't really save anything by fasting since we have a bigger meal after the fast."
3. One Year's Food Supply	"We don't have enough money to have two weeks supply on hand. It wouldn't be so bad once you get the supply on hand, but getting started is the tough part."
4. Genealogy	"I don't know how we would find the time or the money to do the research."
5. Having a Family	"We are waiting and saving until we can give them all the advantages they need to get along, such as a mission, college."

These objections and principles could be discussed with consideration to the following areas:

1. In the light of the Savior's counsel to "Seek ye first the Kingdom of God," which of the foregoing principles should take priority over providing for an adequate home and its necessities?

2. In terms of the objections cited above, what is the significance of the Savior's statement: "For where your treasure is, there will your heart be also." (Matthew 6:21.)

3. The Lord has counseled the prophet in this dispensation that ". . . all things unto me are spiritual, and not at any time have I given unto you a law which was temporal;" (D&C 29:34.) How do each of the principles cited above contribute toward the building of an eternal future together?

What Would Jesus Do?

C arefully review the preceding three statements to ascertain some counsel of the Savior pertaining to the principles of this lesson. Do you really want to apply His teachings to your marriage? Consider then these suggestions:

1. Talk over with your wife her goals, interests and hobbies, and how your marriage could be more companionable by combining your interests and hobbies together. Plan to renew or develop a joint interest or hobby. You could both set aside a time to discuss the mutual goals of your marriage and what preparation and planning is presently being made toward achieving these goals.

2. You could commence a periodic budget analysis where you and your wife jointly plan together how your income is to be saved and spent. You could further discuss with her what provisions you have made in planning for the family's economic security in the event that you are removed from the scene. A good book on planning for financial security could be read together. You could explain the money situation of the household to the children at family home evening and show them what part they play in reference to the family budget.

3. Plan together to live a principle of the Gospel that is needed in the home, such as tithing or a year's supply of food. Through a family council you could announce that it is the intent of you and your wife to live this principle and indicate to the children specifically how you are going to do it. It might be that the family will start their year's supply be getting one or two month's supply.

Ponder the following: D&C 29:34; D&C 132:19.

SPECIAL INSTRUCTIONS TO THE TEACHER

As each spiritual principle and its counterpart economic objection is discussed, care should be taken to avoid controversy. Objections should be discussed in light of the counsel given in the scriptures governing the spiritual principle. There are varied applications suggested in this lesson. Priesthood holders should be encouraged to select the particular application or applications in which he feels the greatest need and make some self-commitment to strive for improvement.

Sharing Your World

LESSON FOLLOW-UP

1. Each class member could indicate on a sheet of paper one or several things he specifically did with his wife in the past week in the following areas:

a. Discussion and/or planning joint interests or hobbies.

b. Discussion and evaluation of the goals in their marriage.

c. A joint budget planning session and/or discussion of family finances.

d. A joint resolve of the husband and wife to live a gospel principle needed in their home to ensure an eternal continuity in their relationship.

2. One or several class members might be called upon to relate briefly their experiment with the challenge of the previous week.

(This discussion should not exceed five minutes.)

LESSON OBJECTIVE

The Priesthood holder should feel motivated to confide in his wife more about his aspirations for the future and to seek her counsel more often in relation to problems.

INTRODUCTION

The following story of an experience that she had while in Los Angeles has been told by Emma Ray Riggs McKay, wife of President David O. McKay:

Last summer on reaching Los Angeles, we decided to have our car washed by one of those "Quickies" on Wilshire Boulevard.

207

As I was watching the last part of the operation from a bench, to my surprise a tiny voice at my elbow said, "I guess that man over there loves you."

I turned and saw a beautiful little curly-haired child with great brown eyes who looked to be about seven years of age.

"What did you say?" I asked.

"I said, I guess that man over there loves you."

"Oh, yes, he loves me; he is my husband. But why do you ask?"

A tender smile lighted up his face and his voice softened as he said, "Cuz, the way he smiled at you. Do you know I'd give anything in this world if my pop would smile at my mom that way."

"Oh, I'm sorry if he doesn't!"

"I guess you're not going to get a divorce," he questioningly remarked.

"No, of course not; we've been married over fifty years. Why do you ask that?"

"Cuz everybody gets a divorce around here. My pop is getting a divorce from my mom, and I love my pop and I love my mom. . . ."

His voice broke, and tears welled up in his eyes, but he was too much of a little man to let them fall.

"Oh, I'm sorry to hear that!"

And then he came very close and whispered confidentially into my ear, "You'd better hurry out of this place or you'll get a divorce, too!"

Then he picked up his papers and walked disconsolately down the street.[1]

LESSON DEVELOPMENT

This poignant story illustrates the tragic effect that divorce has

---

[1]McKay, Llewelyn R., Compiler and Writer, *Home Memories of President David O. McKay*, Salt Lake City, Deseret Book Company, 1956, p. 189.

upon young people. Assuming that this little fellow's parents started their marriage "in love," what are some of the possible causes for the deterioration of the husband-wife relationship that only a divorce is sought as a solution to the problem?

In discussing such causative factors as not being able to communicate, financial problems, etc., the quorum members might further discuss the following:

1. How might some of the more serious difficulties that couples encounter be prevented?

2. What steps can a couple realistically take in our society to help their companionship to grow closer rather than apart?

When a couple begin their married life together, they little realize that there are cultural forces set in motion that tend to separate the couple. The reason for this is that they spend most of their waking hours in two separate worlds. The world of the husband is centered around providing a living for his family. The wife, on the other hand, confines most of her time in the world of the home. Where the couple began marriage "living for each other," they now spend most of their time assuming an independent role in their respective world.

TWO DIFFERENT WORLDS

The culture requires a father to spend his time and energy toward achieving his ambition; thus much of his time is spent away from home putting forward his "best front." The wife is expected to provide a good home, raise the children and care for the domestic situation. As their marriage continues, unless the husband and wife deliberately do something to preserve and safeguard their interest in each other, the expectations of their respective roles will cause them to drift apart so that in time, their two worlds are completely isolated and separated. This may be illustrated by the following diagram.

Placing this illustration, or a similar one, on the board, the quorum members might discuss and list under each of the respective "worlds" of the husband and wife, the factors that make each of their "worlds" different from the other.

If a marriage is to be successful and joyful, not only must both husband and wife be conscious of the forces that tend to

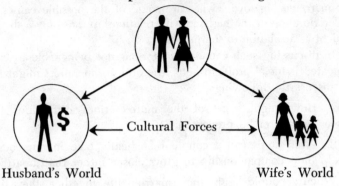

Courtship and Start of Marriage

Cultural Forces

Husband's World

Wife's World

1. Making a Living vs. Homemaking
2.
3.
4.

separate them, but they must take some positive steps to ensure their happiness. The following are three areas that demand continuous attention if the couple is to develop a closer companionship as their partnership progresses:

SHARING HOPES AND AMBITIONS

Every man strives for the "better life," a life that will provide him with self-fulfillment. He entertains a constant hope to achieve a nobler status. It is not sufficient that he entertains a hope for a life beyond this one. Something innately tells him that his heaven cannot exceed his capacity. So he strives to achieve the splendor of his dreams by improving himself in his various responsibilities. Sad, however, is the situation that confronts many men in older age when they come to realize that many of their hopes and ambitions have not been attained, nor is there any prospect for their attainment. In his book, *The Challenge*, Alvin R. Dyer has typified this situation in these words:

> . . . young men grow to be older men, and young women grow to be older women. And in the growth they forget their dreams, their hopes, and their ambitions, surrender-

ing to the average and commonplace their once noble and lofty aspirations.

He then quotes David Thoreau who said:

Youth gets together his materials to build a bridge to
    the moon.
Or perchance a palace or a temple on earth,
But alas, at length, the middle-aged man
concludes to build a woodshed with them.[2]

From a more positive viewpoint, there are those few who have achieved their ambitions and realized their hopes, and who bear witness to the fact that such attainment could not have been accomplished without their wife's encouragement.

It is well also for a husband and wife to realize that generally more important than attaining a goal is the way in which they really try.

A close relationship exists between the Priesthood holder's realizing his hopes and ambitions and the sharing of these aspirations with his wife. Hundreds of cases might be cited throughout the Church where a young man has confided his ambition to his fiancee or new bride and she has unselfishly sacrificed to see that he could go through school in order to attain this objective. (The quorum leader might ask one or two brethren to use their personal success story as illustrative of a sacrificing and understanding wife.) What might have been the case if these hopes and ambitions had not been confided?

DISCUSSING PROBLEMS AND EXPERIENCES TOGETHER

Case Problem Number One

Ben came home from work and flopped on the couch. It had been one of those days when he should have stayed in bed. First, he had arrived at work late and the foreman told him his time would be docked. Later during the day he had misread a blueprint with the result that a number of parts had to be discarded. What a "chewing out" he had got for that. And so when Sandra, his wife, walked in the front room and said, "Hi, Ben, how was your

---

[2]Dyer, Alvin R., *The Challenge*, Salt Lake City, Deseret Book Company, 1962, p. 106.

day?" he growled, "When's dinner going to be ready 'round this crummy place?"

"I thought we might go out for a hamburger tonight. I've been . . ."

"Go out to eat again? That's all you want to do. Now get in the kitchen and get a meal on the table."

"We haven't done anything for two weeks," she pleaded. "Couldn't we just go out tonight, Ben? The kids have been on my nerves all day."

"What do you think we are, millionaires? Now leave me alone, will ya?"

With emotion in her voice, Sandra countered, "I won't have you swearing in this house. If you can't act like a man you can go right back out."

"Shut up and get out of here," Ben ordered. With that, Sandra ran out of the room crying. Ben muttered under his breath, turned over, and tried sleeping it off.

Case Problem Number Two

Today had been one of the days when Don had wished he'd not gone into business for himself. Orders were piling up all over, the secretary had called and said she could not come in today because she was ill, several suppliers had called and wanted payment on their bills. To top it all off, on the way home he got stopped for speeding and was given a citation. This would probably cost him $35.00. When he got home, he was in no mood for the cheerful greeting of his wife, who said: "Hi, Don, guess what?"

"I'm not in the mood for guessing games, Lisa," he said abruptly. "What is it?"

"Nothing," Lisa dejectedly replied.

Don saw immediately that he had hurt his wife's feelings. "Look, honey. I'm sorry. I had a bad day today. Let me wash up; then let's sit down together and you tell me all about it." He kissed her on the nose, provoked a smile from her, and then asked, "O. K.?"

"O. K." Lisa replied. "I'm anxious to know what made you so grouchy."

SOLVING PROBLEMS BEFORE THEY BECOME CRISES

The foregoing case studies are illustrative of two approaches that the husband uses in normal day-to-day relations with his wife. It is evident which of the two contributes to a better relationship.

1. How does the willingness of a partner to sit down and discuss his or her problems foster a closer companionship between them?

2. What happens to the communication between husband and wife in each case? Why is a person offended when they're ignored or "cut off"?

3. In the second case problem, what attributes are evident in Don's character that contribute to better understanding? (Though he offended his wife, when he realized this, he was willing to listen to her rather than vent his own problems.)

SHARING MOMENTS ALONE

Having discussed the factors that tend to separate the husband and wife in their marriage relationship, it is well for members to now discuss the things that can be done to bring their two worlds together. This could be done by adding to the previously used illustration the following diagram and listing under it the factors which will help fuse the two worlds together.

Courtship and Start of Marriage

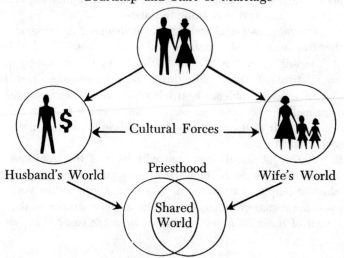

Husband's World Priesthood Wife's World

Cultural Forces

Shared World

1. Same Interests, Faith, etc.
2.
3.

It is necessary that each Priesthood bearer realize that a wife needs constant courting and the feeling that of all the women in the world, she alone matters to her husband. Sharing time as a family is essential, but it is equally important that the husband has shared moments with his wife.

IMPLEMENTATION

This week, in attempting to merge together your "world" with your wife's "world," why not plan to adopt one of the following suggestions in your home situation:

APPLICATION

What Would Jesus Do?

" . . . and they twain shall be one flesh, and all this that the earth might answer the end of its creation." (D&C 49:16.)

Such is the counsel of Jesus pertaining to the unity that should be between a husband and wife. This, of course, implies that there is a concerted attempt to share their world together. Following are several suggestions that may bring this about:

1. The most powerful and significant influence of bringing together the "worlds" of a husband and a wife is the Gospel of Jesus Christ. You might assess with your wife the way this is being applied in your relationship. Specifically, this means your reliance upon the Lord to solve your problems; heartfelt repentance when needed; covenant-making and covenant-keeping; and seeking for and acquiring the gift of the Holy Ghost which brings you to a unity of thought and feeling.

2. You might discuss with your wife some of the ambitions you have toward the fuure, how she is involved in these plans and how she can help you attain them. When was the last time you expressed appreciation to her for her self-sacrifice already in the attainment of these ambitions, if this has been the case? Why not do

it today? If this has not been the case, together you might work toward an understanding of each other's respective world and what each might do in helping bring your two worlds together.

3. The problems and experiences encountered during the week outside the home could be discussed with your wife. Her advice should be solicited and tried. Appreciation for her counsel should not be forgotten.

4. When was the last time that you sat down together and studied the scriptures? Why not set aside a regular time to do this, letting her know that she is as important to you now as she was when you were first married.

Read and ponder: D&C 88:67-68; Luke 14:28-30; Moses 5:1.

SPECIAL INSTRUCTIONS TO THE TEACHER

1. The major emphasis of this lesson should be to help the quorum member to see the Gospel of Jesus Christ as the means of bringing the lives of two people together.

2. Ask quorum members to relate specific illustrations of how they try to share their worlds with their wives and the results it has in their marriage.

"Be Ye Aware . . ."

LESSON FOLLOW-UP

If you are seriously attempting to do what Jesus would do, you should begin to notice some changes in your wife's attitude and disposition toward you. Is it working? Let's determine what you did or didn't do in connection with last week's suggestions.

1. Did you assess with your wife the way the Gospel was being applied in your relationship?

2. Did you sit down and discuss together your hopes and ambitions for the future?

3. Did you solicit your wife's advice or counsel regarding problems you experienced outside the home? Did you accept her advice? Did you express appreciation for it?

What was the result of trying one of these suggestions? This week, let's have a few volunteer their experiences with trying the challenge.

(This discussion should not exceed five minutes.)

LESSON OBJECTIVE

The Priesthood bearer should feel motivated to understand his wife's special needs and ways she is different from him.

INTRODUCTION

Try the following opinionnaire to determine how much you think you know about your wife or women generally. In answering the questions, you should apply the statements to women generally since it is understood that there are exceptions to the statements. The answers will be found at the end of this lesson. Correctness of the response has been determined through several survey interviews of women. Circle a "yes" response if you feel the statement reflects an accurate indication of women generally, and a "no" response if the description is inaccurate.

yes   no   1.   A woman needs to know constantly that she is loved.

yes   no   2.   It is a woman's desire to be like all other women.

yes   no   3.   A woman's needs are significantly different from a man's.

yes   no   4.   A woman stands in need of continuous admiration.

yes   no   5.   A woman's beauty is largely determined by a man's attention.

yes   no   6.   What you, the husband, think of your wife is more important to her than what she actually is.

yes   no   7.   A woman is more satisfied with a compliment on her looks than on an attribute she is attempting to acquire.

yes   no   8.   Whether a woman is cheerful or despondent is largely up to her husband.

yes   no   9.   A woman's confidence is determined from being continually reminded of her positive qualities.

yes   no 10.   A woman is more responsive to a man when he presents her with gifts than when he gives her a look, a touch, or a kind word.

LESSON DEVELOPMENT

HOW A WOMAN DIFFERS FROM A MAN

Many husbands go through married life seemingly oblivious to the very obvious fact that a woman's needs and a man's needs are quite dissimilar. So significantly different are they that unless a husband understands these "need" differences, he will most likely treat his relationship with his wife as he would that of another man. As we consider some of the basic ways a man and woman differ with respect to their needs, it will become apparent why such an approach is devastating to the marriage relationship.

Consider briefly the significant ways your wife will differ from you. (The following areas may be discussed in addition to other suggested need differences.)

1. How does a woman's need for continual love and expression of affection differ from a man's? How does a man's job involvement at times cause him to neglect the expression of love to her?

2. In terms of having a stabilized home situation and job permanency, in what ways does a wife differ from her husband? What effect does it have on the wife's feeling of security to have to move to a new community with a change of job assignment or a situation of unemployment? Is a husband affected the same way?

3. Why are men in many instances less emotionally sensitive than women?

4. In what ways does a man's attitude about a home life situation differ from that of a woman?

What happens when a husband fails to recognize these distinctive needs of his wife? One result is that she then has difficulty in understanding her role as a mother and a wife. Consequently, she may become overzealous in her attention to the home or children with an obsession for cleanliness. Or she may divorce herself from the home altogether and seek security in outside interests. Or, she may become slothful and unconcerned about her personal appearance, her children's appearance, or the appearance of the home.

A WOMAN'S NEEDS DEFINED

Among the needs of women the following are considered the most dominant and important for effective husband-and-wife relationships.

1. *Her Need for Security.* As previously noted in lesson 25, one of the most vital factors of a woman's development is that she feels that as a person she is making an important contribution. When she assumes the role of motherhood, the need is all the more important.

2. *Her Need for Uniqueness.* Closely related to the feeling that she is making an important contribution is her need to feel unique from all other women. She wants to feel distinctive in her personal appearance, the decor of her home, and the way her children are attired.

3. *Her Need for Continuous Admiration and Recognition of Her Virtues:* It is a well-established principle in the area of human relationships that people do better when they are appreciated for their attributes than when they are criticized. So it is in husband-wife relationships. As a wife receives admiration and praise for her positive qualities, she develops more confidence and poise.

Even more important, however, when her positive qualities are emphasized, she develops the courage to attempt reconstruction of her weak character flaws.

The reason for this need of continuous admiration and recognition by her husband of her positive qualities is that it lets her know that she is accepted as an equal in the marriage relationship and has worth to her husband. Criticism for the things she doesn't do, on the other hand, lets her know that she is not accepted and that she only has a conditional worth to her husband. If he pays her small attentions, she will take great pains to make herself all the more physically, emotionally, and spiritually beautiful for him; if he doesn't she feels that he doesn't care.

HELPING HER MEET HER NEEDS

Let's consider practically several things you as a husband can do to help your wife meet her needs:

1. You might begin by expressing appreciation to your wife for the job she is doing as a wife and mother with the children. One husband, who frequently expresses to others his appreciation for his wife's efforts in training his well-mannered children was asked by his wife: "Why haven't you ever told me personally that you appreciate the job I've done as a mother? I've never heard you thank me once."

2. Sincerely commend her for the strong qualities she possesses. For example another husband frequently commends his wife for the effort she is making in being more patient with him and his children. As a result, she strives all the more to live up to his commendation.

3. Be observant of her efforts to be distinctively different from other women on her personal grooming and decor in the home.

4. Rather than criticizing her for any shortcomings she has, attempt to say nothing of these during the forthcoming week. Avoid also any comparison to any other women.

OBTAINING A POSITIVE RESPONSE FROM YOUR WIFE

"I'd give anything if my wife and I could restore the joy we had earlier in our marriage" one husband lamented before his stake president. Anything? It will require considerable effort on the part of the husband because as many authorities in marriage relations have indicated, how the wife thinks, acts, and feels, is primarily dependent upon the husband. "Wait a minute," you say. "You mean to tell me that I determine how my wife is going to act while I've been gone all day?" Yes, to a great extent you do, but before accepting any statements at face value, consider the following elements that will produce a positive response from your wife:

1. *Her emotional temperament is regulated by you.* It is an interesting challenge to each husband to consider that he, in large measure, determines the emotional temperament of his wife. For it is the husband—the knowledgeable husband—that can create within her a cheerful disposition.

In their book, *The Marriage Climate,* Ligon and Smith assert that a wife is sparkling or temperamental, depending on you, the husband. The important factor "is what you, a husband, *think*— not what your wife *is.*"[1]

2. *Her main concern is for what you think, feel and need.* As previously noted, ideally when a woman marries she makes a total commitment of herself to her husband. Her total world is centered in what he, the husband, thinks, how he feels, and what needs he has. This is why the woman is oftentimes very submissive to the husband's will even though he is wrong. This is particularly true of a Latter-day Saint girl who is taught to be submissive to her husband's will as he is submissive to our Heavenly Father's will. But, it doesn't take too much or too long to create a disillusionment within a wife so that she will actually resist in spirit the will of her husband when he unwisely makes excessive demands of her or fails to give her appreciation and attention. When you demand what she is willing to give unconditionally she is robbed of the one major asset she has to contribute to the marriage relationship—looking for new ways to please her husband according to his thoughts, feelings, and needs.

3. *She is more responsive to your look, your touch, your word than your gifts.* In a widely published article, "The Power Men Have Over Women," the author, Maryn Mannes chastises the "silly

---

[1]Ligon, Ernest Mayfield and Smith, Leona Jones, *The Marriage Climate,* St. Louis, the Bethany Press, 1963, pp. 37-38.

male fool" because he is often ". . . unaware of how much a look, a touch, a word, can hold for a woman."[2]

"But," you say, "I know what my wife looks like." You do, but she wants that undistracted look that keeps her secure in the knowledge that she is still the "only one."

SOME "GOLDEN RULES" FOR HUSBANDS

As husbands, if we are wise, we shall seek to practice at least one of the following "golden rules":

1. Permit your wife the freedom of responding to your needs without reminding or demanding it of her.

2. See in your wife a radiant personality. Accentuate her positive side and give her recognition for it. One very charming wife, who is frequently complimented on her beautiful and radiant personality, answers many times in reply, "If you had a husband like mine you couldn't help being charming. He always tells me how beautiful and happy I look so *I can't help being that way!*"

3. Be wise and practice giving your wife that look that attracted her to you, a touch that lets her know she is loved, and a word that assures her how you really feel.

APPLICATION

What Would Jesus Do?

T herefore all things whatsoever ye would that men (wives) should do to you, do ye even so to them." (Matthew 7:12.)
This is the principle by which the Savior would have us govern our relationships with others, especially our wives.

You might this week inventory your wife's personal qualities. Write them down. What has she done for you, the children and the home? Don't weigh these assets against any liabilities.

Read and ponder: I John 3:1-3, 16-18; I John 2:5.

[2]Mannes, Maryn, "The Power Men Have Over Women," *The Reader's Digest,* June 1964, p. 61

1. Even though some may have read the lesson and answers to the quiz before class, give the quiz anyway. This can be done by simply reading questions aloud or even better having it printed on separate sheets to be handed out to be done silently.

2. Opinionnaire responses: Numbers 2, 7 and 10 rate generally "no" with women; the rest, "yes." (See page 217.)

3. Tally the responses and find out if there was one or two on which some gave incorrect answers. Discuss the ones where there were different opinions.

4. Ask quorum members to give some of their own "Golden Rules" for husbands or some they have observed others use that seemed effective.

INSTRUCTIONAL MATERIALS

If possible, have the quiz duplicated on small pieces of paper and have quorum members answer the questions silently before discussion.

Let them use the back of the paper to write a list of their own "Golden Rules" for husbands.

What Kind of Dad Are You?

Last week it was suggested that you inventory your wife's assets as a means of better appreciating her. You were also encouraged to apply the Savior's "golden rule" to your relationship.

One or two quorum members might briefly report on "one interesting development in our home resulting from our Priesthood lesson was . . ."

LESSON OBJECTIVE

The Priesthood holder should feel motivated to better understand his relationship to his children.

INTRODUCTION

It is suggested that the class teacher, on a Sunday or two before this lesson is to be given, ask one or more Sunday School teachers of boys and girls ages 12 or 13 to take five minutes of class time, requesting that class members respond on paper to this: "I like my dad because. . . ." No names should be given with the replies.

Then, to begin this Priesthood lesson discussion, the class teacher could read these anonymous statements from the Sunday School boys and girls.

LESSON DEVELOPMENT

CHILDREN HAVE SPIRITUAL NEEDS TOO

Parents have the obvious responsibility to provide for the physical needs of their children: food, clothing, and shelter. They also have the obligation to assist them in the learning of such basic skills as how to eat properly, how to walk, talk, to wash, and to dress themselves. But children also have spiritual needs, and parents must satisfy these also.

In a familiar revelation the Lord says that if parents teach not their children "to understand the doctrine of repentance, faith in Christ the Son of the living God, and of baptism and the gift of the Holy Ghost by the laying on of the hands, when eight years old, the sin be upon the heads of the parents." (D&C 68:25.) President Joseph F. Smith declared, "The parents in Zion will be held responsible for the acts of their children, not only until they become eight years old, but, perhaps, throughout all the lives of their children, provided they have neglected their duty to their children while they were under their care and guidance, and the parents were responsible for them."[1]

Parents need to understand their responsibilities thoroughly in regard to their children, but in order to succeed in meeting these responsibilities their primary motivation must come from love for their children rather than merely a sense of obligation to them.

Providing for the needs of children is a joint enterprise involving both father and mother.

President Joseph F. Smith also said: "The father, if he is worthy of his Priesthood, has certain rights and authority within his family, comparable to those of the bishop with relation to the ward. Too often amongst us the head of the family, though he holds the higher Priesthood, fails to magnify his calling as the spiritual head of the household. It would be better if every elder who is a father rose to the dignity of his position and officiated in his holy office within his family organization. He may call to his aid any others who are worthy holders of the requisite authority in the Priesthood, but it is his privilege to stand as the head of his household and to perform the ordinances pertaining to his family."[2]

FATHER IS PATRIARCH IN HIS HOME

The worthy father who holds the Melchizedek Priesthood has the priceless privilege of administering the ordinances of the Gospel to his children at the appropriate times and places. He may bless his children as babies and give them the names by which they will be known; similarly he may baptize and confirm them members of the Church, and anoint and bless them in times of sickness.

---

[1]Smith, Joseph F., *Gospel Doctrine* (Fifth Edition), Salt Lake City, Deseret Book Company, 1939, p. 286.

[2]*Ibid.*, p. 291.

Also, when a child is going away from home to go to school, or to work, or on a mission, or has a special problem of some kind, or an especially difficult decision to make, it is the worthy father's right as the patriarch to his family to give that child a special blessing.

In some instances the home teachers, members of the ward bishopric, the quorum presidency, or others may be called in to assist in an administration of some kind. The presence of these persons in no way alters the fact that the father presides in his home. For example, we are told by President McKay: "In the home the presiding authority is always vested in the father, and in all home affairs and family matters there is no other authority paramount. To illustrate this principle: It sometimes happens that the elders are called in to administer to the members of a family. Among these elders there may be presidents of stakes, apostles, or even members of the First Presidency of the Church. It is not proper under these circumstances for the father to stand back and expect the elders to direct the administration of this important ordinance. The father is there. It is his right and it is his duty to preside. He should select the one who is to administer the oil, and the one who is to be mouth in prayer. He should not feel that because there are present presiding authorities in the Church that he is therefore divested of his rights to direct the administration of that blessing of the Gospel in his home. (If the father is absent, the mother should request the presiding authority present to take charge.)"

President McKay then reminds us that we must "keep religion in home life. We should make it obvious, both by our actions and our conversation, that we are seriously interested in religious things and believe in them ourselves: faith in God, in the divine mission of Jesus Christ, and in the restoration of the Gospel . . .

"To give young people the right start in life, we must discuss with our children and friends questions of motive and subjects like birth, love, marriage, death, and destiny. Babson says: 'One of the best things that could happen to America today would be a return to family prayer; the getting together after breakfast or in the evening for five or ten minutes for simple family worship! The saying of grace before meals would be a step in this direction.' I am glad that that practice is general, I hope, throughout the Latter-day Saint homes."[3]

---

[3]McKay, David O., *Gospel Ideals*, Salt Lake City, Deseret News Press, 1953, p. 479.

WHAT DO YOU THINK OF YOUR DAD?

Bryant S. Hinckley tells this story:

Three hundred twenty-six school children of a district near Indianapolis were asked to write anonymously just what each thought of his father.

The teacher hoped that the reading of the essays might attract the fathers to attend at least one meeting of the Parent-Teachers Association.

It did.

They came in $400 cars and $4,000 cars. Bank president, laborer, professional man, clerk, salesman, meter reader, farmer, utility magnate, merchant, baker, tailor, manufacturer, and contractor, every man with a definite estimate of himself in terms of money, skill, and righteousness or looks. . . .

The president picked at random from another stack of papers. 'I like my daddy,' she read from each. The reasons were many: he built my doll house, took me coasting, taught me to shoot, helps with my schoolwork, takes me to the park, gave me a pig to fatten and sell. Scores of essays could be reduced to: 'I like my daddy. He plays with me.'

Not one child mentioned his family house, car, neighborhood, food, or clothing.

The fathers went into the meeting from many walks of life; they came out in two classes: companions to their children or strangers to their children.

No man is too rich or too poor to play with his children.[4]

The Lord has revealed that it is His work and glory to bring to pass the immortality and eternal life of man. (Moses 1:39.) It is part of the stewardship of each father in Israel, as the patriarch to his family, to administer all of the affairs within his own jurisdiction, in such a way as to do all within his own power to accomplish that work of God as regards his own family.

---

[4]Hinckley, Bryant S., . . . *Not by Bread Alone*, Salt Lake City, Bookcraft, 1955, p. 84.

What Would Jesus Do?

N o more sacred responsibility has been laid upon the Priesthood holder than the teaching and watch care of his children.

The teachings of Jesus to parents have been repeatedly emphasized in this manual. (See D&C 68:25-29.)

To assess how you are doing in this responsibility, ask yourself:

1. Do I make a concerted effort to teach my children the Gospel of Jesus Christ?

2. Do we give *all* our children an opportunity to participate in *every* family home evening?

3. Do I ever make things with my children?

4. Have I started a missionary and education fund for each of my children?

5. Do I encourage each of my children to own his own set of standard works?

6. Does our family play together frequently?

7. Do we have family prayers regularly?

8. Am I teaching my children to pay an honest tithe?

Read and ponder: 3 Nephi 25:5-6; D&C 93:39-50; 3 Nephi 18:21; 2 Nephi 25:26.

SPECIAL INSTRUCTIONS TO THE TEACHER

1. Invite quorum to divide into groups of five or six and discuss ways in which they can be a real father, in a patriarchal sense. Afterwards have each group share their results and list them on the board.

2. Challenge each member to do something to get closer to their children.

3. Bear testimony to the importance of their relationship with their children.

INSTRUCTIONAL MATERIALS

Meetinghouse library pictures:
OP252, OQ201, OQ204, OQ244, OQ245, OQ263, OQ269

Wanted: Respect and Honor

LESSON FOLLOW-UP

Class members might be asked to tell of some of the specific things they have done during the week to get closer to their own children.

(This discussion should not exceed five minutes.)

LESSON OBJECTIVE

The Priesthood holder should feel motivated to understand how to establish respect and honor among all members of his family.

INTRODUCTION

One of the prevalent problems of our time is the lack of respect that children have for their parents and elders. More than the lack of respect children show for their parents, however, is the lack of understanding that parents have in earning respect from their children. The father of the family should understand that his children will have respect for him and his wife as they themselves respect the individuality and person of each child. He should also recognize that the respect, trust, and faith that his children will have toward their Heavenly Father is in large measure determined by their mortal father's attitude toward spiritual things.

Recently one of the seminary teachers in the Church was approached by a sister who inquired, "Why is it that you can't teach our children to have more respect for their parents?"

1. What would motivate a parent to ask such a question?
2. In this teacher's place, how would you answer her question?

LESSON DEVELOPMENT

This mother's inquiry is not an isolated instance. Rather, this problem comes to the attention of our church leaders all too often.

GAINING YOUR CHILDREN'S RESPECT

Too frequently parents feel that respect for them and others is gained through moralizing preachments to the children. While moral teachings have their place, more effective means are available to the Priesthood bearer to earn the respect of his children rather than having to demand it. The following questions represent several of the most important factors that contribute to the children's showing respect to their father.

CHILDREN LEARN BY EXAMPLE

What kind of an example am I to my children? Children learn a great many things by imitation. A parent who is disrespectful of others can expect to receive the same in his home. For example, many fathers who criticize those with whom they work in and out of the Church in front of the children cannot understand why their children are so rebellious toward the Church and toward them. One father can't understand why his children are delinquent to the law, yet he prides himself on circumventing the law and refers to the police as the "bulls."

One can tell a great deal about a child's home life by his attitude and respect for sacred things, for it is in the home that this attitude is learned. It should be challenging to every father to know that his children's concept of their Father in Heaven to a very great extent will be determined by the example of their mortal father. If he is patient, kind, and loving, it will be easy for them to understand their Heavenly Father as being patient, kind, and loving. If he is stern, curt, and vengeful with his children, it will be difficult for the children to understand how their Heavenly Father can be any different. In a positive way, the importance of example was brought out at the 1964 Priesthood Conference of the Church when a young Deacon testified:

Until I was trying to prepare this talk I really didn't realize how many things my parents have taught me. Almost everything I do and feel is a result of their teachings and example.[1]

---

[1]Pace, Grant, *Conference Report,* October 2-4, 1964, Salt Lake City, The Church of Jesus Christ of Latter-day Saints, p. 89.

TEACHING CHILDREN TAKES EFFORT

Do I deliberately make an attempt in my home to teach my child so I will earn his respect? One mother was approached one day by another mother who said, "I would give half my life to have a son such as yours," to which the first mother replied, "That's exactly what I did!"

A father who is concerned that his children develop a proper relationship with their Heavenly Father has found an outdoor hike or trip with his children one of the most effective teaching aids. When they are all alone in the beauty of the mountains, he expresses to them how thankful he is for what Heavenly Father has created. He then asks them to join him in prayer after which he invites each child individually to express his appreciation through prayer to their Heavenly Father. He reports that it is always an experience that his children remember.

GIVE YOUR CHILD RESPONSIBILITY

Do I give my children freedom with responsibility? One of the most difficult dilemmas facing a parent in giving the child freedom is in drawing the line between freedom and responsibility. Of course, there is no hard and fast rule on this since each child is an individual apart from every other child, but a general guideline to a father and a mother should be that a child can be given as much freedom as he can responsibly handle. There are two important considerations to helping the child develop responsibility.

1. He needs to know you have faith in his ability. The father who doubts his child's ability to do something right will seldom have it done right without compulsion. A father, on the other hand, who displays confidence in his children's ability will find that they will strive to live up to their parents' confidence. As an example of this, one father gave his twelve-year-old daughter the money to purchase her own shoes. He sat down with her beforehand and explained certain standards and limits within which she was free to buy. Later he went shopping with one of his younger daughters who was not old enough to be given the responsibility of handling her own money. They went to the same shoe store where the former daughter had purchased her shoes. The store manager asked him, "Aren't you the father of that young girl who came in last week

with just $8.00 to spend on a pair of shoes?" He replied he
The manager then said, "I just want to congratulate you on the
way you've trained your daughter. She really gave us an interesting
time! I think she went through every shoe in the place because
she was so concerned about getting the most practical buy for
her dollar."

Showing faith in children's ability has another application.
Older parents are at times so protectively concerned about their
married children that they want to continue to help them financially and otherwise after marriage. Of this, President Hugh B.
Brown has admonished:

> In many cases the cause of divorce can be traced right
> to the doorstep of unwise in-laws. As each new marriage
> craft sets sail, there should be a warning call, which is
> familiar to all ocean travelers, "All ashore that's going
> ashore," whereupon all in-laws should get off the matri-
> monial boat and return only at infrequent intervals and
> then only as invited guests for brief visits. If they are wise
> and polite, they will remember they are merely guests and
> not members of the crew.[2]

2. They need to know that they are trusted. Children raised
in an atmosphere of trust will seldom disappoint their parents.
It also follows that those who are continually mistrusted will not
know how to handle their freedom responsibly and more often than
not will disappoint their parents.

One of the typical problems that parents have in our time is
getting their teenagers to come in at a proper time at night. One
father who has never had any difficulty with this problem has
reported that he and his teenagers have come to a previous agreement on what a "reasonable" hour is at night. When they agree
upon a time, he commits them to their word and trusts them to
observe it. His teenagers have been most conscientious in handling
their freedom since they understand that if they don't handle it
responsibly, their freedom has to be limited.

CONCERN, RESPECT, RECOGNITION AND REMEMBRANCE

Do I take the time to really be concerned about each one of

---

[2]Brown, Hugh B., *You and Your Marriage*, Salt Lake City, Bookcraft, 1960, p. 138.

is not enough to play with the children collectively. ... know that father is concerned with him as an ... one busy father takes at least five minutes each day ... child so that he knows his father is interested in him.

... show respect for the privacy of their world? One of the ... portant things to a young person as he grows up is to feel that he has possessions that he can call his own. He needs to know that this privacy is respected. No father or mother should open the private mail of their children or read an opened letter unless invited to do so. This would also apply to a diary. Out of courtesy, a parent should knock on the closed door to the child's private room before entering.

Do I recognize in each of my children a unique and individual spirit? Each of our children came to us with a spirit begotten by our Eternal Father. They thus have individual qualities, characteristics, and personalities apart from every other spirit son and daughter of our Father. The wise father will therefore not attempt to make each of his children into the same "mold" but will emphasize and capitalize upon that child's strengths. One father had two sons that excelled in school work. The third son excelled in athletics, but did very poorly in school. Rather than compare the achievements of the first two sons scholastically against the failures of the third son, this father capitalized upon the athletic ability of this boy by praising him and giving him recognition for it. Because he felt that he too had something to contribute to the family, this son later developed an interest in his school work and has now received his doctorate degree from a well-known university.

Do I remember that I live a generation apart from my children? One of the problems a father frequently has is that he forgets that the world of his day and his children's day are two worlds apart. How many fathers are guilty of saying, "When I was a boy . . ."? Each dad needs to remember that times and situations change. To most fathers, having a car when he was a boy would be like asking for an airplane today. But to many boys today, this luxury of having a car is commonplace. This comparison should not be misconstrued to mean that all young people should have a car when they reach driving age. The illustration indicates only that a father should understand the gap that exists between the days of his youth and his children's. It should be remembered that the greatest gap that exists between fathers and their children is in relation to goals. A father frequently will think in terms of long-range goals such as "eternal life." A young person typically thinks only of his immediate needs. Just to know the gap exists, however, is not sufficient. If the gap is to be bridged, the father must step inside his children's world. By so doing, he will be conscious of their needs and attempt to help them creatively fulfill these needs.

Another thing that must be remembered by a father is that he must not judge his children's success by his adult standards.

APPLICATION

What Would Jesus Do?

D o you compliment your children? Do you trust them with responsibility and then recognize their limitations? Would you feel good if our Heavenly Father corrected you like you correct your children? Do your children know that you love and respect them? Have you told them? What other ways do you "tell" them? What would Jesus have you do to receive more respect from your children or family members? Here are several suggestions.

1.   Compliment your children's distinctive qualities. For example, you might try to capitalize upon their strengths this week and tell them how these strengthen the family.

2.   Trust your children with a responsibility this week that they are able to handle in accordance with their age and ability. For example, you might sit down and discuss with one of your sons or daughters the purchase of some necessity. Discuss with him or her the limitations in which they are free to buy. Allow then the son or daughter the freedom to make the purchase with the right to make a mistake without chastisement, remembering that mistakes offer sometimes the best opportunities to teach a lesson.

3.   Remind yourself each day of the difference between your experiences and theirs. Make an attempt to understand your children by looking at their world from their point of view.

4.   Let your children understand that they have a part in helping the family make decisions. Let them have a voice in the family council the next time a critical problem arises, and listen to their ideas.

Read and ponder: Ephesians 6:4; D&C 50:40; D&C 93:11-14, 20; Alma 36:1-4.

1. Four brethren may be each assigned during the week a paragraph under the heading in the lesson, "Concern, Respect, Recognition, and Remembeance." They could then report the essence of that paragraph and provide personal examples in their comments.

2. Challenge quorum members to select one of the suggestions in the section, "What Would Jesus Do?" and attempt to apply it during the week with their children.

How Shall They Be Led?

Each quorum member might be given a sheet of paper. On this, he could be asked to record the names of each of his children. He might then note briefly what he did with or for each child that was an attempt to let the child know of his concern. One or several class members could then be asked to briefly report on their success with the challenge, noting briefly which child they worked with and what they did with him last week.

(This discussion should not exceed five minutes.)

LESSON OBJECTIVE

The Priesthood holder should be motivated to apply the concept of discipline as it relates to discipleship in the Gospel.

INTRODUCTION

The teacher should place the term "discipline" on the chalkboard. The quorum members could be asked to give their reaction to the word, the first thing that comes to their mind. After several exploratory reactions, the teacher might ask the quorum members to discuss the following question: What are some other dimensions to disciplining children in addition to punishment?

LESSON DEVELOPMENT

Ligon and Smith in their book, *The Marriage Climate*, contend that punishment and discipline are related only indirectly. Discipline, they say, is a quality the child possesses. Punishment is action of parents. Discipline is related to discipleship. In other words, we discipline only those who are our disciples.[1]

In the light of the foregoing description, how does a father make his children his disciples? (Briefly outline on the board some methods that would accomplish discipleship.) It is interesting that child psychologists have been giving considerable attention to the discipline problem as it affects the parent-child relationship for many years, but the Lord revealed the key for the most effective human relationships many years ago.

THE ELEMENTS FOR MAKING DISCIPLES

In a revelation to Joseph Smith, Jr., while he was in Liberty Jail, the Lord declared to him the principle upon which all Priesthood authority should operate. Each member of the Church has perhaps heard and read this quotation on numerous occasions, but how many have considered each of the elements contained within this revelation to apply to his home situation?

> No power or influence can or ought to be maintained by virtue of the Priesthood, only by persuasion, by long-suffering, by gentleness and meekness, and by love unfeigned;
>
> By kindness, and pure knowledge, which shall greatly enlarge the soul without hypocrisy, and without guile—
>
> Reproving betimes with sharpness, when moved upon by the Holy Ghost; and then showing forth afterwards an increase of love toward him whom thou hast reproved, lest he esteem thee to be his enemy. (D&C 121:41-43.)

1. Making a disciple of your children "only by persuasion."

    a. How did Jesus use the method of persuasion in winning his disciples? (John 1:45-51; 3:1-22.)

    b. Before He persuaded His disciples to follow after Him, why did He give them instruction pertaining to His expectations of them? (See Matthew 19:16-23.)

A significant lesson may be learned by each father from the Master's method. Consideration should be given to the following:

---

[1]See Ligon, Ernest and Smith, Leona, *The Marriage Climate,* St. Louis, The Bethany Press, 1963, p. 55.

c. Why is the technique of understanding and using loving persuasion better in enlisting discipleship of others than making continual demands of them?

d. In correcting our children, why would it be better to explain to them the reason for our expectations of them rather than giving them the common reason, "because I told you so?"

One father who has had good success with his children by using this technique has found that discussing his expectations with each of the children in regard to their household chores, picking up after themselves, time to get in, etc., is the key to a cooperative agreement on the discipline. "What do you feel your mother and I should do if you don't live up to your end of the bargain?" he asks. Usually the children are too harsh on themselves so he must temper their decisions, but the children have an understanding of what will result if the child doesn't live up to his commitment. In the event that a child does not abide by his commitment, the consequences are then explained to the child as the result of *his* action rather than the father's.

As an example: One father and son have an agreement that the son will be in at a specified time. Before the parents retire they set the alarm for that time with the understanding that the son is to turn the alarm off before it rings when he comes home. If it does go off, the son knows that his parents will be waiting for him and further, he will not have the privilege of going out for two weeks. Follow-through on the agreement between them is the key that creates better understanding.

2. Making a disciple of your children "by long-suffering."

a. In the case of Jesus, where He had godlike characteristics of perfection, why was it so important that He exhibit "long-suffering" in winning His disciples? What reasons did He have at times for showing impatience toward Peter?

b. What have you found in your own family to be successful in practicing this quality of long-suffering?

One father has made it a practice to listen to his children's side of the story before he determines what should be done. The important thing for the father to remember is that his children are going to make mistakes and have shortcomings because they are immature. He needs to remind himself continually that his children are not to be judged by adult standards.

3. Making a disciple of your children "by gentleness and meekness."

The quality of gentleness reflects a behavior appropriate for one of noble birth. It is an expression of refinement. This quality is coupled closely with meekness which signifies that one is not inclined to anger or resentment. As we visualize the Savior these qualities emerge as some of his dominant characteristics. In the sense of the definitions given, truly it can be said that He was gentle and meek.

There is another sense in which the word meekness is used. In Hebrew times it referred to a man who was "molded" through his submission to God's spirit. Meekness was not then the weakling, but a person whose strength rested in the Lord.

a. How might a Latter-day Saint father exemplify the qualities of a *gentle* man in terms of the foregoing definitions?

President McKay has stressed frequently in his talks the need for this quality through the usage of such courtesies as "please," "thank you," and "pardon me."

b. How can a father bring these qualities of gentleness and meekness into a very real family situation such as when one child refuses to mind? What part would the father's private and family prayers in behalf of his children have in the expression of these qualities? One father has indicated that he can often discipline his children better through family prayer than when he talks to them face to face since they will listen to his sincere concern for them in the prayer whereas otherwise they regard it as moralizing.

4. Making a disciple of your children "by love unfeigned."

To feign a particular attribute in one's behavior is to convey the impression that one possesses that particular quality when, in fact, the quality is lacking. In other words, feigning an attribute or quality is a deception. Jesus regarded this as one of the sins most detrimental to man because it prevented repentance and inhibited his eternal progress.

How easy is it for children to spot "feigned" love in their father? Have any of us been guilty of representing ourselves before the membership of the Church as a model saint through our church attendance, tithe payment, willingness to help others; when at home we are cross, belligerent, critical and in some cases swear at the family and resort to all kinds of cruelty to the children?

It is clear from the revelation given to Joseph Smith that the quality of "unfeigned love" is the means by which a father can overcome his weaknesses and gain disciples of his children. For the idea of "unfeigned love" to have a meaningful application in dealing with one's children, several suggestions might be considered.

a. It should first be recognized that any pretense with one's children is usually the result of "covering up" an exaggerated ambition or one's sins. Pretense is the mask for inferiority feelings. The first step then to learning an unfeigned love is to recognize the ambitions, pride, and sins that preclude such attainment and have a willingness to change. This may call for a little soul searching.

One father has found that his children will frequently let him know of his weak areas when he asks them at family home evening, "If there was one thing you could change in each member of the family, what would you change about that person?"

b. The next step is to openly acknowledge before the family the idea that their father doesn't have all the answers and sometimes his behavior is regrettable. He could then explain to them that it is for this reason that he and mother pray for guidance in raising them. A father who does this with his children has indicated that when he acknowledges his mistakes and weaknesses and asks his children for understanding and forgiveness they are much more receptive to him. As an example: One dad was asked by his daughter for permission to go to a movie with some of her girl friends. After hearing the name of the movie, he passed judgment on it and declined to allow her to go. He refused to listen to his daughter's pleas and finally reprimanded her by sending her to her room. Later, he found that the film was excellent. He went to his daughter, acknowledged his mistake, asked for forgiveness for his hasty action and *then took her to the film*. What effect do you think this had upon their relationship?

5. Making a disciple of your children by "kindness and pure knowledge."

Many instances are recorded in the New Testament where

the Master gained a disciple through His kind compassion. (See, for example, the account of Zacchaeus, Luke 19:2-8.) Many of His miracles were motivated by this quality. Kindness or compassion and pure knowledge are related to the extent that one does not really show complete compassion to another until he can give to that person the understanding and treatment most essential for their spiritual growth. How does one obtain pure knowledge? One way is to have love and virtue in our lives to the extent that the Holy Ghost becomes our constant companion. (See D&C 121:45-46.) Another way is to work diligently through study, learning, and seeking for the answer to the problem and then go to the Lord for confirmation on the answer we have found.

One leader in the Church who has been successful in having all his children married in the temple attributes this to the fact that he and his wife have prayerfully considered the needs of each of their children and struggled and worked at its solution; in many instances they were given an understanding of that particular son or daughter that assisted them most at that period in their lives. Concerning this important element, President McKay has said:

> The spirit of kindness is as enduring as love itself. Let us go home, and if we have been cruel, either by treating our wives with indifference, or by scolding, or loud talking, if we have been cruel to our children by neglect, or by striking them, let us see if we cannot repent and look introspectively and see whether or not we are not to blame for some of the conditions that arouse these passions.[2]

6. Making a disciple of your children by "reproving . . . when moved upon by the Holy Ghost." There are times when a rebuke or reproof is in order in making a strong disciple.

   a. What were some instances in the life of the Savior when He used this method to win disciples? (Matthew 15:1-10; Luke 9:51-57; 22:31-39.)

   b. How did the reproof challenge them to a renewed determination, greater effort, or more spirituality?

   c. Is there any evidence to suggest that He displayed an increased love after rebuking them?

---

[2]McKay, David O., *Gospel Ideals*, Salt Lake City, Deseret News Press, 1953, p. 490.

One of the difficulties a father is challenged with in disciplining his children is in controlling his emotional anger. In this connection, the quorum or Priesthood group might discuss the following questions:

    d.   When is the best time to discipline a child—at the time the infraction occurs or when emotional anger subsides? How does an agreement beforehand between the father and child on what the consequences should be if an infraction occurs, help in controlling the emotional factor?

    e.   Why is it usually best to reprove a child in private rather than before his friends?

    f.   How can a father display to his children after disciplining them an "increased love"?

APPLICATION

What Would Jesus Do?

A s you consider how the Savior made disciples, you will recall that His great influence was the result of the example leadership. As others saw the principle of the Gospel in His life, they were motivated to follow Him.

Look through the following suggestions that might be helpful to you in making your children your disciples. Check one suggestion that you desire to work with this coming week.

1.   Discuss with each child the expectations that you have in regard to his obligations and duties to the family. Make certain he understands the expectations. This should be discussed when you are not trying to solve a problem, but trying to avoid it from taking place.

2.   You might try to concentrate this week on one shortcoming such as impatience by attempting to be more understanding of your children's immaturities and shortcomings.

3.   Try to reprove the children in the spirit of love. Let them know of their positive attributes, and then indicate the undesirable characteristic that needs improving.

4.   Support your wife in her disciplining of the children. Even if she is not always what you consider right, support her and then discuss the discipline when the child is not present.

5. Try to correct in a positive manner by eliminating all the "don'ts" from your vocabulary. Use instead a positive approach such as, "Please shut the door quietly," "We agreed that you would . . ."

6. You might prayerfully seek understanding of your children's needs in cooperation with your wife.

Read and ponder: I Timothy 4:12. Review Alma's counsel to his sons: Alma 36:42.

SPECIAL INSTRUCTIONS TO THE TEACHER

1. Point out that D&C 121:34-45 constitutes what is known as the Doctrine of the Priesthood. It describes how power and authority are to be administered by the Priesthood, and that no power or influence "can or ought to be maintained" on any other basis.

2. Use examples to illustrate each of the virtues described in the lesson.

Are You the Leader?

LESSON FOLLOW-UP

Last week it was suggested that you select one of several challenges and make a serious attempt to improve in that area. At this time, look back at the suggestion you checked. In consideration of your past week's performance, how would you rate your effort at improving in this suggested area?

_____ I tried hard and felt that I made good improvement!

_____ I tried, but my effort could have been better!

_____ I remembered the assignment, but I had trouble in carrying out my program of action!

_____ I forgot completely, but I'll repent!

(This discussion should not exceed five minutes.)

LESSON OBJECTIVE

Since the inauguration of the family home evening as a vital program in the home, many brethren have indicated the definite need for some suggestions in helping them with this program. Some of the areas where many have indicated a need for help are:

1. How to create a continual interest among their children for family home evening.

2. How to conduct.

3. How to get members of the family involved.

The purpose of this lesson is to provide each member of the quorum or Priesthood group with suggestions that will assist them in creating a more meaningful family home evening.

KEEPING INTEREST IN THE HOME EVENING

"Red" Blake has been active in his quorum only the past two years. Since that time he and his wife have been sealed in the temple, and he has made wonderful progress in the Church. It is now his earnest desire to do everything he can in following the counsel of his bishop and elders' quorum presidency.

Within the past year, "Red" and his wife have attempted to hold the family home evening in their home since they could see the benefits that would come to their two teenagers, David and Jennifer, and their eight-year-old son, Bobby. At first the children were curious to see what the new program was like, so they participated. Now, however, "Red" and his wife have noticed a reluctance on the part of the older children to participate in the home evening. The last few times they were to have their home evening, David complained, "Ah gee, Dad! Are we gonna have to go through this again?" David's attitude has had a very negative effect upon the other children. This situation has been going on for some time now.

"Red" is a fairly successful contractor in his town but feels his inadequacy as a teacher because he never pursued his education beyond high school. His real concern is that his children won't have to go through the same "inactive" period in their Church life as he did; but he is getting pretty discouraged with the attitude of his children toward the home evening.

STEPS FOR GETTING MORE INTEREST

In assisting "Red" in the solution of this problem, the quorum or Priesthood group might consider the following questions:

1. What are some of the reasons that teenagers or younger children might consider the home evening a waste of time, or boring? (These reasons might be listed on the chalkboard.)

2. Which of the reasons listed might be the fault of the father's lack of preparation or not getting the other family members involved in the lesson?

3. In the light of what has been listed and discussed, what

are some of the things that would create greater interest for the children?

This particular lesson would lend itself nicely to a role playing situation. A quorum member, who is successful in involving the members of his family in family home evening, could be asked to conduct a "home evening" presentation. This member could take the role of the father, another brother could be asked to be the mother, and a third might take the part of a rebellious teenager. Several others might take the role of other children of the family. This role playing situation could demonstrate the method this father might use in creating interest in his children for the home evening, and how he would involve them in the program. A variation to this suggestion is to have three or four quorum members briefly demonstrate effective techniques under the areas of (1) conducting, (2) creating interest, and (3) getting involvement from family members.

CREATING INTEREST

One of the contributing factors to boredom on behalf of the children is that the parents frequently feel obligated to give ALL the material in the home evening lesson. The lessons have been prepared so that the broadest possible coverage of any family-type situations can be given. The Family Home Evening manual has been prepared so that the broadest possible coverage of many family-type situations can be given. In planning for each home evening, the parents need to be selective of the lesson that best meets the family needs that week, and then within each lesson they should use only those materials that best fit *their* family situation. Further, they should realize that the presentations need to be kept short. Unless there is an unusual interest, they should be planned to take no longer than twenty to twenty-five minutes.

Four suggested techniques that parents can use in creating more interest in their children for the home evenings are:

1. You should personalize the stories by including the names of your own children in the story whenever appropriate.

2. Use experiences of the family members to make a point.

3. Get involvement of each member of the family, and

4. Use a variety of methods in the presentation of the lessons. One brother, in planning for family home evening, attempts to use a different method of approach each time. He selects from the following techniques:

   a. Give the children a problem and have them try to solve it.

b. Give a case study to the family and discuss it.

c. Have several of the older children conduct a panel discussion.

d. Take a nature hike together.

e. Have children place questions in a question box, and then discuss the questions at the family home evening.

f. Start a lesson from time to time with a brief quiz on the material on the night's lesson.

g. Play an instructional family game together.

h. Give the children a checklist to determine some areas of needed improvement.

i. Have the children give memorized scriptures (Give a reward to the children who do well).

j. Have a "read around" where each member takes a turn reading the scriptures.

k. Have one of the children give a brief talk.

l. Have a role playing situation where the children sometimes take the part of mother and dad and the parents take the role of the children.

m. Have group singing and/or solo performances.

n. Have each member of the family bear his testimony.

o. Have one person give a reading.

p. Have different persons tell a story illustrating the lesson ideas.

q. Show a filmstrip or motion picture.

r. Have a flannelboard or picture presentation.

Wherever possible a father or mother should avoid reading the lesson manual to the children. It is suggested that the lesson manual not be a part of the presentation at all, but all lesson material be written out in advance or outlined. Where scriptures are cited, these should be read from the Standard Works.

WHO SHALL CONDUCT?

Often the father feels that because he is the Priesthood holder, he should do all the conducting of the family home evening. Actually this should not be the case. There is an essential difference between presiding and conducting. As the patriarch of the family, the father *always* presides in that he is the acknowledged spiritual leader of the family, but he may delegate the responsibility of conducting to any other member of the family whom he chooses.

To ensure, however, that an effective home evening is planned, he should sit down with that member of the family who will be conducting, and help him or her with the program.

GETTING FAMILY INVOLVEMENT

One of the most successful ways that a father can keep the interest of each member of the family toward the home evening lesson is to see that each member is personally involved in the lesson. EVERY FAMILY HOME EVENING SHOULD INVOLVE EVERY FAMILY MEMBER! It has been repeatedly reported by young people throughout the Church that the thing they would like to change most about the family home evening is that "Dad talks too much!" To those dads that may be talking "too much" but are holding the home evening, they are to be congratulated on getting their families together for the home evening. The suggestions that follow are intended to give further help to these fathers so that they might understand their children's complaints and be more prepared to meet the needs of their children. The key, as will be seen, in averting criticism is to get the children involved!

1. A definite time and date should be set that is agreeable to each member of the family. Since Monday evening has been kept free from other Church-related activities, this may be the most appropriate evening. The family should understand that nothing else is to interfere with this time and evening.

2. The parents should plan out carefully each program in advance, or the father should plan each program with the person who is to conduct. He should give particular guidance to this person.

3. Any assignments should be given at least a week in advance, and the parents should periodically check to see that these assignments are being carried out. This caution should be particularly observed with younger children.

4. Assignments to read particular passages of scripture should be rotated among the members of the family. The mother can be of help in assisting younger children in memorizing a particular passage for the home evening.

5. The older children could be given the responsibility to help the younger ones since many times, when the parents attempt to "reach" the younger children, the older ones complain that this is "kindergarten stuff."

6.   The children should be given a voice in solving the family problems. One dad, whenever a decision has to be made that will have any bearing on the family, calls his family together during the family home evening and considers the opinions of each member of the family relative to that decision. He has reported that often some of the best suggestions have come from his children.

7.   Periodically, it is well to hold a "complaint" session at the conclusion of the family home evening. Teenagers particularly need to tell their parents what is bothering them. One father who does this finds that when his daughter can express her "complaint" without fear of being reprimanded, her whole attitude and behavior are greatly improved.

What Would Jesus Do?

I t is evident that since the Savior places such stress on the importance of parents teaching their children correct principles of His Gospel that He would have effective home evenings being held in all Latter-day Saint homes.

You might sit down and review the following check list with your wife or the person who is conducting the next family home evening. This list should help you quickly review your strengths and weaknesses in your lesson presentations. As you determine your weak areas, place a check ($\checkmark$) by them. You could then attempt to improve your lessons by incorporating some of the suggested techniques that were discussed in this lesson. The number in brackets beside each of the statements will refer you back to the page in the lesson that provides you with a helpful suggestion on the improvement of that item.

LESSON INTEREST

_____   The length of our lessons is within twenty-five minutes. (p. 245)

_____   We attempt to personalize our lessons by using personal experiences and the names of our own children in the stories we use. (p. 245)

_____ We attempt to vary each lesson by the use of a different approach such as a family skit, a role-playing situation, a flannel board presentation, special musical numbers, etc. (pp. 245-246)

_____ We make it a point never to read the lesson manual to our children. (p. 246)

_____ We prepare our lessons in advance so that everyone knows specifically his or her assignment in connection with that lesson. (p. 247)

CONDUCTING

_____ As the Priesthood leader in my home, I always preside but allow others to conduct. (p. 246)

_____ I make an attempt each week to assist the person conducting in planning the program. (p. 247)

FAMILY INVOLVEMENT

_____ In giving the lesson to the family, I make it a point not to lecture, but try to get each family member involved. (p. 247)

_____ We have a definite time on Monday evening for our family home evening. (p. 247)

_____ We check periodically during the week with each member of the family to see that he or she is carrying out their assignments. (p. 247)

_____ In reading the scriptures during the family home evening lesson, we try to rotate the opportunity. Also, we make an attempt to see that our children are memorizing the scriptures. (p. 247)

_____ We make an attempt to have our older children teach the younger ones during the family home evening lesson presentation. (p. 247)

_____ We attempt to give each of our children a "voice" in the family council. (p. 248)

_____ We allow our children to express their feelings during the family home evening. (p. 248)

ASSIGNMENTS

_____ Prior to each lesson, we carefully review the objective and plan our assignments to reach this goal. (p. 247)

_____ We make a sincere attempt to have each member of the family suggest to us the assignment that would be most helpful to him. (p. 247)

_____ As a family, we make a conscious effort to follow through on the assignments that are given. We periodically remind each other of the assignment. (p. 247)

_____ At the beginning of each new lesson, we try to follow up on the previous week's assignment to determine how we did.

Read and ponder: 2 Nephi 31:3; 2 Nephi 33:1; Mosiah 4:14-15.

SPECIAL INSTRUCTIONS TO THE TEACHER

In addition to discussing the suggestions for improving family home evening that are found in the manual, ask class members to share personal successes they have had as a family in each of the areas discussed in the lesson:

a. Creating and sustaining interest
b. Conducting the meetings
c. Involving each family member
d. Making meaningful assignments to family members

The Spirit in Our Homes

Class members could be invited to tell what they have done specifically during the past week to improve their family home evenings in view of the discussion last week.

(This discussion should not exceed five minutes.)

LESSON OBJECTIVE

The Priesthood holder should feel motivated to create a home atmosphere wherein the Lord's spirit can abide continually.

LESSON DEVELOPMENT

GOALS ARE LIKE BLUEPRINTS

Our main goals can be likened to the blueprints for a house or a recipe used in cooking because they have an important influence in determining what the final product will be. It seems to be true of most individuals that their goals are acquired unconsciously; they become conditioned to behaving the way they do by imitating others. They do not take the time to think seriously about whether the aims of the groups to which they belong are the right aims or not.
are the right aims or not.

But we cannot afford to leave such important matters to an unconscious process. We should take the time—whatever time is necessary—to understand thoroughly the goals that our Heavenly Father has in mind for each of us. They then serve the same function as the roots of a tree or the hub of a wheel. They are the guidelines around which all our activities take place.

The Lord has indicated that the family is an *eternal* organiza-

251

tion in His plan of Salvation. But if any individual is to experience fully the satisfaction and joy that a family can bring to him, he must abide by the conditions upon which such satisfaction and joy are based. This means that he would be married by the authority of the Priesthood and would live so that his marriage could be sealed by the "Holy Spirit of Promise," that is, by the Holy Ghost. He would thus *become* a son or daughter of our Heavenly Father in the sense that he would be worthy to live in His presence.

MANY CHALLENGES TO OUR GOALS

Each person is confronted with a difficult problem in trying to carry out the goals given us by our Heavenly Father because in this world we have not only His plan of living but many others as well. Various groups have ways of behaving which are sometimes at variance with those taught us by the Gospel. The world in general may consider the Sabbath primarily as a day for recreation instead of a day of rest and worship. Adults in many countries use tobacco, alcohol, tea, and coffee in ways which are in direct contrast to the teachings of the Lord. Many people exploit their fellow human beings on the grounds that "business is business" or "the union" demands that he behave this way. Many husbands and wives justify disloyalty to their marriage vows on the basis of the "new morality."

One way to solve the problem of living in "the world" and yet not participating in activities which are not approved by the Lord is to constantly keep in mind our ultimate goals. Many organizations other than the family make demands upon us. We have certain "deadlines" which must be met, such as meetings to attend, reports to make, and appointments to keep. It is often easy to let the family and its members suffer when faced with such demands from other organizations. A young man who was executed in one of our state penitentiaries for committing a murder said shortly before his execution, "When I was a child, I idolized my father. As I grew up, there were so many times that I wanted to do things with him. But he was always saying to me, 'I'm sorry, son, I have a meeting to attend, but we'll do it some other time.' But we never did. I saw clearly from his *behavior* that I wasn't as important to him as his profession."

AN ACTIVITY FOR CLASS MEMBERS

Members of the class may want to analyze their own behavior toward their wives and children. Do they give a significant and meaningful part of their time, energy, and devotion to their families? Once a group of people came to see a general authority and wanted to spend some time in talking to him. He replied that he would be very happy to talk to them, but at this time he had an appointment with members of his family. They had planned an activity together. "You see," he said, "my family is as important to me as anything in my life." How many class members would have answered as this general authority did? Would members of the class consider it as important to carry out a family home evening in which an important principle of the Gospel should be studied as it is to attend a meeting of their occupational organization? If one of their children asked them a question of importance to the child, would they give the child the same consideration as they would if the president of their occupational organization would ask a question of similar importance?

DO WE MAKE VICTIMS OF FAMILY MEMBERS?

How Do We Behave at Home? In many and varied activities outside the home we often develop mental and emotional tensions. We are often misunderstood by others. We fail to achieve some of the objectives we set for ourselves. When we come home at night, it is very easy to make family members the victims of our disappointments and frustrations. Our tensions need to be released, but in legitimate ways. Some release tension by playing golf or tennis. Others listen to beautiful music. Still others cultivate a garden or participate in a creative activity which is *different* from the work they normally do for many hours of the day.

We pay a tremendous price when we "take out" our problems on the members of our families. The price is that they come to resent us. When this happens, we lose a great opportunity to teach them the principles of the Gospel. When people resent us, in most cases they do not accept the idea we are trying to teach them. But if a child *knows* and *feels* that his parents love him and are *sensitive* to his feelings, he will listen to his parents' teachings.

DO WE COMPLIMENT OUR CHILDREN?

Often parents can easily see the immaturity of their children. Again, it is very easy to point out these immaturities and faults to our children. *But how often do we compliment our children for the things they do well?* It is true that we can get people to behave the way we want them to behave by "negative" as well as "positive" measures. A child will sit still in church because he is afraid of the spanking he will get if he doesn't. But we accomplish a greater thing when the child sits still because he is thinking of the Savior and His meaning in his life. Every time a parent can find a legitimate reason to compliment his child, he is establishing a positive reason for the child to want to continue in a desirable behavior pattern. Napoleon was said to have finally realized that in the long run the love demonstrated and emphasized by the Savior was much more powerful than the force and harshness which had characterized so much of his own behavior.

APPRECIATION IS POWERFUL

Appreciating and complimenting our wives will also improve relations in the home. In one of the first lessons of the Family Home Evening Manual, members were asked to indicate one desirable trait which each one of the other family members possessed. When the members of one family carried out this activity, the husband told his wife how much he appreciated her handling of their finances. When he told her this, she began to cry and told him how much she appreciated his telling her. What she didn't tell him was that this was the *first* time in twenty years of married life that he had ever expressed such appreciation. Good relations are enhanced by people honestly and sincerely letting others know of their gratitude.

Another point about behavior in the home needs to be stressed. Many adults do not understand that children, especially young children, are imitating their parents' behavior. It is sometimes characteristic of a parent to "let down" and become careless in what he does. For example, perhaps someone calls on the telephone asking for an assignment that should have been completed some days ago. The parent says, "Tell him I'm not in." His observant five-year-old child hears his statement. What does the child conclude about telling the truth?

The holder of the Priesthood should make a personal commitment to the Savior, who extended the authority of the Priesthood to him, to represent in the best way he knows how in all of his actions the principles upon which that authority is based.

WE NEED TO LEARN TO BE AWARE OF OTHERS

Attitudes Toward Others. A child is often concerned only with his own personal welfare. As these lessons have indicated, as he grows up he has to learn to appreciate others. If he develops the love for them advocated by the Savior, he will be "born again"; the Holy Ghost will help influence his behavior.

When a person has reached such a state of development, he dedicates himself to helping others to know the same joy that he himself knows. He does not see them primarily as his competitors but as his brothers and sisters. He is pained when he sees them sin. Since he is in command of his own emotions, he demonstrates mature behavior even when others are behaving immaturely. He does not try "to get even" with others when they wrong him. He tries to teach them.

He realizes that no two of us are exactly alike. We may differ in age, experience, sex, knowledge, or wisdom. But each of us is a child of the same Father in Heaven and as such deserves the respect of that status.

APPLICATION

What Would Jesus Do?

The spirit which generally characterizes our homes is the final result of the principles discussed in this manual. These are the principles that Jesus Himself exemplified in a perfect way, and that which He would have all men do who bear His authority. These principles might be summarized in specific ways by the following check list.

A CHECK LIST EMPHASIZING SPECIFIC THINGS THAT PRODUCE A DESIRABLE SPIRIT IN OUR HOMES

1. If I ask my child to perform a favor for me, do I say "please"?

2. If I make a mistake in my relationships with my child, do I consider apologizing to him?

3. Do I unjustly shout at my child?

4. If I spank my children, what effect do I think it has upon my relationship with them?

5. Do I generally "preach" to my children ("You ought to do this because I said so") or do I try to give them an understanding of the principle involved by discussing it in terms of their understanding and from their point of view?

6. Do I regularly study a principle of the Gospel with my children?

7. Do I regularly compliment my wife and children for things they do well?

8. Do I honestly listen to family members when they speak? Do I really understand what they are saying and *why* they are saying it?

9. Do my children regularly confide in me? If not, why not?

10. If I have to make a decision involving our whole family, do I consult my wife and let her freely express her views? Do we then try to reach an *agreement* about what we should do? Is it my practice to present our tentative decision to the Lord in the manner prescribed in the ninth section of the Doctrine & Covenants?

11. Do I, as a holder of the Priesthood, bless members of the family?

12. Do we have family prayers?

13. At Christmas time do we emphasize the importance of the Savior in our lives or do we emphasize Santa Clause as a symbol of commercialization—a symbol of "receiving" from others?

14. Do we try to select favorable conditions to discuss our family problems? (When we are tired, hungry, sleepy, or depressed, it is hard to make wise decisions.)

15. In our home do we follow the practice of having only one person speak at a time?

16. Does each member of the family understand his family responsibilities? (One family outlines the specific duties of each child at the beginning of the week. These are placed upon a bulletin board. To obtain variety, the responsibilities are changed each week.)

17. Do I keep my promises to my children and my wife?

18. Do I punish my child for *his* sake or *my* sake?

19. Do I permit my children to participate in some kinds of

decisions with the thought in mind of preparing him to make decisions when he is no longer in my home?

20. How often have I told my wife and my children in one way or another that I love them?

Read and ponder: D&C 88:119; D&C 31; 9; D&C 121:45-46.

SPECIAL INSTRUCTIONS TO THE TEACHER

1. Discuss with class members what can be done to apply in their families in the foregoing principles as they relate to (a) their families, (b) their wives and (c) their children.

2. Allow quorum members to cite personal experiences where they have improved family relationships.

3. Discuss the need for seeking the assistance of the Holy Ghost in your family associations.

TO ANYONE USING THIS MANUAL:

Would you be so kind as to take a moment and write us?

1. What did you find in this manual of *most value* to you?

2. What did you find in this manual of *least value* to you?

3. Any additional comments: (Use reverse side if necessary.)

Please write or clip this sheet and send your comments to:

Melchizedek Priesthood Committee
The Church of Jesus Christ of Latter-day Saints
47 East South Temple
Salt Lake City, Utah 84111
Attention: 1973-74 Manual Committee

(Clip here)